"Robert Simonson's take on essential [...] told with that great combo of wry wit [...] edge. From the bars and barkeeps to finely tuned recipes, his well-observed entries made me an instant expert in all things booze."

—*Alice Feiring,* author of *To Fall in Love, Drink This* and *Natural Wine for the People*

"*The Encyclopedia of Cocktails* is a crucial addition to any drink aficionado's library. From Adonis to Zombie, every page of Robert Simonson's opus is filled with insightful, amusing histories of the cocktails, bars, and people who transformed drinking culture. I loved it."

—*Kevin Alexander,* James Beard Award–winning author of *Burn the Ice: The American Culinary Revolution and Its End* and coauthor of bestsellers *California Soul* and *The Lemon*

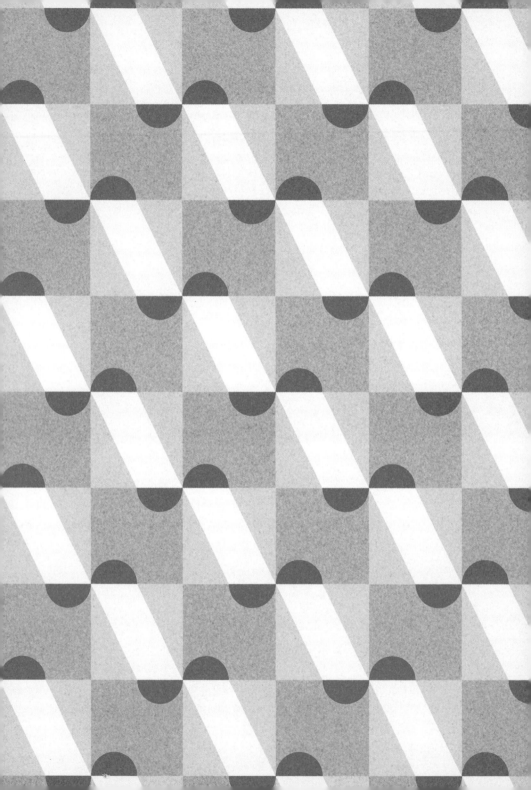

The
ENCYCLOPEDIA
of COCKTAILS

The
ENCYCLOPEDIA
of COCKTAILS

The PEOPLE, BARS
& DRINKS, *with* MORE
THAN 100 RECIPES

Robert Simonson

ILLUSTRATIONS BY
Suzanne Dias

TEN SPEED PRESS
California | New York

To every bartender who has ever served me a cocktail

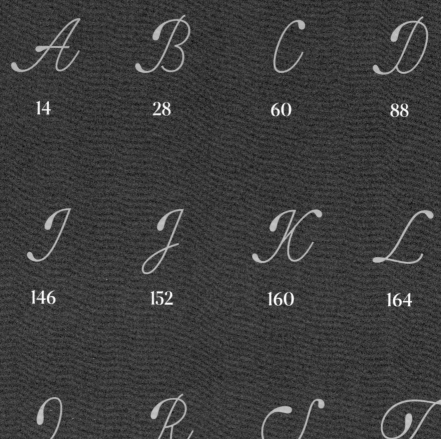

CONTENTS

RECIPES

INTRODUCTION

The name of this book was chosen carefully. This is an encyclopedia of *cocktails.* Its focus is cocktails, just as mine has been for nearly twenty years. Every entry, be it of a spirit or a particular historical bar or a notable person or a professional tool, is written with a view of how that spirit, bar, person, or tool played a role in the history, progress and proliferation of cocktails and cocktail culture. So, the entry on rye whiskey, for instance, does not dwell overly long on how rye is made or who makes it—information better left to books whose subject is whiskey or the making of spirits, of which there are many—but rather how it is used in cocktails, and how that use has changed over time. In other words, I wrote this book wearing cocktail-colored glasses, and you should read it with the same frames.

The time frame covered by this book ranges from the earliest days of mixology to the current day. There are classic cocktails and modern classics; bars that live in legend only and bars that operate today; bartenders famous in their day and famous today.

Regarding the tone of the text, I have tried to write a popular, people's history of cocktails. During my years as a cocktail historian, the texts I have enjoyed best and gotten the most out of, be they books or individual pieces of journalism, were the ones written with a point a view and heavy dollops of opinion. That sort of attitude is, I believe, natural. It's almost impossible to sample a drink or experience a bar without developing almost instant impressions of them. The urge to express those impressions follows almost immediately after. I've tried to follow in that outspoken tradition in these pages. Throughout, one of the models I kept in mind was Samuel Johnson's *Dictionary of the English Language* from 1755. I don't pretend to Johnson's greatness, but I have admired since college his decision to inject humor and opinion into his definitions. (Classic example: "Oats: a grain which in England is generally given to horses, but in Scotland supports the people.") When's the last time you laughed, or even smiled, while reading a reference book? I hope you will at this one.

That air of playful bias extends to the entries themselves, which number more than three hundred. All were selected by me and me alone. Some choices were obvious. Of course, I had to include the Martini, Jerry Thomas, El Floridita, and gin. If not, there would have been hell to pay. But mixed in between expected topics from absinthe to Zombie you will find more than a few wild cards.

ABSINTHE (BAR)

A French-style brasserie that opened in 1997 in the Hayes Valley neighborhood of San Francisco. The bar was managed by Marcovaldo Dionysos, an up-and-coming bartender and ardent student of cocktail history. Dionysos put that knowledge to work. His innovative menu not only was littered with neglected classic cocktails but listed each drink's place and date of origin—a novelty at the time. The Ginger Rogers—a mixture of gin, lemon juice, ginger syrup, ginger ale, and mint based on the Favorite, an old cocktail published in 1914 by Jacques Straub—proved to be the bar's breakout drink. Dionysos left Absinthe after three years.

ABSINTHE (SPIRIT)

An herbal liqueur with a strong flavor of anise that has enjoyed an important, almost romantic, and certainly dramatic role in cocktail history. Originating in Switzerland and associated with late-nineteenth-century Paris, where it was a favorite of artists and the bohemian set, absinthe has played the starring part in drinks like the Absinthe Drip and Absinthe Frappe, which were quite popular in the late nineteenth century, particularly in New Orleans, a city whose love of the spirit has never died. (Shout-out to the Olde Absinthe House on Bourbon Street!) But more often, it was used as an important accent flavor in innumerable cocktails that had other spirits as their base, including the Blackthorn, Turf Club, Tuxedo, Monkey Gland, Morning Glory, De La Louisiane, Corpse Reviver No. 2, Remember the Maine, and, most famously, the Sazerac.

Absinthe's life in cocktails was cut short by a virtual ban on the spirit in the United States in 1912, the result of a global demonization of the liqueur, which was defamed as the cause of mayhem and madness. Substitutes like Herbsaint and Pernod stepped in while absinthe was off the market. The absinthe ban remained in effect for nearly a century, much to the frustration of mixologists, who required it to recreate dozens of old cocktail recipes. Its repeal was largely the work of a Louisiana chemist named Ted Breaux, who was inspired by Barnaby Conrad III's book on the subject. He collected old bottles of absinthe and tested them for thujone, the chemical compound that detractors said led to hallucinations and violent behavior. The experiments revealed nothing potentially deleterious about the liquid. Breaux wrote scientific studies and, with the help of Viridian Spirits, succeeded in having the absinthe ban repealed in 2007. Similar bans were repealed in other countries around the same time. Viridian and Breaux then collaborated on the first new mass-market brand of absinthe in nearly a century, Lucid. More brands followed, as did absinthe-themed cocktail bars. In New York, a New Orleans–style bar called Maison Premiere opened in Brooklyn, and Sasha Petraske opened White Star in Manhattan. The first succeeded, the second didn't. Ultimately, absinthe-obsessed bartenders overestimated the public interest in the product. A dismissive 2009 article in the *New York Times* captured the mood at the time: "It tasted like licorice. Remember: licorice jellybeans are always the last to go." Eventually, absinthe returned to its former role as a modifier used in dashes or small measurements.

But for a time in the late aughts, every cocktail bar in the nation proudly displayed an absinthe drip device on its bar top. The theater of the preparation was much of the appeal of an Absinthe Drip: cold water drips through a sugar cube set on an ornate, slotted absinthe spoon perched atop a glass filled with absinthe. This slowly results in a louching of the mixture—as the clear spirit turns opaque, it takes on a dreamy, pale-green hue. A few bartenders came up with significant new cocktails that called for absinthe, among them the Paddington at the trailblazing New York cocktail bar PDT and Joy Division at Death & Co.

ADONIS

A blend of sherry, sweet vermouth, and orange bitters, the Adonis is one of the three classic sherry cocktails, the others being the Bamboo and the Sherry Cobbler. The Adonis was named after the 1884 Broadway musical *Adonis,* which was a sensation in its time, running more than five hundred performances. If the Bamboo was the world's Sherry Martini, this was its Manhattan. The drink all but disappeared in the latter twentieth century as sherry, as well as low-ABV cocktails, went out of fashion. Sherry-loving mixologists brought it back in the twenty-first century. The ratios of sherry to vermouth vary widely in early recipes, and the style of sherry is never specified, leaving modern bartenders a lot of latitude in how to best present the drink.

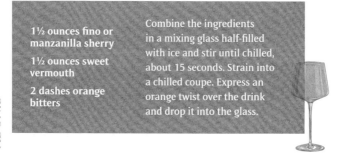

ADONIS

1½ ounces fino or manzanilla sherry

1½ ounces sweet vermouth

2 dashes orange bitters

Combine the ingredients in a mixing glass half-filled with ice and stir until chilled, about 15 seconds. Strain into a chilled coupe. Express an orange twist over the drink and drop it into the glass.

ALASKA

A relative of the Martini that uses yellow Chartreuse instead of vermouth. The drink first appeared in the 1910s and was sometimes made with Old Tom gin. Later on, as Old Tom became less available, London dry gin became the norm. Modern mixologists gave the drink a mild revival in the 2010s.

ALASKA

2¼ ounces Old Tom gin

¾ ounce yellow Chartreuse

1 dash orange bitters

Combine the ingredients in a mixing glass half-filled with ice and stir until chilled, about 15 seconds. Strain into a chilled coupe.

ALEXANDER

A classic cocktail made of gin, crème de cacao, and cream, and sometimes an egg white. It began to appear in cocktail books in the 1910s. By the mid-century, the Brandy Alexander, in which brandy stood in for the gin, exceeded it in popularity to the point that few people today are aware of the original Alexander. In some books from the 1930s, the brandy version was simply called Alexander No. 2. The Brandy Alexander is typically a dessert cocktail, and in the Midwest is usually made as an ice cream drink.

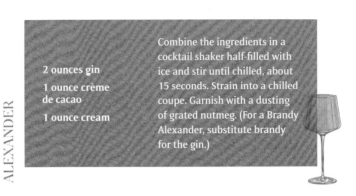

ALEXANDER

2 ounces gin
1 ounce crème de cacao
1 ounce cream

Combine the ingredients in a cocktail shaker half-filled with ice and stir until chilled, about 15 seconds. Strain into a chilled coupe. Garnish with a dusting of grated nutmeg. (For a Brandy Alexander, substitute brandy for the gin.)

ALEXANDER, CATO

One of New York's first celebrity bartenders, Alexander ran a tavern on the old Harlem Road in the country to the north of the city, which, in the early nineteenth century, occupied only the southern tip of Manhattan. A Black man born into slavery in 1780, he gained his freedom in 1799. As a young man he waited on George Washington; as a bar owner his clientele included some of the elite of the city, including the renowned Irish stage actor Tyrone Power (an ancestor of the twentieth-century movie star of the same name), who admired Alexander's way with a Mint Julep. "Everyone went there," wrote the *New York Daily Herald* years later. "It was the rage and the fashion." He amassed a fortune over the years, but then lost it in being too generous in his loans to patrons who promptly forgot their debt to the barkeeper. After opening a short-lived oyster bar downtown, he retired. He died in poverty, largely forgotten. Upon his death in 1858, the *Daily Herald* wrote, "Cato seemed to have a peculiar gift for hotel keeping. His larder was of the best, and his liquors were the boast of connoisseurs."

AMARO

A category of herbal liqueur associated with the aperitivo and digestive drinking culture of Italy, but also made in Germany, France, and elsewhere. It is characterized by a potpourri of botanicals, roots, barks, herbs, and spices that leans toward the bitter and astringent. (Amaro means "bitter" in Italian.) Traditionally consumed for their perceived qualities in helping with digestion and as a general health tonic, amari are also drunk for pleasure and, beginning in the twentieth century, became a popular component in cocktails. There are literally hundreds of amari produced in Italy, most of them regional beverages. A few have achieved national and—with the advent of the cocktail renaissance—international reputations. Among those are Averna (from Sicily), Montenegro (Bologna), Nardini (Veneto), Sibilla (Marche), Braulio (Lombardi), Amaro Nonino (Friuli, from a family of grappa makers), Ramazzotti (Piedmont), and Lucano (Basilicata). Within the amaro world are a host of subcategories, including fernet, which are more sharply bitter, Fernet-Branca being the more prominent example; carciofo, made with artichoke, of which Cynar is the leading brand; rabarbaro, made with rhubarb, including the brand Zucca (Milan). Alcohol content varies considerably and recipes are closely held family or company secrets. In Italy, amari are usually drunk neat, on the rocks, or with water. In the U.S., amari were little known or drunk outside of Italian communities, such as that in San Francisco. Occasionally they would find their way into cocktails. The Hanky Panky, which calls for Fernet-Branca, is a famous example. And Amer Picon, made in France, was often mixed, leading to famous potions like the Picon Punch. The twenty-first century saw mixologists, entranced by heritage elixirs and challenging flavors, clutch amari close to their collective chest. The liqueurs were worked into a wide variety of new cocktails. Some became popular, like the Black Manhattan, which uses Averna; Little Italy, made with Cynar; the Hard Start, composed of Fernet-Branca and Branca Menta; and the Paper Plane, which contains Amaro Nonino Quintessentia. Some American bars became famous for specializing in amari, including Amor y Amargo in Manhattan and Billy Sunday in Chicago. Consequently, more brands of amari became available in the U.S. than in any time in history, and multiple American distillers began creating new amari.

AMERICAN BAR AT SAVOY HOTEL

An art deco bastion of mixological art, situated in London's most famous hotel, and one of the most influential and long-lasting cocktail bars in history. It has been managed by a series of bartending legends over the years, including Ada Coleman, Harry Craddock, Joe Gilmore, and Peter Dorelli. It opened in the 1890s or early 1900s, depending on the source, as one of the first places to introduce American-style cocktails to Europe, hence the bar's name. It has attracted many famous patrons over the years, including Mark Twain, Charlie Chaplin, and Winston Churchill, and was a popular gathering spot for visiting Americans, both famous and not. Craddock made permanent the bar's influence when, in 1930, he published *The Savoy Cocktail Book,* which has been a bartending bible for nearly a century. The White Lady is the bar's signature cocktail.

AMERICANO

An Italian-born drink consisting of Campari, sweet vermouth, and soda water, and a direct precursor to the boozier Negroni. The drink came back into vogue in the United States with the low-ABV trend of the 2010s and today.

1 ounce Campari
1 ounce sweet vermouth
Soda water

Add Campari and vermouth to a collins glass filled with ice. Fill with soda water. Briefly stir. Garnish with an orange twist.

AMOR Y AMARGO

A small, innovative bar that opened in the East Village neighborhood of Manhattan in 2011 with a strict focus on bitter elixirs, including dashing bitters, Italian amari, and fortified wines. No shaken cocktails were served, and fresh juice played no role on the menu. The program was headed by bartender Sother Teague. Signature drinks included the Sharpie Mustache (Amaro Meletti, Bonal, gin, rye, Bittermens tiki bitters, and orange twist) and the eight-amaro Sazerac, which is exactly as advertised.

ANDERSON, JULIAN

Only the second Black American bartender (after Tom Bullock of St. Louis) to publish a cocktail book. Anderson's parents were slaves, and he believed he was born in Hamburg, Germany, where his parents moved after the outbreak of the Civil War. Upon returning to the United States, Anderson worked in hotels and bakeries in Washington, DC, Colorado, and Wyoming, before being hired in 1893 as a bartender at The Montana Club, an exclusive men's club in Helena. He stayed there for sixty years, serving the occasional dignitary like Mark Twain and Theodore Roosevelt, and becoming a local legend in the process. In 1919, he authored *Julian's Recipes,* a brief volume of roughly sixty recipes. Among them was Anderson's Mint Julep, an ornate creation using whiskey, brandy, and rum, for which he was celebrated. The mint, which he claimed to have brought to Montana from Virginia, came from his own backyard. He died in 1962 at the age of 102.

JULIAN ANDERSON

ANGEL'S SHARE

A pioneering Japanese-style speakeasy, Angel's Share was founded in New York City's East Village neighborhood in 1993 by Japanese-American entrepreneur Tadao "Tony" Yoshida, the same man behind the vegetarian restaurant mainstay Dojo and many other businesses that brought Japanese food and culture to the East Village. No other cocktail bar that opened in the 1990s had a greater influence on the future of the coming cocktail revival in that city and beyond. The bar was located on the second floor of a building on Stuyvesant Street, behind a door at the back of a Japanese izakaya ("stay-drink-place"). Yoshida, while initially inspired by the 1988 movie *Cocktail*, sought to replicate the sort of intimate and formal cocktail bars—dedicated to service, tradition, and meticulous craft—that could be found in Tokyo and were largely unfamiliar to the American public. The bartending staff would go on to include influential figures such as Shinichi Ikeda, Shingo Gokan, Shigefumi Kabashima, Gn Chan, Takuma Watanabe, Ben Rojo, and Nana Shimosegawa. They all worked with great ceremony and exacting precision beneath a vast mural painted by a Spanish street artist, which depicted cherubim and angels (the central angel was a portrait of Yoshida's infant son). The bartenders produced not only classic cocktails but also original drinks using Japanese ingredients like shochu and shiso leaf, sometimes bought from the next-door Japanese supermarket Sunrise Mart, also owned by Yoshida. The bar may have been the first in New York to employ block ice, each cube used in a drink being hand carved. Angel's Share had posted rules of etiquette, did not allow standing, and did not accept large parties. Because of the cultural divide between the staff and the customers, few bartenders or bar owners followed Angel's Share's example; the bar remained a singular entity within the city's drinking community. It did, however, produce one important acolyte. Sasha Petraske, a regular, would adopt much of the Angel's Share blueprint when he opened his bar Milk & Honey on the Lower East Side. As other cocktail bars came and went in the following years, Angel's Share endured. In 2019, the owner finally branched out, opening the bar Oldies in the Industry City complex in Brooklyn. In March 2022, Angel's Share closed its original location following a rent dispute with its landlord, Cooper Union. Yoshida's daughter, Erina, reopened the bar in 2023 in Greenwich Village as the sole owner.

ANKRAH, DOUGLAS

An influential London bartender and key figure in the city's 1990s cocktail revival. Born in Ghana, Ankrah cofounded the London Academy of Bartenders, a bartending school that ultimately failed, but not before it spun off LAB, a massively popular party bar in Soho where drinks were theatrical creations and bartenders were celebrities. He went on to open Townhouse in Knightsbridge in 2002, where he debuted his most famous creation, the provocatively named Porn Star Martini, a florid blend of vanilla vodka, vanilla syrup, passion fruit puree, and, on the side, a shot of champagne. Over time, it became one of the most ordered cocktails in the UK. He came out with his own ready-to-drink version in 2017. Ankrah died in 2021 at age fifty-one.

APEROL SPRITZ

The most successful corporate-created cocktail since Galliano executives got behind the Harvey Wallbanger in the early 1970s. A typical recipe consists of Aperol, Prosecco, and soda water.

2 ounces Aperol
3 ounces Prosecco
1 ounce soda water

Build the ingredients in a large goblet filled with ice. Stir briefly. Garnish with an orange slice.

APEROL SPRITZ

APTE, ANU

A native of Utah, Apte opened the craft cocktail bar Rob Roy in Seattle in 2009 and quickly became a force in the small but influential Seattle cocktail scene. She went on to open the tropical bar Navy Strength and a beer bar called No Anchor, later reopened as Trade Winds Tavern.

AQUAVIT

A Scandinavian spirit whose informing flavors are caraway and cumin, it is typically served chilled and with food. The Trident, by Robert Hess, is a rare cocktail where aquavit has a starring role. Aquavit has never been a huge player in the cocktail world, though certain valiant bartenders have fought mightily to alter that fact. But, like fetch, it's not going to happen.

ARNOLD, DAVE

The cocktail universe's own Mr. Science, who has applied advanced technology and science with the goal of making drinks better tasting and more consistent, at his own bars and in service of countless others. The techniques he helped popularize include the use of liquid nitrogen to chill glassware, employing rotary evaporators to distill and extract flavors, the application of forced carbonation, and acid adjustment for citrus juices. Arnold was a philosophy major at Yale and

DAVE ARNOLD

received an MFA in performance sculpture from Columbia. Ever a tinkerer in the field of food and drink, he was introduced to the food world by writer and editor Michael Batterberry and was eventually hired to head the first-of-its-kind Culinary Technology department at the French Culinary Institute, where he basically pursued whatever ideas intrigued him. He discussed his experiments on his blog *Cooking Issues* and compiled his findings in the book *Liquid Intelligence.* Arnold put his money where his mouth is in 2011 when he opened the high-concept cocktail bar Booker and Dax in collaboration with chef David Chang. During its five-year run, Booker was one of the few exemplars of molecular mixology in the United States. He tried again in 2018 with Existing Conditions, a collaboration with bar idea man Don Lee and entrepreneur Greg Boehm. Acclaimed for its easygoing way with innovation, the bar nonetheless closed in 2020, a victim of the Covid-19 pandemic. Arnold's longest-lasting ambition is the Museum of Food and Drink, which he first conceived of in 2005. It has produced several exhibitions but is still in search of a permanent home.

ARTESIAN

A posh London bar inside the Langham Hotel on Regent Street. For a time in the early 2010s, under the leadership of Czech-born Alex Kratena and Simone Caporale, an Italian, it was one of the world's hottest, most awarded cocktail bars. Well funded by liquor companies, the bar realized every drink at great expense, usually involving a custom vessel and some level of theatricality. The Forever Young, for example, was inspired by *The Picture of Dorian Gray* by Oscar Wilde. It was served in a silver cup hidden behind a small mirror and accessed through a straw that pierced the looking glass. Drink lists were planned far in advance. The effort paid off; soon the Artesian was topping every best-of list, usually competing with Dead Rabbit in New York for the title of world's best cocktail bar. Its brief blaze of glory ended in 2015 when Kratena and Caporale suddenly left. It has since drawn on a revolving door of head bartenders from a host of different countries but never quite won back its prominent role in the cocktail world.

ATLANTIC BAR AND GRILL

A splashy, multilevel, subterranean nightclub with multiple bars that opened in 1994 on Glasshouse Street in the Piccadilly section of London. It quickly upended the city's drinking scene. It was opened by nightlife and liquor entrepreneur Oliver Peyton, who found himself in possession of a rare license to stay open until 3 a.m. He hired Dick Bradsell, the city's leading bartender, to head up one of the bars, which eventually was called simply Dick's Bar. He thus afforded both Bradsell and craft cocktails a showcase from which to coax Londoners away from their pints. The atmosphere was scene-y, with lots of celebrities, the lavish décor often likened to that of a 1930s ocean liner, but the club moved the needle in terms of cocktails and English drinking life. Bradsell left after six months but was followed by others who would become leaders in the British cocktail scene themselves, including Angus Winchester, Alex Turner, Douglas Ankrah, Jamie Terrell, and Dré Masso.

AVIARY

A temple of high-end molecular mixology founded in Chicago in 2011 by Grant Achatz, one of the few celebrity chefs to take a serious interest in cocktails. There was no bar where customers could sit, but instead a walled-off laboratory of sorts where cocktails were prepared for guests, who waited at tables in a plush, curtained lounge. Drinks were treated like hybrids of science and art projects, engineered down to the last molecule. They arrived in every liquid, solid, and gaseous form imaginable, housed within the confines of custom-made vessels of various shapes and sizes. Example: In the Rock, an Old-Fashioned encased inside an ice orb that was shattered by the guest with a sort of slingshot attached to the glass. Achatz considered Aviary not a bar, but a drinking extension of his restaurant, Alinea. Head bartenders included, successively, Craig Schoettler, Charles Joly, and Micah Melton. An outlet in Manhattan, meant to be the first of many worldwide, was not successful and closed after two years.

AVIATION

A blend of gin, lemon juice, maraschino liqueur, and a touch of crème de violette, the Aviation first appeared in print in Hugo Ensslin's *Recipes for Mixed Drinks* in 1917. The drink became a cause célèbre in the aughts, when maraschino liqueur and crème de violette returned to circulation and cocktail bartenders embraced the cocktail as a forgotten classic. A decade later, however, its star had fallen, a victim of premature overpraise and the prevailing opinion that the drink tasted like dish soap.

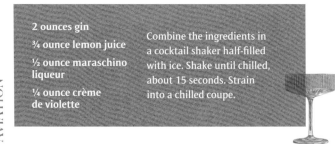

2 ounces gin
¾ ounce lemon juice
½ ounce maraschino liqueur
¼ ounce crème de violette

Combine the ingredients in a cocktail shaker half-filled with ice. Shake until chilled, about 15 seconds. Strain into a chilled coupe.

AVIATION

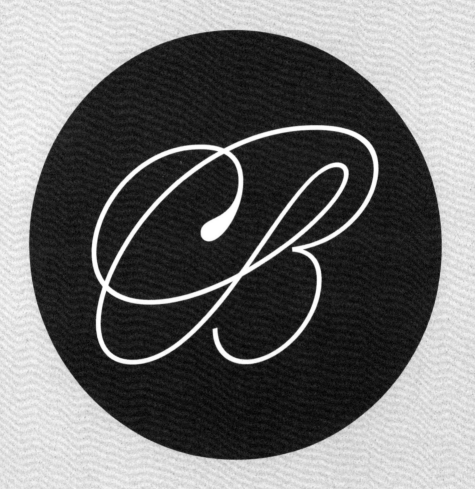

BAKER, CHARLES H., JR.

A high-living, globe-trotting food and drink enthusiast who managed to gig out his hedonistic hobbies into a living as a writer. Baker was born on Christmas Day in 1895, and every day thereafter was like Christmas for him. In 1932, he met and married mining heiress Pauline Elizabeth Paulsen while on a cruise ship for which he was publicist. When he wasn't at their house in Coconut Grove, Florida, he was traveling the world, living the good life, soaking up the food and drink of various cultures, discovering bars, collecting recipes, and writing about it all for magazines like *Esquire*, *Town & Country* (where he was food editor), and *Gourmet* (where he was drink editor). *Esquire* knew whom they had hired. "If you ever wondered whose oyster the world is," the magazine wrote in 1954, "meet Charles H. Baker, Jr." His

CHARLES BAKER, JR.

books, full of colorful tales, included *The Gentleman's Companion: Being an Exotic Drinking Book or Around the World with Jigger, Beaker and Flask* and *The South American Gentleman's Companion*. He was a friend of the likes of Hemingway and Faulkner, to whom he was known as "Bake." He died in 1987 and was largely forgotten until, in the early twenty-first century, the cocktail community took a renewed interest in him and his recipe collection. One bartender in particular, St. John Frizell, took up Baker as his preferred subject, writing about him often and promoting his drinks. Frizell even went so far as to trace some of Baker's steps. Margaria Fichtner, writing about Baker in the *Miami Herald* in 2002, described the man well: "Oh, he was grand, and rightly so—yachtsman, raconteur, amateur botanist, friend of the famous, famous himself in certain circles, a small-town Florida Cracker who knew (or smoothly could find) his way around the world." Baker's recipes are generally acknowledged to be frequently flawed and unbalanced, but gems have been extracted, including the now acknowledged classic Remember the Maine.

BAMBOO

An austere, elegant mix of sherry and dry vermouth with dashes of orange and Angostura bitters and a lemon twist garnish. Though some early recipes called for Italian vermouth (that is, sweet), dry vermouth became the accepted ingredient in this drink. It was created by American hotel manager Louis Eppinger at The Grand Hotel in Yokohama, Japan, in the 1890s. The Bamboo was being served in the United States by 1900. The drink made a comeback in the twenty-first century. Whatever the original Bamboo tasted like, the modern standard has become a drink pale in color, dry in character, with a touch of salinity and nuttiness from the sherry, and a pleasing, if subtle, complexity.

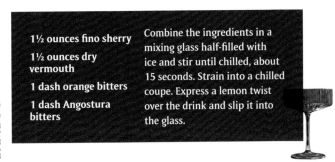

1½ ounces fino sherry

1½ ounces dry vermouth

1 dash orange bitters

1 dash Angostura bitters

Combine the ingredients in a mixing glass half-filled with ice and stir until chilled, about 15 seconds. Strain into a chilled coupe. Express a lemon twist over the drink and slip it into the glass.

BAMBOO

BAR AGRICOLE

A sprawling bar and restaurant opened in 2010 by Thad Vogler, a San Francisco bar director. The bar was a reflection of Vogler's exacting preferences, which hewed toward artisanal and heritage spirits of small scale and unimpeachable character, and classic cocktails workshopped down to the smallest detail. Both the back bar and cocktail list were tight, featuring only spirits Vogler approved of and could vouch for. Corporate liquor concerns held no sway at Bar Agricole—a rare stance among big-city bars at the time. There were few original cocktails on the menu—Vogler considered such drinks products of ego—yet the classics were often hard to recognize. The Old-Fashioned was made with cognac, because Vogler didn't particularly trust the provenance of American bourbon; and the Jack Rose was made with his beloved calvados. Campari was ash-canned in favor of a preferred red bitters out of Colorado. Ti' Punch, which may be the most pared down and spirit-true of cocktails, was an emblematic mainstay. Despite Vogler's hard-headed approach, Bar Agricole was typically cited as having the best cocktails in the city, and was nominated for many honors. The bar closed in 2020, as did all other Vogler ventures, felled by the Covid pandemic, but it reopened in a new form in August 2022.

BAR BASSO

A famous cocktail bar in Milan known for serving the Negroni Sbagliato, which was created by bartender Mirko Stocchetto and is made with Prosecco instead of gin. The bar was founded in 1947 by Giuseppe Basso as one of the first bars in Milan to focus on American-style cocktails. Stocchetto, a veteran of Harry's Bar in Venice, bought the bar in 1967, after which Basso's golden age truly began. The bar is frequented by members of the fashion industry. Beginning in the 2010s, Bar Basso's influence grew when bartenders all over the world began to serve the Negroni Sbagliato at their bars. Stocchetto died in 2016.

BARREL-AGED COCKTAILS

An enduring fad of the twenty-first century, kicked off in 2009 by Jeffrey Morgenthaler, a Portland, Oregon, bartender. Inspired by London bartender Tony Conigliaro's experiments with aging cocktails in glass vessels, Morgenthaler did the same, but he traded the glass jars for small oak barrels, which imparted their woody flavors to the spirit within and sped up the aging process. The result quickly became a national sensation after he served barrel-aged Negronis and the like at his bar, Clyde Common. Within a year, dozens of bars were offering barrel-aged cocktails of nearly every sort. The general impression is that the barrel-aging softened the edges of a drink and contributed to the blending of the various liquor components.

BARSPOON

A long spoon used to stir cocktails, typically made of metal and with a threaded stem, which allows the tool to move fluidly between one's fingers. It usually measures about eleven inches in length, but there are theatrical versions that stretch far longer. Some have a small muddler or fork at the other end, making them multitask tools. The bowl of the spoon is often used to measure liquids used in small amounts. Mainly a bar tool before Prohibition, barspoons became common household items after repeal, when home bartending was on the rise. They became less common, however, behind the bar, as many post-Prohibition bartenders switched to shaking all drinks, regardless of the cocktail's contents. With the cocktail revival of the twenty-first century, barspoons came back into wide use.

BARTENDER'S CHOICE

A gambit invented during the early days of the cocktail renaissance in New York, in which a customer left the choice of cocktail up to the bartender. The stratagem was hatched at Sasha Petraske's bar Milk & Honey, somewhat out of necessity, as the bar had no menu and every order began with a conversation between staff and patron. The interrogation usually went, "What kind of spirit would you like?" "Light or boozy?" "Up or on the rocks?" "Sweet or bitter?" and so on. The approach was advantageous on both sides: The customer got to test the acumen of the bartender, and the bartender had a guinea pig to whom they could serve something unusual or a favored drink. With the opening of Petraske's Little Branch, which *did* have a menu, Bartender's Choice was in print as a selection for the very first time. Thereafter, Bartender's Choice made the leap to other bars around the world and became an industry norm in craft cocktail bars. There is a downside to Bartender's Choice: Jaded bartenders tend to make the same choice again and again.

BARTENDER'S HANDSHAKE

Nickname for a spirit or cocktail preferred within, and proffered by, the insider-y coterie of cocktail bartenders. A liquid bond, mutually ingested. Often, it's something that's hard to take. Fernet-Branca is the classic example and was indeed the first handshake shared by in-the-know bartenders in the early years of the cocktail revival. Drinks that enjoyed handshake status in the past include the Aviation, Last Word, CIA, and Fifty-Fifty Martini.

BAUM, JOE

Arguably the most influential American restaurateur of the twentieth century, Baum is also a legitimate contender for the title of Father of the Cocktail Revival. The restaurateur's claim to the throne lies mainly in one hire: Dale DeGroff, a former actor whom he tapped to man the many bars at the Rainbow Room, the sky-high art deco restaurant he reopened in Manhattan in 1987. DeGroff executed Baum's vision of bringing back the classic cocktails of the pre-Prohibition era, working off a copy of Jerry Thomas's 1862 bar manual, which Baum ordered the barman to find and read. The Rainbow Room wasn't Baum's first foray into cocktails. He knew his drink history and mixed a little of it into all of the many restaurants he opened in postwar New York. There were Pisco Sours at La Fonda del Sol; tiki drinks at the Hawaiian Room. He had DeGroff train at his restaurant Aurora before bringing him into Rockefeller Center. The Rainbow Room made DeGroff the most famous bartender in the United States and the de facto leader of what would become the cocktail renaissance. Baum died in 1998.

BAX, MATTHEW

A Sydney-born artist turned bar owner who, as the owner of Der Raum and other bars, had an outsized impact on the Melbourne cocktail revival in its earliest days. As an accountant and would-be artist in Munich, Bax passed the time at places like Schumann's Cocktail Bar. Inspired, he returned to Melbourne and opened Der Raum in the city's Richmond neighborhood. Quickly overwhelmed by the realities of running a bar, Bax went all-out experimental, toying with molecular mixology, using pill presses and liquid nitrogen to complete drinks, and—following an art exhibit in the bar—leaving the back bar's bottles suspended from the ceiling by bungee cords. It was a cocktail bar as conceived by a conceptual artist. As Der Raum became known and praised, Bax attempted to open a second location in Munich. That quickly imploded, and shortly after, in 2012, the original Der Raum closed. Bax soldiered on, however, opening the rum bar Bar Economico in the former Der Raum space and, in 2011, the tiny, exquisitely designed Italian apertivo bar Bar Americano. Bax continues to work as an artist.

BEATTIE, SCOTT

The San Francisco cocktail revival's first star, Beattie was an evangelist of the West Coast garden-to-glass style. He established his name at Cyrus, a Napa Valley restaurant opened by Nick Peyton and Douglas Keane in 2005. Mirroring the practices of the kitchen, Beattie became as much a forager as a bartender, creating verdant culinary cocktails and sourcing their citrus, other fruit, and herbs from local farmers, gardens, and orchards. Picturesque as well as fresh, Beattie's rococo cocktails featured wheels of citrus pressed against the glass and crowns of luscious garnish, often pushing spirits into the role of blank canvas, as opposed to flavor base. One writer described Beattie's drinks—which could be composed of up to a dozen ingredients, many of them fresh—as Chartreuse in a glass. The press soon caught on to his eye-catching style, and in 2008 Beattie became one of the first craft cocktail bartenders to publish a book, *Artisanal Cocktails.* Beattie left Cyrus and went on to work and consult at a variety of restaurants. Given the difficulty of Beattie's approach to drink building, his style was not adopted by many, but what followers he had were devoted.

BELLINI

A simple cocktail, named after the artist of the same name. Composed of champagne or Prosecco and white peach puree, it is credited to Giuseppe Cipriani and his famous Venice establishment Harry's Bar. It was invented sometime in the 1940s, and reports of the Bellini's popularity began to hit the press in the 1950s. Accounts of celebrities from Tennessee Williams to Andy Warhol downing the Bellini lent the cocktail a sort of glamour. To this day it remains a must-order at the posh boîte. Elsewhere, it reigns as a brunch fallback, though never enough to knock the Mimosa or Bloody Mary off their thrones.

BEMELMANS BAR

A classic, ur–New York cocktail den, nestled inside the confines of the Carlyle Hotel, the Upper East Side haven of wealth, fame, and influence. The walls of the amber-hued cove were designed by illustrator Ludwig Bemelmans, who gave the bar its name. The bar's peaceful slumber as a quiet-drinking sanctuary was jostled into relevancy in the early aughts when Dale DeGroff was hired to spruce up the drinks program. He was later succeeded by protégé Audrey Saunders, who coaxed the union bartenders into executing her craft cocktail menu, which included her own Old Cuban. For half a century, until 2012, Tommy Rowles bartended here, becoming a local legend in the process. With the Plaza's beautiful Oak Room seemingly closed for good and the Algonquin modernized into meaninglessness, Bemelmans is the last of the grand old New York hotel bars, along with the King Cole Bar in the St. Regis Hotel.

BÉNÉDICTINE

A benchmark herbal liqueur made in France, but of international reputation and utility. It's one of the most myth-mongering spirits of all time, as the company has long promoted the idea that the liquor's formula is many centuries old and derived from a sixteenth-century recipe by Benedictine monks. In truth, it was brought into commercial life in 1863 by Alexandre Le Grand and has never been made by monks, though many still believe it is. The formula—a secret, as is the norm with such liqueurs—involves twenty-seven botanicals. Bénédictine found a warm welcome in cocktails from the beginning and is an important element in several famous drinks, including Widow's Kiss, Bobby Burns, Chrysanthemum, Creole, Vieux Carré, De La Louisiane, and Singapore Sling, and, of course, the B&B, a mix of Bénédictine and brandy that the company starting bottling in 1938.

BENTON'S OLD-FASHIONED

The most popular drink at New York's PDT, and the most famous example of the fat-washing technique in the cocktail canon. Inventor Don Lee combined melted fat from Benton's bacon—a renowned meat out of Tennessee—with Four Roses

Bourbon, resulting in an impressively smoky, savory spirit. This he sweetened with maple syrup and accented with Angostura bitters. The drink has consistently been the top seller at PDT since it debuted on the menu in 2007 and inspired hundreds of other fat-washed cocktails across the globe.

2 ounces Benton's Bacon Fat-washed Four Roses Bourbon*

¼ ounce maple syrup

2 dashes Angostura bitters

Combine the ingredients in a rocks glass filled with one large cube of ice. Stir until chilled, about 15 seconds. Garnish with an orange twist.

*BENTON'S BACON FAT-WASHED FOUR ROSES BOURBON

1½ ounces (by volume) Benton's bacon fat

750 ml Four Roses Bourbon

To make the fat-washed bourbon, warm the bacon fat in a small saucepan over low heat, stirring until it is melted, about 5 minutes. Combine the melted fat with the bourbon in a large freezer-safe container and stir. Cover and let sit at room temperature for 4 hours, then place the container in the freezer for 2 hours. Remove the solid fat from the surface of the bourbon and discard. Strain the bourbon through a terry cloth towel or a double layer of cheesecloth into a bottle and store in the refrigerator for up to 2 months.

BENTON'S OLD-FASHIONED

BERG, MONICA

A Norwegian bartender who became a force in London bartending in the 2010s. Berg entered the service industry at an early age, working at Aqua Vitae in Oslo. In 2013, she moved to London and served as head bartender at Pollen Street Social in London and Himkok in Oslo. In 2016, alongside partner Alex Kratena (Artesian), Berg cofounded P(our), a nonprofit symposium focused on bartending culture based in Paris. In 2019 she and Kratena opened the London bar Tayēr + Elementary, which went on to receive many accolades.

BERMEJO, JULIO

The son of a San Francisco restaurant owner, he took control of the bar at Tommy's Mexican Restaurant and, beginning in the late 1980s, transformed it into a tequila mecca. In addition to stocking dozens of brands of tequila, he educated his clientele through tequila tasting clubs and trips to Mexico. After attracting attention within the bar industry, Bermejo converted many a bartender, both in the United States and the United Kingdom and beyond, to the virtues of tequila as a spirit equal in quality to any other. Perhaps his most lasting achievement was the creation of Tommy's radical house Margarita. Composed solely of 100 percent agave tequila, agave syrup, and fresh lime juice, it came to be known worldwide as the Tommy's Margarita.

BERRY, JEFF

The man who rescued tiki and tropical bar culture in the United States in the twenty-first century, and the only modern cocktail historian who took his research and knowledge and converted it into a practical, brick-and-mortar reality, opening the acclaimed bar Latitude 29 in New Orleans in 2014. Without Jeff Berry and his dogged diligence in tracking down former bartenders from Trader Vic's and Don the Beachcomber and prying from them the drink recipes secreted in their brains, the current tiki revival simply never would have happened. Over the last few decades, he has steadily produced the most comprehensive modern library of tiki scholarship there is. Beginning in 1998 with a volume called *Beachbum Berry's Grog Log*—published by Slave Labor Graphics and available mainly in comic book stores—his works bear titles like *Intoxica!* and *Sippin' Safari*. The canon culminated in 2013 with the coffee table–worthy

JEFF BERRY

Potions of the Caribbean. Born to New Yorkers and raised in Southern California, Berry became besotted by Polynesian restaurant culture at an early age. As an adult working in the film industry, he spent his free time hanging out in California's remaining tiki bars, talking to old veteran bartenders who had worked at Trader Vic's and Don the Beachcomber, trying to suss out the secrets of the drinks they served. Recipe by recipe, he gathered his knowledge, transforming himself into the tiki-culture expert nobody in the bar world knew they needed. The American cocktail revivalists were immune to tiki's charms in the aughts, so Berry—like a Dexter Gordon for the cocktail world—took his talents to Europe, where tropical drinks weren't shunned, lecturing on the subject in Ireland, Italy, and Germany.

But by 2008 or so, attitudes in New York and elsewhere had changed, and bartenders were willing to listen to Berry's gospel that tiki drinks were good drinks—if made correctly. His archeological achievements are many. He has published dozens of lost or unknown cocktail recipes. He discovered the original formula for the Zombie, a famous drink whose recipe had been muddled and confused over the years. He uncovered drinks that have since become tiki staples, including Three Dots and a Dash and the Jungle Bird. His literature has made it possible for acclaimed tiki bars like Smuggler's Cove in San Francisco and Three Dots in Chicago to open and flourish. His opening of Latitude 29 was the cocktail-world equivalent of legendary acting teacher Lee Strasberg taking on the role of Hyman Roth in *The Godfather Part II.* It was the backstage guru stepping up and showing the youngsters how it's done. After opening the bar with his wife, Annene Kaye, Berry continued on the entrepreneurial track, collaborating with bar and barware mogul Greg Boehm on both custom tiki barware and publications, and a franchise of tiki-themed Christmas pop-up bars called Sippin' Santa. Typically dressed in a wide straw hat and tropical shirt, he acquired the professional handle "Beachbum" Berry, a sobriquet of his own choosing, initially meant as a joke, but one that stuck. The move has ample historical precedence: In the mid-twentieth century, nobody knew who Ernest Raymond Beaumont Gantt and Victor Jules Bergeron Jr. were. But they sure knew Don the Beachcomber and Trader Vic, the identities taken on by those two titanic entrepreneurs in all things faux tropical.

BITTERS (DASHING)

A wide genre of medicinal brews, made up of various herbs, spices, and botanicals, usually steeped in alcohol. Originally devised to aid stomach maladies, they are today used exclusively to accent cocktails. Broadly speaking, bitters are the salt and pepper of cocktails, tying the flavors of a drink together. The first bitters emerged in the 1700s. They were often administered by dashing a few drops into alcohol. Eventually, that practice got flipped on its head, as health concerns were forgotten, and bitters were used to balance and improve a cocktail's taste. The earliest definition of the cocktail—spirits, sugar, water, and bitters—is dependent on the inclusion of the product. Early prominent brands that found a place in the bar include Boker's, Abbott's, and Stoughton's. Over time, many brands disappeared, most put out of business by Prohibition.

Surviving and dominating the scene for a century has been Angostura bitters, created by German doctor Johann Siegert in the 1820s and produced in Trinidad. Angostura is the Heinz ketchup of bitters, generally mixing well with most anything, and critical to some of the most famous cocktails in the canon, including the Old-Fashioned and Manhattan. Second in prominence, and a distant second at that, is Peychaud's bitters, a New Orleans product invented by pharmacist Antoine Peychaud in the 1830s, and an essential ingredient in the Sazerac. Those two brands—and the lonely regional Fee Brothers company, which quietly made bitters year in and year out in Rochester, New York—were the whole ball game until the twenty-first century, when bartenders bent on recreating old cocktails demanded more variety.

Critically missing from the arsenal were orange bitters, an ingredient in early Martinis and many other cocktails. Writer Gary Regan solved that issue when he came up with Regan's Orange Bitters No. 6 in 2005. After that came the deluge. Bitters companies sprang up overnight around the world, producing bitters of every flavor and conception under the sun, most with little immediate utility in the real world. Every fruit flavor was represented, including lemon, peach, rhubarb, grapefruit, and plum. With the rise in popularity of agave spirits, several brands of mole bitters proved popular and useful. And the various types of celery bitters found their place in Bloody Marys. Occasionally, bitters will play more than a dashing role in cocktails, applied by the ounce in such drinks at the Gunship Fizz (2 ounces of Peychaud's) and Trinidad Sour (1½ ounces of Angostura). However, the high cost of such cocktails—bitters ain't cheap—precludes the spread of such stunt mixology.

BITTERS (DIGESTIF)

A wide range of potable liqueurs, primarily from Italy, that offer a bittersweet flavor profile and are drunk by themselves, over ice, with soda water or other mixers, and in cocktails. The term is roughly interchangeable with amaro, although in terms of mixology, it's most commonly applied to the subset often referred to as "red bitters," because category members are usually vividly red. Prominent representatives include Campari, Aperol, Cappelletti, and examples created by the Italian distillers Carpano, Galliano, Luxardo, Nardini, Contratto, and Bordiga. In recent years, other countries, notably the United States, have gotten into the red bitters game. Most every red bitter has found its way—or is desperately trying to find its way—into the Negroni market.

BLACK MANHATTAN

A simple Manhattan variation created by San Francisco bartender Todd Smith in 2005. The Italian amaro Averna takes the place of the typical sweet vermouth, and the bitters is split between Angostura and orange. It was created at the restaurant Cortez but received a boost in profile when Smith commanded the drinks program at the cocktail speakeasy Bourbon & Branch. By the late 2010s, it was an established modern classic.

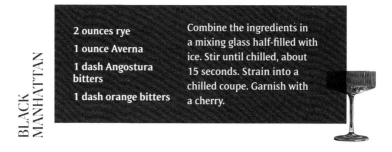

BLACK MANHATTAN

2 ounces rye

1 ounce Averna

1 dash Angostura bitters

1 dash orange bitters

Combine the ingredients in a mixing glass half-filled with ice. Stir until chilled, about 15 seconds. Strain into a chilled coupe. Garnish with a cherry.

BLACK PEARL

One of the most prominent and enduring of the modern-era Melbourne cocktail bars, Black Pearl was founded in 2002 by Tash Conte. Situated in the Fitzroy neighborhood, the two-story bar effectively balanced being both a local favorite and a bar of international reputation that raked in accolades. It also developed a reputation for fostering bartending talent. Its best-known drink is the Death Flip, an unlikely mélange of intimidating ingredients, including a whole egg, Jägermeister, Chartreuse, and tequila.

BLOOD AND SAND

An equal-parts mixture of scotch, sweet vermouth, Cherry Heering, and orange juice. The drink is named after the 1922 Rudolph Valentino film of the same name and first appeared in the *Savoy Cocktail Book* in 1930. It is a rare cocktail that calls for scotch as its base spirit, as well as one in which Cherry Heering plays a major role. In recent years, as mixologists have made it their business to drag old drinks out of the shadows, the Blood and Sand has engendered a fair share of enduring controversy, with some critics declaring it utterly unpalatable while others stand by it as a deserving classic. Seemingly impervious to argument, the drink has persevered—never fully embraced, yet never wholly abandoned. A rum drink by the same name has been a house specialty at The Dresden Room in Hollywood for decades.

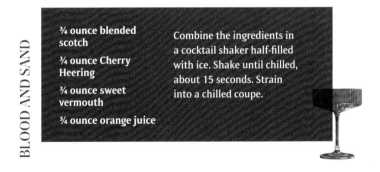

BLOOD AND SAND

¾ ounce blended scotch

¾ ounce Cherry Heering

¾ ounce sweet vermouth

¾ ounce orange juice

Combine the ingredients in a cocktail shaker half-filled with ice. Shake until chilled, about 15 seconds. Strain into a chilled coupe.

BLOODY MARY

The ultimate day-drinking cocktail, a brunch-time behemoth, and the drink that brought vodka to the masses and gave tomato juice a reason to be behind the bar. Origin stories abound, but the generally accepted history is that French bartender Fernand Petiot created the prototype of tomato juice and vodka while working at Harry's New York Bar in Paris, and brought it with him when he came to New York in 1934 to work at the King Cole Bar in the St. Regis Hotel, refining it to contain

BLOODY MARY

salt, black pepper, cayenne pepper, Worcestershire sauce, and lemon juice—every ingredient that we now associate with the drink. It was called the Red Snapper at the St. Regis and still is today. But the world came to know it as the Bloody Mary, though how that name came about is a disputed matter. Other ingredients commonly found in the cocktail include hot sauce and celery salt. A celery stalk is a common garnish, but the Bloody Mary is perhaps the most heavily garnished cocktail in history. Even modest versions will sport cherry tomatoes, cheese cubes, sausage, and pickled peppers. In recent years, the sky has been the limit in terms of garnishes, with some drinks boasting a virtual cornucopia of foodstuffs atop the actual drink. Wisconsin, where the drink is typically served with an accompanying snit of beer, is particularly gung-ho in this respect. At places like Sobelman's in Milwaukee, versions are topped with hamburgers and whole roasted chickens, eliminating the need for a food order. Common variations include the Bloody Maria (made with tequila), the nonalcoholic Virgin Mary, and the Caesar, a rendition using the clam-tomato juice Clamato, which constitutes the national drink of Canada.

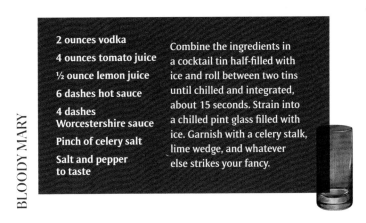

BLOODY MARY

2 ounces vodka
4 ounces tomato juice
½ ounce lemon juice
6 dashes hot sauce
4 dashes Worcestershire sauce
Pinch of celery salt
Salt and pepper to taste

Combine the ingredients in a cocktail tin half-filled with ice and roll between two tins until chilled and integrated, about 15 seconds. Strain into a chilled pint glass filled with ice. Garnish with a celery stalk, lime wedge, and whatever else strikes your fancy.

BLUE BLAZER

A theatrical nineteenth-century toddy in which a mixture of whiskey, hot water, and sugar is warmed by being lit on fire and passed back and forth in dramatic fashion between two tankards. The drink is closely associated with Jerry Thomas, who included it in his 1862 bartender's guide.

BOADAS COCKTAILS

One of the most influential, long-lasting, and beloved cocktail bars in the world, Bar Boadas, located just steps off Barcelona's famous La Rambla, was founded in 1933 by Miguel Boadas, who first learned his trade at El Floridita in Havana. Small, triangular in shape, and art deco in design, the bar is famous for its habit of "throwing" cocktails; that is, tossing them theatrically from one tin to the next, a style of mixing you'll see only in Cuba, Spain, and a few other isolated places in the United States and Europe. The bartenders are dressed in tuxedos. Miguel, who died in 1967, was succeeded by his daughter Maria, who passed in 2017. After that, it was run by longtime bartender Jerónimo Vaquero. In 2022, the bar was bought by Italian-born bartender Simone Caporale, who made his name at

BOADAS COCKTAILS

London's Artesian bar. The Boadas family opened a second, even-smaller bar around the corner in 1974, the rum-themed Caribbean Club. It is currently run by Boadas alumni Juanjo González.

BOBBY BURNS

A cocktail composed of scotch, sweet vermouth, and Bénédictine. It is named after the Scottish poet Robert Burns. Early recipes varied, but by the late 1910s the defining element in this Rob Roy variation—Bénédictine—had appeared, and that has remained the formula ever since. Like the Mint Julep, the Bobby Burns gets major play only once a year, on Burns Night, January 25, the poet's birthday.

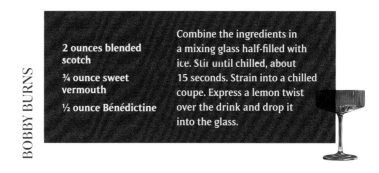

2 ounces blended scotch

¾ ounce sweet vermouth

½ ounce Bénédictine

Combine the ingredients in a mixing glass half-filled with ice. Stir until chilled, about 15 seconds. Strain into a chilled coupe. Express a lemon twist over the drink and drop it into the glass.

LA BODEGUITA DEL MEDIO

A long-standing restaurant and bar in Havana, Cuba, with an undying reputation as a Hemingway haunt and as the novelist's preferred purveyor of Mojitos. That Hemingway ever went there or even liked Mojitos has been largely debunked by writer Philip Greene, who is both a cocktail and Hemingway authority. That La Bodeguita del Medio makes oceans of Mojitos, most of them sucked down by busloads of tourists, cannot be denied. After the preeminent El Floridita, it is probably the most famous and visited bar in Havana. Founded in 1942, it was originally called La Casa Martinez, after the founding family. The name later changed to La Bodeguita del Medio, meaning "the small store in the middle," after its location on the street, and it began serving meals and Mojitos. Over the years, it was a favorite hangout of various writers, artists, and other celebrities. It's virtually impossible to have anything resembling a normal bar experience there anymore. It is always crowded, the walls are covered with graffiti, there is usually live music playing, and nobody drinks anything but Mojitos, which the bartenders make twenty or thirty at a time.

BOILERMAKER

The descriptive term for the long-standing composite quaff of a shot and a beer. The format was reembraced by mixologists in the 2010s, resulting in a wide variety of fanciful and high-concept pairings, such as aquavit and Belgian ale or tequila and Tecate. Many bars now have entire boilermaker menus. There is considerable debate on how to drink the simple serve. Some down the shot and then move to the beer; others prefer going back and forth between the two; and still others drop the shot in the beer.

LA BODEGUITA DEL MEDIO

BOOKER AND DAX

A bar that, for a short time, provided the cocktail world's resident lab director and mysterious barroom Thomas Edison, Dave Arnold, with a platform from which to implement the various scientific drink techniques he had developed in his time at the French Culinary Institute. Cocktails were chilled using liquid nitrogen, heated up with a long device called a red-hot poker, pre-mixed-and-diluted, carbonated, clarified by a centrifuge, and distilled down to their essence via a rotary evaporator. Arnold's desire was not to convert mixology into science, but to use science to produce better cocktails. Booker and Dax—named after Arnold's two sons, and opened in collaboration with chef David Chang at the back of Chang's restaurant, Momofuku Ssäm Bar—opened in 2012 and managed to attract a devoted clientele through a combination of excellent drinks, lack of pretension, and just the right amount of showmanship. Chang's renovation of Ssäm Bar ended Booker's short reign in 2016.

BOOMERANG

A sealed drink ferried by clandestine courier from one bar's bartender to another bar's bartender as a show of friendship or solidarity. What goes around comes around.

BOOTHBY, WILLIAM

The dean of pre-Prohibition San Francisco bartenders. Boothby was born in San Francisco in 1862. He tried his hand at many things—acting, dancing, insurance, tailoring, politics—before settling in 1884 into the profession that made him "Cocktail Bill," the most celebrated San Francisco bartender of his day. He worked at many bars in and around San Francisco, most famously at the Pied Piper Bar in the Palace Hotel, where he reportedly invented his signature cocktail, the Boothby, a Manhattan topped with champagne. He is remembered today chiefly because in 1891 he published a cocktail manual titled *The World's Drinks and How to Mix Them.* The book enjoyed several editions after that, including ones in 1900 and 1908. Prohibition ended Boothby's career, forcing him to serve soft drinks. He retired in 1925 and died five years later.

BOOTHBY COCKTAIL

2 ounces rye or bourbon

1 ounce sweet vermouth

2 dashes Angostura bitters

1 ounce chilled champagne

Combine all the ingredients but the champagne in a mixing glass half-filled with ice. Stir until chilled, about 15 seconds. Strain into a chilled coupe. Top with the champagne. Garnish with a cherry.

BOULEVARDIER

An equal-parts mixture of bourbon, sweet vermouth, and Campari invented by Erskine Gwynne, an expatriate writer, socialite, and Vanderbilt family relation who founded a literary magazine called the *Boulevardier* in 1927; and, as such, one of the few Vanderbilt contributions to the common good. The recipe first appeared that same year as a footnote in Harry MacElhone's cocktail book *Cocktails and Barflies* (which contained an advertisement for the magazine). The drink was largely forgotten until the twenty-first century, when it rode back into visibility on the coattails of the Negroni revival. It found a particular advocate in writer-bartender Toby Cecchini, who serves perhaps the most famous version of the drink at his Brooklyn bar, Long Island Bar. Beginning in the 2010s, many cocktail bartenders started making the drink with rye.

BOULEVARDIER

1 ounce bourbon

1 ounce sweet vermouth

1 ounce Campari

Combine the ingredients in a rocks glass filled with one large ice cube. Stir until chilled, about 15 seconds. Express an orange twist over the drink and slip it into the glass.

BOURBON

A corn-based, barrel-aged American whiskey that is all but the United States' official spirit, so closely is it associated with the nation's history, so dearly is it loved, and so widely is it consumed, both on its own and in cocktails. While it can legally be distilled anywhere in the nation, its ancestral home is Kentucky. Indeed, 95 percent of the bourbon distilled comes from that state, though neighboring Indiana kicks in its share in its own industrial way, dispensing good stuff, but without the charm and romance that the spirit is typically wrapped up in. Laws passed in 1964—among the most stringent in spirits—require that it be distilled from at least 51 percent corn, aged in charred new white oak barrels, and bottled at a minimum of 80 proof. The rest of the mash bill is made of rye, wheat, or malted barley, depending on the distiller's recipe. Bourbons with a significant rye content are referred to as "high-rye" and are generally more spicy in flavor. Bourbons with a high wheat content are softer and called "wheated." Brands that specialize in the latter style are fewer in number but include some of the biggest names in the business, such as Maker's Mark and Pappy Van Winkle. Straight bourbon must be aged at least two years.

The history and origins of bourbon are a jumble of myths and theories that stretch back to the late eighteenth century. Many of the stories are tied up with a collection of names, many of whose deeds and accomplishments in the advancement of American whiskey-making are clouded by the perpetual self-interested marketing efforts of various bourbon brands who have tied their fortunes to a famous name. (A lot of bourbon brands are named after historical figures.) Also unknown is how bourbon got its distinctive name. Bourbon was used in cocktails beginning in the mid-1800s, running neck and neck with rye as the base of mainstay drinks like the Old-Fashioned, Manhattan, and Whiskey Sour. Bourbon is perhaps most famous as the foundation of the Mint Julep, a drink that began as an all-spirits-welcome affair but settled into a bourbon mode by the 1930s.

The bourbon boom of the twenty-first century, which has seen demand, selection, and prices rise, owes a great deal to the cocktail renaissance. The spirit had been in the dumps for decades, ignored and unappreciated by the vodka-drinking public of the late twentieth century. As bartenders brought old whiskey drinks back to the forefront, they also invented all sorts of new vehicles for bourbon, such as the Gold Rush, Paper Plane, Benton's Old-Fashioned, Whiskey Smash, Kentucky Buck, and Revolver. Soon enough, the cheap, plentiful, old, and good stuff bartenders were using to make their drinks had become expensive, scarce, less old, and not as good. Bars dedicated to bourbon began to open in cities besides Louisville. In the process, bourbon left its old status as a regional Southern beverage behind for good and ever. Bourbon belongs to the world now.

BOURBON AND BRANCH

A San Francisco speakeasy pointedly patterned after Milk & Honey in New York. It wasn't the first important cocktail bar in the city, but it blew the Bay Area cocktail scene wide open when it arrived in 2005. For better or worse, the bar introduced to the city various earmarks that became synonymous with the cocktail revival, including reservations, neo-Prohibition chic, mixologist imperiousness, lengthy cocktail menus, and, of course, cocktails of exacting excellence. With a cocktail program led by Todd Smith, the bar initially employed nearly all of the best cocktail bartenders in the city. It did not invent but helped popularize such cocktails as the Revolver and Black Manhattan. Eventually, it expanded to accommodate demand, opening several adjoining spaces.

BRAMBLE

A gin sour made with lemon juice and simple syrup, served over crushed ice, and topped with crème de mure, which is floated picturesquely on the surface of the completed drink. It was invented in the early 1990s at the private London bar Fred's Club by Dick Bradsell, who at that point had not yet achieved the title of godfather of the British cocktail revival. The drink quickly achieved widespread popularity.

BRAMBLE

2 ounces gin
¾ ounce lemon juice
¾ ounce simple syrup
½ ounce crème de mure

Combine the first three ingredients in a cocktail shaker half-filled with ice and shake until chilled, about 15 seconds. Strain into a rocks glass filled with crushed ice. Float the crème de mure on the surface of the drink. Garnish with a blackberry and a lemon wedge.

BRANDY CRUSTA

BRANDY CRUSTA

One of the most elaborate classic cocktails in the canon, involving cognac, bitters, sugar, and curaçao, all held by a goblet with a thickly sugared rim, the inside of which is lined by a long strip of lemon peel that encircles the bowl. The drink was invented by New Orleans bartender Joseph Santini, who owned a bar called Jewel of the South. The drink gained considerable fame outside of New Orleans, thanks to being included in Jerry Thomas's 1862 cocktail manual. Because of the ornate, pain-in-the-neck preparation, the Brandy Crusta never caught on. Nonetheless, cocktail experts believe that the Crusta opened the door for many of the sours to come, not least the Sidecar. In 2018, Chris Hannah opened a new bar called Jewel of the South in New Orleans, showcasing the Brandy Crusta.

BRANDY CRUSTA

2 ounces cognac

½ ounce lemon juice

½ ounce curaçao

¼ ounce maraschino liqueur

2 dashes Angostura bitters

Wet the rim of a small wine glass with lemon juice, then dip the rim into sugar. Cut a long, continuous peel from a lemon and position it in a spiraling pattern inside the prepared glass. Combine the ingredients in a cocktail shaker half-filled with ice and shake until chilled, about 15 seconds. Strain into the glass.

BRANDY OLD-FASHIONED

The preferred form of the Old-Fashioned in the state of Wisconsin, where it is prepared using domestic California brandy, muddled cherry and orange slice, and topped with a spurt of either a citrus soda like Sprite (in which it is termed "sweet"), a grapefruit soda like Squirt ("sour"), or a mixture of Sprite and soda water ("press"). Garnishes range from additional cherry and orange to olives, pickled mushrooms, and pickled Brussels sprouts. In recent years, however, the traditional whiskey Old-Fashioned has crept up in popularity in Wisconsin.

BRANDY OLD-FASHIONED

2 ounces domestic brandy

1 barspoon simple syrup

2 dashes Angostura bitters

Orange slice

Cherry

Sprite or Squirt soda

Combine the simple syrup, bitters, and orange slice and a cherry at the bottom of a rocks glass. Muddle gently. Add brandy and stir. Add several ice cubes and stir until chilled, about 10 seconds. Top with a splash of either Sprite ("sweet"), Squirt ("sour"), or a combination of Sprite and soda water ("press"). Garnish with another orange slice and cherry or, instead, an olive or pickled mushroom or pickled Brussels sprout.

BREAKFAST MARTINI

The signature cocktail of Salvatore Calabrese, the Italian-born bartender who became one of the most prominent bartenders in London in the years leading up to the cocktail revival in that city. A mixture of gin, lemon juice, curaçao, and marmalade, it was one of the more sophisticated entries in the ongoing 'tini craze of the 1990s, and an early cocktail to employ jam as an ingredient—a trick that became commonplace by the mid-aughts. The Breakfast Martini made its debut at the Library Bar in the Lanesborough, a hotel in London's posh Belgravia neighborhood. Calabrese brought the drink to all his subsequent bar posts in London.

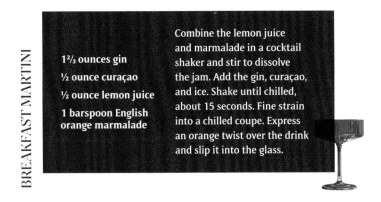

BREAKFAST MARTINI

1²/₃ ounces gin
½ ounce curaçao
½ ounce lemon juice
1 barspoon English orange marmalade

Combine the lemon juice and marmalade in a cocktail shaker and stir to dissolve the jam. Add the gin, curaçao, and ice. Shake until chilled, about 15 seconds. Fine strain into a chilled coupe. Express an orange twist over the drink and slip it into the glass.

BRONX

A mixture of gin, dry and sweet vermouths, and orange juice that became a sensation in the first two decades of the twentieth century, but, following repeal, never scaled those heights again. There are multiple origin stories, the best-known coming from Albert Stevens Crockett, historian of the Waldorf-Astoria Hotel, who said it was created by bartender Johnnie Solan. The drink surely had as good a press agent as any in cocktail history, such was its notoriety. In 1911, a New York newspaper wrote, "In this city, the Bronx cocktail has worked its way insidiously into the barroom, the café and the steam radiator sideboard." It was still famous enough to rate a mention from bibulous detective Nick Charles in the 1934 film *The Thin Man*. Its popularity plummeted in the following decades, and the cocktail renaissance lifted not a finger to save it. It is held in near universal disdain by modern bartenders, who regard it as weak and flabby and believe there is no method within their talents to make the drink palatable. The memory of it is clung to mainly by those who wish for every New York borough to possess a legitimate cocktail of its own.

BROTHER CLEVE

The cocktail godfather of Boston. Born Robert Toomey, Brother Cleve grew up in a cocktail-drinking family (Mom, daiquiri; Dad, Rob Roy; Grandma, Manhattan) in Medford, Massachusetts, a half-dozen miles northwest of Boston. His unusual nickname was taken partly from his involvement with the Church of the

BROTHER CLEVE

SubGenius, a parody religion founded in Dallas in the 1970s, and partly from an on-air personality he adopted as a radio host in Boston. In the 1980s, he began crossing the nation as a keyboardist with various bands, most notably Combustible Edison and the Del Fuegos. He ordered cocktails at every diner, restaurant, bar, and club, and over the years, drink by drink, he became an expert. By the mid-1990s, his cocktail acumen was on par with his musical bona fides. A *Boston Globe* article published in 1999 called him "the only D.J. in town who can mix music and a martini simultaneously." In 1998, he was drafted to help open the B-Side Lounge in Cambridge, which would usher in the city's cocktail revival. He has proven a mentor for many of the important bartenders to come up during the cocktail revival in Boston, including Jackson Cannon and Misty Kalkofen. He continued to keep one foot in music, the other in drink, DJing regularly, and in 2022 cofounding a Manhattan bar called Lullaby. He died suddenly in September 2022.

BROWN DERBY

A bourbon sour made with grapefruit juice and honey, invented in Los Angeles in the 1930s. A weird example of a cocktail named after one restaurant that was purportedly created at a *different* restaurant, the Vendome Club. The Brown Derby restaurant did not return the favor.

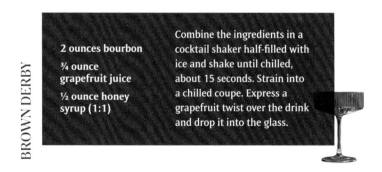

BROWN DERBY

2 ounces bourbon

¾ ounce grapefruit juice

½ ounce honey syrup (1:1)

Combine the ingredients in a cocktail shaker half-filled with ice and shake until chilled, about 15 seconds. Strain into a chilled coupe. Express a grapefruit twist over the drink and drop it into the glass.

BROWN, DEREK

The leading figure in the Washington, DC, cocktail world, Brown opened The Columbia Room, a ten-seat drinking enclave hidden inside the more populist The Passenger, and the city's first foray into haute mixology. Opened in

2010, the bar moved to more lavish digs in 2016 and closed in 2022. Brown also opened early examples of bars dedicated to whiskey and sherry—Southern Efficiency and Mockingbird Hill, respectively—though both were short-lived. More recently, he has become an advocate for "mindful drinking" and non-alcoholic drinks.

BRYANT'S COCKTAIL LOUNGE

The most lasting Milwaukee cocktail presence in a city better known for beer consumption. It is both ardently traditionalist—in its mid-twentieth-century décor, covered windows, and dim lighting—and idiosyncratic in its capacious catalogue of custom drinks and lack of a menu. Opened by bartender Bryant

BRYANT'S COCKTAIL LOUNGE

Sharp in 1936, it was imbued with new relevance when, in 2008, it was taken over by John Dye, a Montana native with a passion for the past. Dye has since assumed control over two additional Milwaukee institutions, the jazz club Jazz Estate and onetime Bryant's rival At Random, which specialized in ice cream drinks.

BUENA VISTA, THE

A long-standing café that has been the spiritual home of the Irish Coffee since 1952, when San Francisco columnist Stanton Delaplane introduced the drink (born at Ireland's Shannon Airport) to the American public. Originally a boardinghouse, the building's ground floor was converted into a saloon in 1916. Perennially popular with both locals and tourists, each day the Buena Vista sells as many as two thousand Irish Coffees and goes through a hundred bottles of Irish whiskey.

BULLDOG

A crude but popular concoction, also called a Mexican Bulldog, in which a bottle of beer (typically Corona) is upended and buried in a frozen Margarita. As the cocktail is sipped through a straw, more beer slowly trickles in. In the mid-2010s, cocktail bartenders took inspiration from the model, combining a variety of mini-bottles of various liquors with assorted host drinks, at bars such as Genuine Liquorette and Mother of Pearl, both in New York, and the Broken Shaker in Miami.

BULLOCK, TOM

The first Black American bartender to publish a cocktail book, *The Ideal Bartender,* in 1917. Born in Louisville, Bullock (1872–1964) worked at the city's Pendennis Club. He later tended bar for many years at the St. Louis Country Club. Bullock was celebrated anew when his book was reprinted in 2015 by Cocktail Kingdom, a Manhattan publisher that specializes in resuscitating old drinks manuals. The book's introduction was written by George Herbert Walker, a club member and both the grandfather and great-grandfather of a

TOM BULLOCK

chief executive. His book is additionally valuable as a historical document, since it came out not long before the Volstead Act came crashing down on drinkers' heads.

CABLE CAR

A rare modern spin on the Sidecar, in which the brandy is replaced by spiced rum and the usual sugar rim is supplemented with cinnamon. Created by San Francisco bartender Tony Abou-Ganim in 1996 and first put on the menu at the swanky Starlight Room atop the Sir Francis Drake Hotel. He later took the drink with him to the Bellagio Hotel & Casino's many bars in Las Vegas.

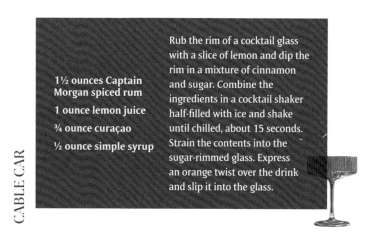

1½ ounces Captain Morgan spiced rum

1 ounce lemon juice

¾ ounce curaçao

½ ounce simple syrup

Rub the rim of a cocktail glass with a slice of lemon and dip the rim in a mixture of cinnamon and sugar. Combine the ingredients in a cocktail shaker half-filled with ice and shake until chilled, about 15 seconds. Strain the contents into the sugar-rimmed glass. Express an orange twist over the drink and slip it into the glass.

CABLE CAR

CACHAÇA

The national spirit of Brazil, distilled from fermented sugar cane juice. It can be made only in that country, where it has been manufactured for centuries and is produced in great volume. A 2013 agreement with the United States declared cachaça a distinctive Brazilian product, after which the U.S. stopped using the phrase "Brazilian rum," a term that had miffed Brazilians not a little over the years. (Other rums, like rhum agricole, are also made from sugar cane juice.) Cachaça consciousness outside of Brazil did not begin until the late twentieth century and was helped along by the cocktail revival. In the United States, the spirit is primarily consumed in the form of a Caipirinha, a simple mixture of cachaça, sugar, and muddled lime wedges. Cocktail bars have dreamed up dozens of other drinks using the spirit, but none have challenged the Caipirinha in popularity or name recognition. In recent decades, artisanal cachaças, made in pot stills and aged in a variety of woods, have attempted to counter the spirit's lingering image as a fiery industrial product lacking in subtlety or nuance.

CAIPIRINHA

The national mixed drink of Brazil, and the delivery system by which most of the rest of the world experiences the spirit cachaça. (That's right! Two cachaça entries in a row!) The drink is of the family of cocktails using the holy trinity of rum, lime, and sugar, found throughout South America and the Caribbean, of which the daiquiri and Ti' Punch are members. Lime wedges are muddled with raw sugar in a glass, which is then filled with cachaça and ice. For much of its life, the Caipirinha was little known outside Brazil. But beginning around the turn of the twenty-first century, it began to be more widely enjoyed.

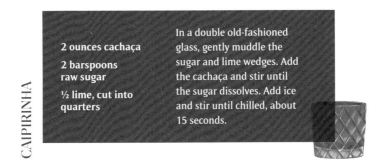

CAIPIRINHA

2 ounces cachaça

2 barspoons raw sugar

½ lime, cut into quarters

In a double old-fashioned glass, gently muddle the sugar and lime wedges. Add the cachaça and stir until the sugar dissolves. Add ice and stir until chilled, about 15 seconds.

CALABRESE, SALVATORE

One of the most celebrated London bartenders of the 1990s and early twentieth century. Calabrese moved from his native Amalfi Coast to London in 1980 and landed a job at the tiny bar at Dukes, an exclusive hotel off St. James Street. There he perfected what became known as the Dukes Martini, an ice-cold, Sahara-dry, undiluted piledriver of a Martini, reportedly at the behest of American newspaper columnist Stanton Delaplane. Calabrese moved from Dukes to the Library Bar in the Lanesborough hotel (where he created the Breakfast Martini) to London's Playboy Club. Calabrese is one of the few old-school London cocktail bartenders (he was president of the stodgy UK Bartenders Guild) to seamlessly adapt himself to the new wave of modern mixology. The author of several cocktail books, he is known for amassing vintage spirits and making expensive one-off cocktails with them. Elegant, loquacious, and charmingly vainglorious, Calabrese refers to himself as "The Maestro."

SALVATORE CALABRESE

CALVADOS

An ancient apple brandy, made for centuries in the Normandy region of northern France. It is distilled from cider made from any of dozens of different varieties of apples, and sometimes pears, grown in the area and then aged in barrels. Like certain wines, calvados is governed by an administrative order-on-consent (AOC) system of regulations that protect the integrity of production. Beginning in the late nineteenth century, calvados was occasionally called for in cocktails, but the domestic American applejack was more commonly reached for.

   With the advent of the cocktail revival in the twenty-first century, certain bartenders declared that calvados made for a better drink in cocktails that called for apple brandy. Thad Vogler, who sourced barrels of calvados directly from French producers to use in the cocktails at his San Francisco bars, was a prominent voice in this regard. But, given that the flavors of American applejack and French calvados are so different from one another, the true result of such experiments was not necessarily a better cocktail, but a different cocktail. Moreover, the high price of calvados generally keeps it out of cocktails. The Conference by Brian Miller and the Tantris Sidecar by Audrey Saunders are two well-known modern cocktails that use calvados.

CAMACHO SANTA ANA, TONYA LENELL

The founder and owner of an influential, if short-lived, liquor store in the hard-to-get-to Red Hook section of Brooklyn. In 2003, Alabama native LeNell Smothers (as she was then known) opened her one-room spirits and wine shop and quickly developed a reputation for stocking quality goods, as well as obscure and hard-to-find liqueurs, amari, bitters, and whatnot. The selection made LeNell's an instant destination for ambitious bartenders looking to re-create old cocktails or create exciting new ones. She bottled her own rye and carried Peychaud's and Underberg bitters when no one else did. A rent dispute with the landlord forced LeNell's to close in 2009. By then, dozens of boutique liquor stores had copied her business model. In 2018, she opened a second liquor store in Birmingham, Alabama.

CAMPARI

The supreme leader of the Italian red bitters and—as an ingredient in the Negroni, Americano, Boulevardier, Old Pal, Jungle Bird, and countless modern cocktails—one of the indispensable bottles of the bar world. The liqueur was invented in 1860 by Gaspare Campari, who was from Novara, Italy. He sold it, at first, out of his café. Campari's first plant was near Milan, which remains its home base. Its distinctive bright red color originally came from carmine dye from cochineal insects. The company decided in 2006 to discontinue the use of cochineal in most of its bottlings in favor of artificial colors, because of what it called the "uncertainty of supply of the natural colorant." The rest of the ingredients are a proprietary mix of herbs and spices. The ABV of Campari varies depending on the country in which it is sold. The family was an innovator in advertising and worked with many Italian artists to create some iconic images. For a long time, it was drunk mainly in Italy and countries with large Italian populations, like Argentina. Consumption of the bittersweet aperitivo in the U.S. was limited to Italian enclaves like that in San Francisco. Campari knew this. Poking fun at its unpopularity, a string of 1973 ads across the United States read, "A great American tradition since 1983."

The liqueur's fortunes did not reverse until the twenty-first century, with the slow rise of the Negroni cocktail. With the popularity of the Negroni and Boulevardier, and the proliferation of new red bitters, many bartenders played around with the traditional recipes, substituting other red liqueurs for Campari. Some insisted their choice of bitters was superior, in terms of either taste or natural makeup, as Campari's color today is achieved through artificial methods. But, as nothing else tastes exactly like Campari, the spirit retains an edge. Gruppo Campari, a multinational liquor conglomerate, owns many liquors in every category, including products that might otherwise be considered competition for Campari, like Aperol and Cynar, as well as items in the needed-for-Negronis family, including various Italian sweet vermouths.

CAROUSEL BAR

A unique, rotating, twenty-five-seat circular bar located just off the lobby of the Hotel Monteleone in New Orleans's French Quarter. It is, indeed, designed like a carousel, and like a carousel the seats go around, completing a leisurely rotation about once every fifteen minutes. This, amusingly, requires bartenders and standing guests to keep regular track of seated drinkers. It opened in 1949, conceived by hotelier Frank Monteleone as a way to stand out among the hundreds of other New Orleans bars. It has undergone design changes over the years, always retaining some sort of circus aura. The hotel's claim to mixological fame is the Vieux Carré, which was invented by Monteleone bartender Walter Bergeron in the 1930s. The bar attained wide notoriety beginning in 2002, when the cocktail convention Tales of the Cocktail chose to set its festival at the hotel, thus exposing bartenders from all over the world to the old hotel bar.

CAROUSEL BAR

CECCHINI, TOBY

A Wisconsin native, he moved to New York to write, but found his métier in mixology. Within a year of working behind the bar at the Odeon restaurant, he had invented the Cosmopolitan, which eventually became an international standard, largely thanks to its being featured on the television series *Sex and the City.* After leaving Odeon, Cecchini ran the bar program at the SoHo restaurant Kin Khao and founded the eclectic Chelsea art bar Passerby. His 2003 memoir, *Cosmopolitan,* told of these years. He also wrote a drinks column for the

New York Times for many years. In 2013, he transformed an old, long-shuttered Brooklyn luncheonette into the Long Island Bar, a neighborhood bar with global cachet.

CHALKER, VERNON

One of the founders and shapers of the modern cocktail scene in Melbourne, Australia. In 1997, Chalker took advantage of newly changed liquor licensing in Melbourne and opened Gin Palace, a plush, dimly lit bar hidden away on one of the city's small laneways. Gin Palace counterintuitively featured gin and gin drinks in a vodka-drinking age. Against all odds, it succeeded. Far in advance of the coming worldwide gin craze, the bar's collection of gins grew from fifteen to two hundred. Chalker went on to open additional bars, including the rooftop, garden-party-themed Madame Brussels and Bar Ampere. Flamboyant and mercurial, he fully embodied the nightlife that was his trade. He died at age fifty-five in 2020.

CHAMPAGNE COCKTAIL

One of the oldest, simplest, and classiest of cocktails. It was what the writers of *Casablanca* had Victor Laszlo order to signify his urbane virtuousness. Simply a sugar cube soaked with bitters and topped with champagne, it is basically a Champagne Old-Fashioned but, based on appearances, seems to belong more to the French 75 fluted family. It was established enough by 1862 to appear in Jerry Thomas's seminal cocktail book. His version used a spoonful of sugar and cracked ice. Harry Johnson went a more opulent route, filling his Champagne Cocktail with an orchard of fruit. But over the years, a simpler style prevailed, as did the use of a drier champagne and a sugar cube. Part of the appeal of the drink is the show: The champagne slowly eats away at the sugar cube at the bottom of the glass, sending a continuous line of fine bubbles to the surface. It has always been a high-toned drink, as champagne ain't cheap. It hasn't enjoyed a rebirth during the cocktail revival, mainly because most bartenders prefer a glass of unadulterated champagne, as opposed to one sugared up. But, as Kingsley Amis wrote, "Everyone seems to think this is an overrated drink, but it keeps going all the same."

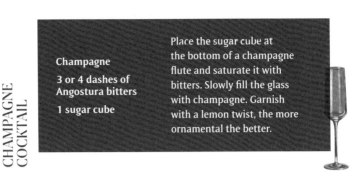

CHAMPAGNE COCKTAIL

Champagne

3 or 4 dashes of Angostura bitters

1 sugar cube

Place the sugar cube at the bottom of a champagne flute and saturate it with bitters. Slowly fill the glass with champagne. Garnish with a lemon twist, the more ornamental the better.

CHARTREUSE SWIZZLE

An audacious modern classic cocktail invented by San Francisco bartender Marcovaldo Dionysos. Built on a base of 1½ ounces of green Chartreuse, it reflected mixologists' obsession with challenging heritage spirits during the early years of the cocktail revival. The vaguely tiki-esque cocktail is filled out by pineapple juice, lime juice, and falernum, which was little known and hard to locate at the time. Dionysos created the drink for a 2002 Chartreuse competition in San Francisco and won, making the Chartreuse Swizzle a rare cocktail-competition-winning drink to achieve lasting fame. This drink and the Last Word helped recast Chartreuse as a cocktail mixer in the aughts.

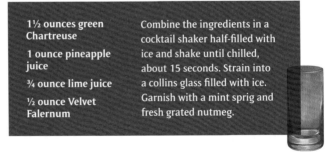

CHARTREUSE SWIZZLE

1½ ounces green Chartreuse

1 ounce pineapple juice

¾ ounce lime juice

½ ounce Velvet Falernum

Combine the ingredients in a cocktail shaker half-filled with ice and shake until chilled, about 15 seconds. Strain into a collins glass filled with ice. Garnish with a mint sprig and fresh grated nutmeg.

CHETIYAWARDANA, RYAN

A pioneering London bartender, bar owner, and all-around entrepreneur who rose to prominence in the 2010s on the strength of innovative approaches to drink creation, sustainability, branding, and marketing. Chetiyawardana (pronounced

Chay-thee-a-WARD-thun-a) studied art, biology, and philosophy on his way to becoming a bartender, and brought a bit of each discipline to the bar. Raised in Birmingham, he worked at Bramble in Edinburgh and then under molecular-mixology maven Tony Conigliaro before striking out on his own. His first bar, White Lyan, opened in East London in 2013. The bar faced the customer nearly unarmed: It was equipped with no ice, no cocktail shakers, and very few bottles of liquor. White Lyan used its own house spirits, which it bought directly from distillers. White spirits were made to specifications. Aged stock, like whiskey, was blended and then diluted with White Lyan's own water: filtered London tap water spiked with a custom mineral content. For all its accolades and press, White Lyan had a brief life, closing in 2017. Thereafter began Chetiyawardana's pattern of opening bars at a rapid rate and closing or reinventing them just as quickly. Dandelyan (all his bars have "lyan" in the name), a botany-focused bar, opened in the Mondrian Hotel in 2014 and closed in 2018, immediately before being named the top bar by the World's 50 Best Bars organization. Other bars included Superlyan in Amsterdam, Silver Lyan in Washington, DC, and Lyaness in London. He also published a book, *Good Things to Drink,* in 2017, put out a line of bottled cocktails, and embarked on corporate partnerships with various liquor brands.

CLARITO

A variation of the Martini found only in Argentina—simply a gin Martini with a sugar rim, appearing in *Tragos Magicos,* a 1950 cocktail book by Santiago Policastro, one of the most famous bartenders in Buenos Aires in his day. The drink would have been lost to time had it not been for bartender Federico Cuco, who rediscovered and promoted it through a "Save the Clarito" campaign. Over time, the sugar rim was dispensed with, leaving a straightforward gin Martini with a lemon twist. The Clarito can still be ordered at bars throughout Buenos Aires.

2¼ ounces gin

¾ ounce dry vermouth

Rub the rim of a cocktail glass with a slice of lemon and dip the rim in sugar. Combine the gin and vermouth in a mixing glass half-filled with ice and stir until chilled, about 15 seconds. Strain into the prepared glass.

CLOVER CLUB

CLOVER CLUB (BAR)

A cocktail bar opened in 2008 by Julie Reiner, of Flatiron Lounge and Pegu Club fame, that brought craft cocktails to Brooklyn, then uncharted territory for fancy drinks. Though ornately appointed, Clover Club was considerably less formal than Manhattan cocktail bars, catering to the relaxed attitudes of the borough. Bartending alumni include some of the best in the business, such as Giuseppe González, Thomas Waugh, Nicholas Jarrett, Brad Farran, Lucy Hawkins, Ivy Mix, Franky Marshall, and Katie Stipe. Bartender and partner Tom Macy ran the bar for many years. The bar is named after a famous pre-Prohibition Philadelphia drink (which itself was named after a Philadelphia men's club). Reiner's Gin Blossom and Slope are the bar's house Martini and Manhattan. González claims to have invented the Trinidad Sour while at the bar.

C

CLOVER CLUB (COCKTAIL)

A cocktail consisting of gin, lemon juice, raspberry syrup, and an egg white. Its heyday, which was not long, was in the first decades of the twentieth century. Its memory was revived by mixologists in the current century. In the past, as often as not, grenadine was used instead of raspberry syrup, which results in a drink of significantly less interest.

CLOVER CLUB

1½ ounces gin	Combine all the ingredients in a cocktail shaker. Shake until integrated, about 15 seconds. Add ice. Shake until chilled, about 15 seconds. Strain into a chilled cocktail glass.
½ ounce lemon juice	
½ ounce simple syrup	
½ ounce raspberry syrup	
1 egg white	

CLYDE COMMON

A bar and restaurant housed inside the Ace Hotel that, under the guidance of bartender Jeffrey Morgenthaler, became the leading cocktail destination in Portland, Oregon, until its closure in 2020 during the Covid-19 pandemic. Starting in 2014, a second bar, Pépé le Moko, operated in the basement, specializing in improved versions of unfashionable cocktails like the Amaretto Sour and Grasshopper.

COBBLER

An elegant category of cocktail in which a spirit or wine is combined with sugar and served over crushed or "cobbled" ice and usually adorned with fruit. Cobblers were quite popular in the mid- to late nineteenth century. There were many types, but the indisputable king of the genre was the Sherry Cobbler, one of the most famous drinks in cocktail history. "The great feature of city civilization is—Sherry Cobbler," declared an 1844 newspaper, which went on to describe the drink build: "to lay sparkling crystals of ice beneath delicious sherry, and to flavor the liquid with sharp slices of lemon, and then to imbibe it, not by coarse Thracian draughts, but gently, lightly and playfully through a rustic straw." The Champagne Cobbler was another popular item of the time. The whole family of cobblers largely disappeared after repeal, being too ornate an affair for the workaday bartenders and simple hard-drinkers of postwar America to mess around with. But the drinks returned with the cocktail revival, particularly the Sherry Cobbler. Some bartenders invented new cobblers. The most valiant effort to bring the cobbler back to glory was at Bellocq, a New Orleans hotel bar that opened in 2011 and made the ice-laden, fruit-crested breed of cocktail its calling card. The bar would draft a cobbler out of any liquor on the back bar. Bellocq did not, however, last long.

COCKTAIL

The thing this book is about. Originally just one of many categories of mixed drinks. In 1806, it was defined in print as a mix of spirit, sugar, water, and bitters. Over the years, however, "cocktail" became a synonym for any mixed drink. The word also connotes a whole vibe of sophistication and fun and has been applied to all sorts of terms, items, and phrases, including the cocktail hour, cocktail shakers, cocktail dresses, cocktail music, cocktail glasses. As to the origin of the word—which, we must all admit, is one of the weirdest in the English language; it's a miracle that we all utter it with ease on a daily basis without blinking an eye or dissolving into laughter—there are many theories, about horses' doctored tails, mistreated roosters, French mispronunciations, and many more, none of them 100 percent provable. We've lived with the word for more than two hundred years now, so perhaps it's time to pack away all the theories. Let it suffice to say that a cocktail is a cocktail, and we all know what that is.

COCKTAIL SHAKER

A ubiquitous piece of bar equipment used to shake cocktails with ice. There are a few distinct forms. A Boston shaker is composed of a metal tin and a shaker glass or a smaller metal cup, which fit together to create a sealed mixing cavity. This type has no built-in strainer, so a Hawthorne or julep strainer is required to complete the drink. The Cobbler shaker, also called a three-piece shaker, consists of a metal cup, a top containing a built-in strainer, and a cap.

COCKTAIL SHAKER

Cobbler shakers are favored in Japanese bartending. The Parisian, a two-piece metal shaker, offers a middle ground between the Boston and Cobbler. Cocktail shakers were a relatively late addition to the bartender's arsenal of tools. In the early decades of mixology, bartenders compounded cocktails by tossing ingredients from one glass or mug to the other, until the drink was well integrated and chilled. Cocktail shakers began to be common sights in the 1870s. By the early twentieth century, bartending and cocktail shakers were inextricably linked, and the clinking of ice in a shaker was a sound heard in every bar the world over. After Prohibition, when drink mixing became a household art, cocktail shakers became a sought-after consumer commodity. Shakers became an expression of style and fashion, designed in every form imaginable. In the late twentieth century, shakers assumed a lesser role behind the bar as the bartending art was on the decline, and bartenders mixed up cocktails in whatever way was most efficient. With the cocktail revival, stylish shakers came back into use, as did distinctive and theatrical shaking techniques.

COCKTAIL STRAINER

A small, circular metal bar tool with a handle that aids the transfer of a mixed cocktail's liquid ingredients from a cocktail shaker or mixing glass into the waiting cocktail glass. There are two basic styles: the Hawthorne strainer and the julep strainer. The Hawthorne is by far the more ubiquitous and all-purpose, being a flat, perforated metal disk equipped with small "ears" that keep it in place over a glass or shaker, and trimmed with a coiled spring that effectively strains out the solids used in shaken and muddled drinks, primarily juice pulp but also fruits and herbs. The julep strainer, consisting of a perforated metal bowl, is suitable only for stirred drinks made solely of spirits and is used to separate the cold liquid from the ice that chilled it. It was the advent of the use of ice in drinks that brought the necessary strainers into existence in the mid-nineteenth century.

The julep strainer came first. It was often left in the glass, allowing the customer to drink the cocktail through the strainer. The Hawthorne came about in the late nineteenth century. It was invented by Bostonian William Wright and named after Boston's Hawthorne Café. Until recently, the julep strainer had nearly passed out of existence and was little seen. Most bartenders in the late twentieth century shook every cocktail, making the julep obsolete. Only the demands of the revived cocktail bartending community, who began stirring cocktails again, brought it back from the dead. In the early twenty-first century a Boston cocktail bar was named the Hawthorne in honor of the strainer. Around the same time, Montgomery Place, a popular cocktail bar in London, served their julep old style, with the julep strainer in the glass. In the aughts, many cocktail bartenders got in the habit of "double-straining," pouring a shaken drink through both a Hawthorne and a mesh strainer to achieve a higher clarity in the resultant cocktail.

COCKTAIL WRITER

Previously a hobby of the drinking dilettante, writing about cocktails had few full-time practitioners until the twenty-first century, when, thanks to the cocktail renaissance and the public interest it provoked, it became a full-fledged profession and a niche segment of food and drink journalism. In the past, most full-time writers who dabbled in drink journalism published a book and then walked away from the topic to pursue other interests; examples include Bernard DeVoto, Kingsley Amis, David A. Embury, William Grimes, and Eric Felten. The globe-trotting bon vivant Charles H. Baker Jr. was a rare example of someone who kept at the beat over the years. With the advent of the cocktail revival, that all changed. Just as wine and beer had its devoted scribes, now so did cocktails. Ted Haigh, a graphic designer, counts as the movement's first historian, publishing the influential work *Vintage Spirits and Forgotten Cocktails* (2004). The British-born Gary Regan transitioned from a life behind the bar to a writing career, producing multiple volumes, the most notable by far being *The Joy of Mixology* (2003). Beginning in the mid-aughts, David Wondrich, a columnist for *Esquire* and former comp lit professor, emerged as the leading historian in the field, focusing on pre-revival cocktail history and producing two influential textbooks, *Imbibe!* (2007) and *Punch* (2010). Wayne Curtis, whose previous beat was the outdoors, wrote *And a Bottle of Rum* (2007), thus becoming an overnight rum expert, and for many years maintained a drinks column in the *Atlantic.* Camper English made his native San Francisco his bailiwick and adopted a comic gadabout approach to his subject, though he reserved a special seriousness for the subject of ice. The conscientious Paul Clarke, based in Seattle, began as the author of a well-read blog, *The Cocktail Chronicles,* before settling in as a traditional-media eminence as the editor of *Imbibe* magazine.

Kara Newman, working as the spirits expert at *Wine Enthusiast,* proved a dogged reporter with a prodigious output for many outlets. Brad Thomas Parsons positioned himself as an authority on the subjects of bitters and amaro, among other things.

There were still those for whom cocktail writing was an enthusiastic sideline, who kept other day jobs, including M. Carrie Allan, the cocktail columnist for the *Washington Post,* who worked for the Humane Society; and Philip Greene, author of several cocktail books, including a popular one on Hemingway, who works at the Pentagon as a lawyer. Other notable cocktail writers include Emma Janzen, Alia Akkam, Amy Zavatto, Maggie Hoffman, Christine Sismondo, Amanda Schuster, and Alice Lascelles. And, as in the late nineteenth century and early twentieth century, many bartenders have tried their hand at cocktail book authorship, including Toby Cecchini, Dale DeGroff, Jeffrey Morgenthaler, Toby Maloney, Julie Reiner, Jim Meehan, Natasha David, Martin Cate, Sother Teague, Ivy Mix, Thad Vogler, Eric Alperin, Frank Caiafa, and the bar teams at Death & Co. and Dead Rabbit. A sub-genre of writers devoted solely to whiskey emerged in the 2010s, including Dave Broom, Aaron Goldfarb, Fred Minnick, Liza Weisstuch, Noah Rothbaum, Heather Greene, Clay Risen, Robin Robinson, and Lew Bryson.

COGNAC

Many impediments have kept back cognac, the most famous brandy in the world, as a cocktail base over the years, not least the producers of the French brandy, who seem averse to the very idea of mixing their precious spirit with other liquids. But it has found a home in bars here and there, particularly during the nineteenth century. The Sidecar is the spirit's most renowned cocktail. Other name cocktails that have been home to the French brandy from time to time include the Brandy Crusta, early versions of the Mint Julep, late versions of the Sazerac, Japanese Cocktail, Coffee Cocktail, Saratoga, Stinger, Vieux Carré, Brandy Alexander, French 75 (depending on your tastes), and the usual all-spirits-welcome genres of flips, fizzes, fixes, and daisies. Modern cocktails that use it include the Conference, Ritz, and Tantris Sidecar. It is often a part of many punches, both historical and contemporary, as well as holiday treats like Tom and Jerry and eggnog. The spirit has its fervent advocates among modern American bartenders, but they are held back by a general lack of enthusiasm about the spirit as a mixer, and the relative high pour cost as compared to other spirits.

COLEMAN, ADA

The first female head bartender at the American Bar in the Savoy Hotel in London and until recently, when Shannon Tebay was appointed to the post in 2021, the only one. She worked the bar from 1903 to 1926. Her nickname was Coley, and she served drinks to the likes of Mark Twain, Charlie Chaplin, and the Prince of Wales. As popular as she was with her clientele, Coleman was eventually pushed out in favor of Harry Craddock. She is best remembered today for having invented the Hanky Panky cocktail. Coleman was known to have created other popular drinks, but they have been lost to time. Born in 1874, she died in 1966 at the age of ninety-one. In recent years, Coleman has proven an important inspiration to female bartenders within the cocktail community.

ADA COLEMAN

COLLINS, WAYNE

An influential figure in the early years of the British cocktail revival of the 1990s and aughts, both as a mixologist (the White Negroni is his invention), educator, and television personality. A native Londerer, he got his start as a teenager working at a relative's pub. He took to cocktails early on and honored the classics in the bar menus of the many London bars he helped launch. His peak as a bar director was at High Holborn, which had a brief but influential run beginning in 2000. From 2002, he headed Mixxit, the bartending training arm of Maxxium UK, a liquor concern. Collins died in February 2023.

CONNAUGHT BAR

The bar in the posh hotel of the same name in the Mayfair section of London. It was revitalized in 2008 when management drafted two hotshots from the London cocktail scene: Erik Lorincz, a Czech Republic native who was a student of Japanese bar techniques; and the Italian-born Agostino Perrone, a veteran of the celebrated cocktail bars LAB, Montgomery Place, and Trailer Happiness. The reinvented bar caught the public's attention with such drinks as a Bloody Mary made with chilis from India and celery foam and, most famously, a Martini cart that allowed the drink to be made tableside with a selection of six different bitters. After a slow start, the Connaught won acclaim and led the way in reviving London's once-glorious hotel-bar culture.

CONRAD, BARNABY, III

The son of a famed San Francisco novelist, artist, and amateur bullfighter, who owned the restaurant Matador, Conrad went on to write early and influential books on absinthe (1988) and the martini (1995). The former inspired chemist Ted Breaux to begin his historic effort to resurrect the production of absinthe.

COOPER, RON

A New Mexico artist who played a large role in popularizing mezcal in the United States in the early twenty-first century and is the force behind the Del Maguey line of "single-village" mezcals (the term is Cooper's coinage) that were the first mezcals most modern mixologists ever tasted and mixed with. While living and working in Mexico in 1990, Cooper became acquainted with mezcal and began to seek out and befriend the various families that made it. He eventually became possessed by a need to bring the artisanal juice of these small producers to the American public. He began with bottlings from two mezcalaros. In time, he teamed up with Steve Olson, an American bartender and wine director with connections in the restaurant and bar world. After a few years, Del Maguey introduced Vida, a low-priced mezcal specifically intended for mixing into cocktails. By 2010, Del Maguey was well known in drinking circles and presaged what would become a tidal wave of mezcals on the U.S. market.

CORPSE REVIVER NO. 2

A cocktail made of gin, lemon juice, Lillet, Cointreau, and a dash of absinthe, first seen in Harry Craddock's *Savoy Cocktail Book.* Corpse Reviver was previously a broad term winkingly applied to any number of drinks taken in the morning to blow the cobwebs out of your head. But Craddock's is the version that has achieved the most lasting fame. The drink did not get much play in bars until the turn of the twenty-first century, when it was given a big bear hug by the modern mixology community. It has since become a classic. Its popularity among bartenders was such that the Corpse Reviver No. Blue, using taboo blue curaçao, was created in jesting response to it.

CORPSE REVIVER NO. 2

¾ ounce gin
¾ ounce Cointreau
¾ ounce Lillet blanc
¾ ounce lemon juice
Absinthe for rinsing glass

Combine the ingredients in a cocktail shaker half-filled with ice. Shake until chilled, about 15 seconds. Strain into a chilled glass that has been rinsed with absinthe. (For a Corpse Reviver No. Blue, simply substitute blue curaçao for the Cointreau.)

COSMOPOLITAN

The most popular original cocktail of the last decade of the twentieth century and the early aughts and a genuine sensation owing to its featured role in the television show *Sex and the City,* whose four female protagonists couldn't get enough of the tart-sweet pink things. It is a simple sour made of lemon-flavored vodka, lime juice, cranberry cocktail, and Cointreau. Its origins have been a subject of controversy for decades; the only story that has held water over time is that of bartender Toby Cecchini, who said he invented the cocktail in 1988 as a shift drink for the staff at Odeon, a swanky Manhattan restaurant where he worked. He claimed that he was working off the recipe for a California cocktail with the same name, improving on it.

It was created the same year Absolut Citron came on the U.S. market. (A counter claim from a Florida bartender named Cheryl Cook, who said she created it earlier than 1988, persists to this day, primarily because it was promoted by influential bartending mentor Gary Regan.) The drink traveled fast and by the early 1990s was seen at other New York bars. Some places came up with their own riffs on the recipe. Dale DeGroff, working at Rainbow Room, did much to popularize the Cosmo—as it was called for short—by serving it at his high-profile perch. But *Sex and the City* kicked it into the stratosphere, and many Carrie Bradshaw wannabes adopted it as their signature tipple.

The inevitable backlash came when high-minded mixologists refused to make the drink, because (1) it called for flavored vodka and sweetened cranberry cocktail, two things they abhorred, and (2) worse sin, it was popular with the masses. Cecchini himself also disowned the Cosmo for a time, tiring of the responsibility of a cocktail so loved by some and so hated by others. In time, though, he came to wear the achievement with pride, doing brand work with Absolut, Cointreau, and even Ocean Spray. And though he never put the Cosmo on the menu at his Long Island Bar, he did sell a frozen Cosmopolitan. An acknowledgment of sorts.

COSMOPOLITAN

2 ounces Absolut Citron vodka

1 ounce Cointreau

1 ounce lime juice

1 ounce Ocean Spray cranberry cocktail

Combine the ingredients in a cocktail shaker half-filled with ice. Shake until chilled, about 15 seconds. Strain into a chilled coupe. Express a lemon twist over the drink and slip it into the glass.

COUPE

A stemmed cocktail glass, usually with a gently curving, shallow bowl. Dating back to the 1700s, it was previously associated with champagne. Most cocktails that were served "up" in the latter twentieth century were served in the ubiquitous conical martini glass, particularly during the 'tini craze of the 1990s. But with the cocktail renaissance, bartenders turned against the martini glass, which was oversized and unwieldy, and began serving their creations in the more delicate coupe. Dale DeGroff's adoption at the Rainbow Room of the retro coupe that came to be called the Nick & Nora did much to speed along the coupe's comeback, as did Audrey Saunders's use of the same glass at Bemelmans Bar and Pegu Club.

COUPE

COUPE ICE

A trendy practice that emerged in the 2010s, in which a large ice cube is placed in the center of a cocktail in a coupe glass. *See also* BAD IDEAS.

CRADDOCK, HARRY

An English bartender who ranks as among the most influential of the twentieth century by virtue of having published, in 1930, *The Savoy Cocktail Book,* a drink manual that went on to influence generations of bartenders all over the world, but particularly in the UK and United States. Coming out during Prohibition, the book was particularly valuable in preserving recipes and information then being lost in the U.S. Decades later, when the cocktail revival began to gather steam in the early twenty-first century and few historical cocktail books were still in print, the volume proved an important text for yet another crop of young bartenders hungry for knowledge and pre-Prohibition cocktail recipes. The White Lady and Corpse Reviver No. 2, as they appear in the *Savoy,* are accepted classics.

Craddock was born in Stroud, Gloucestershire, in 1876. Because he moved to the United States in 1897 and worked as a bartender in Cleveland and New York—where he bartended at the Knickerbocker Hotel and Hoffman House—a misconception spread, both before and after his 1963 death, that he was born in the U.S. With the advent of Prohibition, Craddock moved to England and joined the team at the Savoy. His tenure as head bartender at the American Bar at the Savoy ran from 1925 to 1938, where his skills in mixing American-style cocktails—with an American accent, to boot—were very much appreciated by expats and the Yankee press alike. By 1927 he was called "the most celebrated of all London cocktail mixers." Between his efforts behind the bar and as author of the book (much of which he nicked from older cocktail books), Craddock must be credited as one of the saviors of American cocktail culture during the long, tortuous Noble Experiment. In the later 1930s he moved to the Dorchester, where a bar was built specially for him, and stayed there for nearly a decade. Craddock died in poverty and obscurity. Since around 2000, however, his reputation and legacy have been thoroughly revived by the cocktail community.

HELEN CROMWELL

CROMWELL, HELEN

A bawdy, unashamed tavern owner and brothel madam known to one and all as
"Dirty Helen," owing to her capacity for blue language. Born in Indiana in 1886,
she ran brothels everywhere from Cincinnati to Chicago to Superior, Wisconsin.
But she found her greatest fame in Milwaukee, where her no-frills saloon—
officially called the Sunflower Inn, but popularly known as Dirty Helen's—began
as a speakeasy in 1926 and grew into a popular hangout of politicians and the
occasional celebrity. There were no stools; if customers tired of standing, they

sat on the sawdust floor. And she served only House of Lords scotch and Old Fitzgerald bourbon. For many years the bar was one of the best accounts for Old Fitzgerald whiskey. Old Fitz distiller Julian Van Winkle, impressed with Cromwell's business, once footed the bill for her to take a taxi from Milwaukee to Louisville. Cromwell lost the bar in 1959 and died in 1969. Her autobiography, written with Robert Dougherty, was published in 1966. The Great Lakes Distillery in Milwaukee named a bourbon bottling after her in 2019, and the Barley Island Brewing Company in Noblesville, Indiana, gave her name to a brown ale.

CUBA LIBRE

A highball composed of rum and cola, usually Coca-Cola, often with a squeeze of lime juice, with origins in Cuba in the early 1900s. It quickly jumped the water and found a home in the States, helped immensely by the Andrews Sisters, who had a massive hit in 1944 with a song called "Rum and Coca-Cola." "Rum and Coke" is how most of the world came to know and drink it, though the original name came back into fashion with the cocktail revival of the current century. Some insist that lime is the factor that separates a Cuba Libre from a mere Rum and Coke. And indeed, it makes a world of difference. It almost makes it a cocktail.

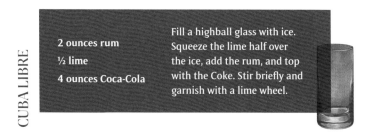

CUBA LIBRE

2 ounces rum
½ lime
4 ounces Coca-Cola

Fill a highball glass with ice. Squeeze the lime half over the ice, add the rum, and top with the Coke. Stir briefly and garnish with a lime wheel.

CURAÇAO/TRIPLE SEC/ORANGE LIQUEUR

One of the most ubiquitous, and annoyingly confusing, of liqueurs. It goes by multiple names and subcategories, but is required in countless classic cocktails, among them Pegu Club, Margarita, Sidecar, Brandy Crusta, Pousse Café, Prince of Wales, Long Island Iced Tea, and Corpse Reviver No. 2, as well as modern classics like the Breakfast Martini, Lemon Drop, Jasmine, Seelbach, Tantris Sidecar, Cosmopolitan, and Cable Car. It was also a go-to liqueur that many late-nineteenth-century bartenders relied on to add a dash of zip to just about any cocktail. When cocktails were "improved," they were often improved with curaçao. The original spirit was made with the peels of a very bitter but very fragrant breed of orange (the laraha) found on the island of Curaçao. As the Dutch controlled Curaçao, the spirit's origins lie within Holland and that general area. In the nineteenth century it became a very popular drink, sipped on its own. Over time, distillers used other sorts of oranges in the production of the spirit, and the term curaçao became a generic one. Today, there is only one curaçao distillery operating on the island of Curaçao.

Triple sec emerged in the 1800s. The origins of the name, which means "triple dry," are disputed. It is usually made with neutral grain spirit and is generally regarded as an inferior category of orange liqueur, almost always used for mixing and almost never for drinking on its own. Both curaçao and triple sec, however, are not protected appellations, have no legally binding definitions, and have been used nearly interchangeably for many years, leading to endless consumer—and cocktail writer—confusion. The differing terminology is needlessly tedious at this point. Curaçao and triple sec are essentially meaningless terms; just think of both as orange liqueur. The spirit is usually clear, but a blue variety appeared in the 1930s, and its colorful novelty led to a popular role in tiki drinks and other gimmicky libations. The range of orange liqueur brands is wide and the quality extremely variable. Cointreau, which has become for many a synonym for orange liqueur, is a prominent French brand of triple sec that uses sweet and bitter oranges and a beet sugar spirit base. Many bartenders favor the brand when making classic cocktails. Grand Marnier, another legacy French product, uses a blend of triple sec and cognac, making for a very rich expression. Both Cointreau and Grand Marnier distinguish themselves in one way beyond overall quality—both are expensive.

CURE

The first important modern craft cocktail bar in New Orleans, a city that never abandoned its cocktail culture but tended to stick to long-established local favorites like the Sazerac and Ramos Gin Fizz, when it was not indulging in the anything-goes liquid debauchery of Bourbon Street. Cure was opened by Neal Bodenheimer in 2009 in the then-dicey Freret neighborhood. Bodenheimer, a New Orleans native who had bartended in Manhattan, brought his New York ideas to the city, including a dress code that didn't go over well. The opening staff represented the pick of the litter of young New Orleans cocktail bartenders, including Kirk Estopinal, who had worked at The Violet Hour in Chicago, Maksym Pazuniak, Danny Valdez, Ricky Gomez, and Rhiannon Enlil. Cure's impact was secured when Estopinal and Pazuniak self-published *Rogue Cocktails,* a collection of bitters-heavy, counterintuitive, apple-cart-upsetting drink recipes during the bar's opening year. The book, and its follow-up *Beta Cocktails,* became underground hits. Bodenheimer went on to open Bellocq, a bar dedicated to cobblers; Cane & Table, a bar and restaurant inspired by Cuba and the Caribbean; and Peychaud's, a bar dedicated to New Orleans–born cocktails. There is another cocktail bar called Cure in Rochester, New York, equally prominent in its city.

CYNAR

An Italian bitter aperitif invented by Angelo, Amedeo, and Mario Dalle Molle in 1952 in Padua. As it is for all such Italian liqueurs and amari, the recipe of thirteen botanicals and herbs is a secret. The one declared ingredient, revealed on the label, is artichoke; Cynar is, in fact, the last major man standing in what was once a whole genre of amaro: carciofi. And yet, the liquor doesn't taste of artichoke. It was bought by the Campari Group in 1995. The liqueur has a long history of popularity in Argentina, where Cynar Juleps are more common than Mint Juleps. In the United States, for a long time it was known primarily in Italian-American communities, where it was drunk neat or on the rocks or as part of a Spritz. The cocktail revival brought the obscure liqueur out of the shadows, with mixologists using it as a modifying agent in new cocktails such as the Little Italy (rye, sweet vermouth, Cynar), Bitter Giuseppe (Cynar, sweet vermouth, lemon juice, orange bitters), Trident (Cynar, aquavit, sherry), Art of Choke (Cynar, rum, Chartreuse, lime juice, mint, sugar), Eeyore's Requiem (Cynar, Campari, blanc vermouth, gin, Fernet-Branca, orange bitters), and CIA (Cynar and applejack). In 2015, Cynar launched the first line extension in the product's history: Cynar 70. The higher-proof version of the liqueur was meant to cater to mixologists' thirst for liquors with a bigger kick. The product, however, has never caught on with bartenders the way the original had.

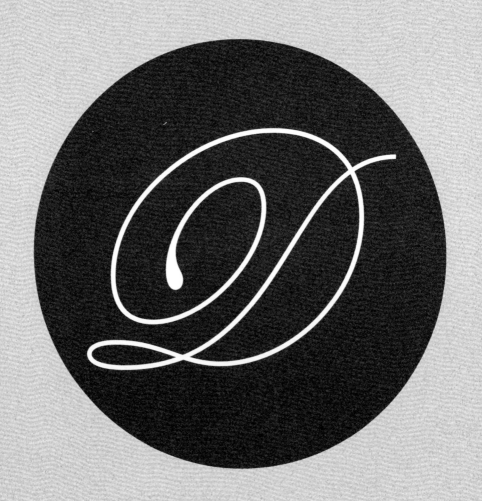

DAIQUIRI

A simple sour composed of rum, sugar, and lime juice, this drink somehow extracts power, poetry, and a party atmosphere from that simple equation and stands as the finest and fullest employment of that holy trinity of cocktail ingredients. It is the favorite drink of many a bartender, and millions of people agree with that assessment. The daiquiri is named for a town in Cuba where Jennings Cox, a rotund, bow-tie-sporting American mining engineer worked at an iron mine around the time of the Spanish-American War. A jolly entertainer, Cox would serve large batches of his own liquid invention, a just-so blend of light-bodied white rum, lime, and sugar. Cox took his daiquiri to a couple of upscale bars he hung out at in nearby Santiago de Cuba: the Hotel Venus bar and the private San Carlos Club. According to Jeff "Beachbum" Berry, a bartender to whom Cox introduced the drink began mixing it in single servings that he poured over shaved ice in a cocktail glass. From Santiago the recipe traveled to Havana. Over the next couple of decades, a perfect storm of circumstances conspired to make the daiquiri a border-crossing hit. Prohibition was passed, instilling in thirsty Americans a sudden urge to travel to Cuba, where liquor still flowed freely. Anyone drinking in Havana was bound to encounter a daiquiri at some point.

In the 1930s, the drink was given an added boost by the one-man publicity machine known as Ernest Hemingway, who had decamped to Cuba and ended up spending as much time drinking at the Havana bar El Floridita as writing. Hemingway's fame rubbed off on the drink. On a wave of rum that flooded the States following Prohibition's repeal, the daiquiri swept the country. The words *frozen* and *daiquiri* were never quite strangers. Those chilly potions Hemingway guzzled at El Floridita were served on piles of shaved ice. In the 1928 work *When It's Cocktail Time in Cuba,* Prohibition-era writer Basil Woon cautioned that the drink "must be drunk frozen or it is not good."

When the Waring blender was introduced to America in 1937, encouraging people to make smoothies out of everything, the daiquiri was transformed, as Wayne Curtis puts it in *And a Bottle of Rum,* into "something to be eaten with a spoon." Postwar America's love of mechanical convenience and the need for speedy service in the discos and singles' bars of the 1970s sealed the drink's slushy fate. In 1971, Dallas resident Mariano Martinez paired up with inventor Frank Adams to make the first frozen drink machine, and the daiquiri, in a rainbow of fruity new flavors, returned to batch proportions.

By the turn of the twenty-first century, the daiquiri had a not-terribly-dignified reputation as a fruity, frothy, adolescent concoction, made for injudicious college drinking and the "specialty cocktail" page at chain restaurants, and all too often impregnated with artificial colors and flavors. Then mixologists rediscovered the drink. Using careful techniques and artisan rums, they pared the drink down to its bones and started pouring daiquiris of beauty and balance. Through their efforts, the sour is now regarded as one of the four or five greatest cocktails of all time, and certainly the sour held in highest estimation in cocktail circles. It was the favorite drink of cocktail renaissance architect Sasha Petraske.

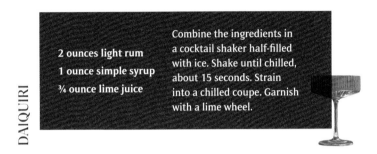

DAIQUIRI

2 ounces light rum
1 ounce simple syrup
¾ ounce lime juice

Combine the ingredients in a cocktail shaker half-filled with ice. Shake until chilled, about 15 seconds. Strain into a chilled coupe. Garnish with a lime wheel.

DANTE

An influential New York bar that borrowed its drinking blueprint from the aperitivo style of drinking intrinsic to Italy. It was opened by a collection of Australians, making it a truly sui generis cocktail-world mash-up. It opened in the space of the former Caffe Dante, a century-old bastion of Italian culture in Greenwich Village, from which it borrowed its name. Against all odds, Dante succeeded in its mission massively, and it helped kick off multiple trends, including aperitivo bars, day drinking, Negroni culture, and low-ABV drinking. The bar is owned by Linden Pride and his wife, Nathalie Hudson, while the drink program was initially headed by Naren Young. There was an early emphasis on the Negroni, and Dante offered several variations, resulting in a full Negroni menu. It also emphasized the Spritz and vermouth, and resurrected the Garibaldi, a little-known mix of orange juice and Campari, as a favored house drink. Eventually, the menu expanded to all genres of drinks, but the emphasis on classic styles of lighter drinking remained. Two other Manhattan locations, Dante West Village and Dante Seaport, were later added.

DARK AND STORMY

A highball made of dark rum, ginger beer, and sometimes a squeeze of lime. It is thought to have been invented in Bermuda sometime around World War I and remains a popular drink there. Traditionally, the drink was made with two Bermudian products, Gosling's Black Seal rum and Barritt's ginger beer. The Gosling company has owned a registered trademark for the name "Dark 'n Stormy" (only one apostrophe, for some reason) since 1991. Since then, they have acted as industry killjoy, preventing any bar from using the name if they don't put Gosling's rum in the cocktail. This has caused the simple drink to be sold under any number of aliases.

DARK AND STORMY

2 ounces dark rum
½ ounce lime juice
3 ounces ginger beer

Combine the rum and lime juice in a highball glass filled with ice. Top with the ginger beer. Stir briefly.

DEAD RABBIT, THE

A would-be nineteenth-century New York tavern, founded in lower Manhattan in 2013 by two Irishmen, Sean Muldoon and Jack McGarry, and one of the most famous and awarded cocktail bars in the world. The odd name comes from a notorious street gang that prowled the streets of early-nineteenth-century Gotham. Occupying three floors of a narrow, historical brick building on Water Street, it served modern spins on classic cocktails, as well as punch. It took special pride in its Irish whiskey collection and developing a respected Irish Coffee recipe. For several years, Dead Rabbit fought it out with Artesian in London for bar accolade spoils. It was an early pioneer among cocktail bars in the field of branding, creating a line of merchandise, clothing, and books, and inventing a mascot of a muscle-bound, mean-tempered, rabbit-human therianthrope who starred in a series of comic-book-like menus. The notoriety paid off: The bar is rarely not busy. As the years went by, it began to more closely identify with its Irish leanings than with its original pre-Prohibition personality. The bar rebounded from both a 2018 fire and the Covid pandemic. In 2022, Muldoon and McGarry split up. Muldoon moved to Charleston to open his own bar with Dead Rabbit beverage

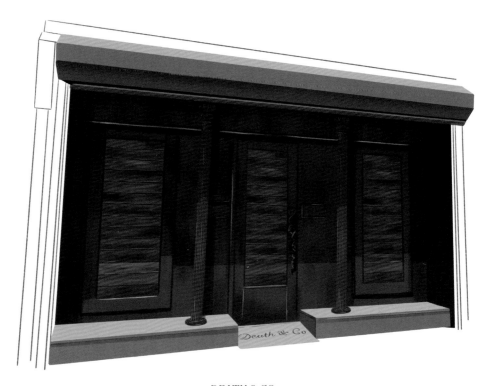

DEATH & CO.

director Jillian Vose. McGarry headed up an ambitious plan to franchise Dead Rabbit throughout the country, while at the same time giving the bar a more family and traditional Irish pub orientation. The duo also opened the equally ambitious Blacktail, an old-school Cuban-style cocktail bar, in 2016, but that outlet was felled by the pandemic.

DEATH & CO.

A bar critical to the evolution of the New York cocktail scene. Death & Co. was opened in 2007 by David Kaplan and Ravi DeRossi. The opening bartending staff featured much of the line-up from nearby Pegu Club, including Phil Ward, Brian Miller, and Jim Kearns, who left Pegu to join the enterprise. Kaplan let the bartenders run the show. The space was dark and low-ceilinged; the menus long and ambitious and frequently changed; the bar popular and difficult to get into. The staff, unbridled, used expensive spirits in their cocktails with abandon. Death & Co. helped pioneer the intense, "brown, bitter, and stirred" style of drink that became New York's de facto style in the late aughts. The bar also introduced punch to New Yorkers, after Kaplan and Ward were inspired by a visit to Hawksmoor in London. Famous drinks born there include the Oaxaca Old-Fashioned, Kingston Negroni, Naked and Famous, and the Conference. Death & Co., easily one of the best-known names in the cocktail world, later opened branches in Denver; Washington, DC; and Los Angeles, launched a line of merchandise, and published a series of cocktail books.

DEGROFF, DALE

An actor, born in Rhode Island, who unexpectedly became the figurehead of the American cocktail renaissance, beginning in the late 1980s, and is still arguably the most famous bartender in the world. While pursuing an acting career, DeGroff took bartending gigs at the Hotel Bel-Air in Los Angeles and Charley O's in New York. A job in the mail room of New York ad agency Lois Holland Callaway (LHC) put him in the sightlines of Joe Baum, the powerful head of Restaurant Associates, an LHC client. Baum put him in charge of the bar program at Aurora, which was ultimately a training ground for Baum's resurrection of the defunct art deco gem the Rainbow Room. His work there got him the Rainbow gig in 1987, where Baum charged him with creating a menu composed of classic cocktails, most of them forgotten and rarely served in New York in those days. Baum also told him to find a copy of Jerry Thomas's long-out-of-print 1862 bar manual, a move that kicked off the book's long journey back to relevancy in bartending circles. Dressed in smart red jackets and serving up Sidecars, Sazeracs, and Champagne Cocktails, DeGroff and his crew made a splash and received copious media coverage, rendering DeGroff an instant expert on cocktail culture virtually overnight. His innovations in the revived art of fine bartending were many. He popularized the bravura touch of the flamed orange twist garnish; he advocated for and found lost cocktail ingredients such as falernum and pimento dram; he reinstituted the old practice of stirring drinks that contained only alcohol (most bars shook everything); he kept his back bar curated with an eye toward quality, often denying space to major brands; and his search for period-correct cocktail glasses brought into being the Nick & Nora coupe, now ubiquitous.

DALE DEGROFF

DeGroff found time to create a few noteworthy new drinks, always based on classics, such as the Ritz, Fitzgerald, and Whiskey Smash. He also published *The Craft of the Cocktail* in 2002, an early and influential text of the aborning cocktail revival. His stay at the Rainbow Room ended in 1999, after which he opened the short-lived Blackbird. After that, he settled into a long career as consultant, lecturer, performer (he sings), guest bartender, instructor (he cofounded the Beverage Alcohol Resource program), entrepreneur (he produced a bitters brand and a Café Brûlot set), and all-around éminence grise. Throughout his career, DeGroff has always been a supporter and champion of other bartenders and has had a direct influence on the careers of many important figures, such as Audrey Saunders, Steve Olson, Sasha Petraske, Julie Reiner, David Wondrich, Paul Harrington, Tony Abou-Ganim, and more. His wife, Jill DeGroff, is an artist whose portraits of bar figures are worn as badges of honor by their recipients.

DE LA LOUISIANE

A forgotten New Orleans whiskey cocktail, brought back to health by the curious bartenders of the cocktail revival. Sometimes referred to as the A La Louisiane, or just La Louisiane, it was the house cocktail at the New Orleans hotel and restaurant of the same name. Like most New Orleans cocktails—and very like its kissing cousin, the Vieux Carré—it is big and boozy, the rye paired with sweet vermouth and Bénédictine, with touches of absinthe and Peychaud's just to prove it hails from NOLA. The Hotel De La Louisiane did business at 725 Rue Iberville in the French Quarter from 1881, when it was founded by Louis Bezaudun and his wife, Ann, until 1996, when it finally went under. (The building still stands.) It's unclear when the drink was invented, but, given the presence of absinthe, it would likely have been before the substance was banned in 1912. The cocktail was locally famous enough by the 1940s that an illustration of it graced the front of the menu, and it sat at the top of the cocktail list. The cocktail would likely have been lost to time if Stanley Clisby Arthur hadn't put the recipe in his 1937 book, *Famous New Orleans Drinks and How to Mix 'Em.* It was there that modern bartenders found it and began to mix 'em again.

DE LA LOUISIANE

2 ounces ounce rye

¾ ounce sweet vermouth

¾ ounce Bénédictine

2 dashes Peychaud's bitters

2 dashes absinthe

Combine the ingredients in a mixing glass half-filled with ice. Stir until chilled, about 15 seconds. Strain into a chilled coupe. Garnish with a cherry.

DE SOTO, NICO

Perhaps the best-known mixologist of the modern era to come out of Paris. De Soto rose up in the Experimental Cocktail Club empire—working at the original Paris location as well as the London and New York outfits—before opening his own bar, Mace, with Greg Boehm, in the East Village neighborhood of New York in 2015. A bar with as many lives as a cat, Mace subsequently moved to a larger space in the East Village and then, during the pandemic, to an even bigger space in the middle Village. At each, de Soto's intricate and complex cocktails were named after, and built around, specific spices, which he sources from around the world. Though mace was, of course, among those spices, de Soto became most famous for his work with pandan, a tropical herb native to Southeast Asia that lends a nutty flavor to drinks. De Soto, whose mania for travel knows no rival in bartending circles, is nearly single-handedly responsible for the global use of pandan in cocktails. He also owns a bar in Paris, Danico. The Mace location carries with it another significant footnote in cocktail history: In late 2014, before the bar was ready to open, the bar owners decided to stage a holiday-themed pop-up bar called Miracle on Ninth Street. It was such a whopping success that it returned each subsequent year and spawned a global franchise in seasonal Miracle bars.

EL DIABLO

A tequila cocktail from the 1940s that enjoyed a resurgence in the 2020s, riding on the coattails of the agave-spirits boom of that time. The origins of the El Diablo are typically traced back to Trader Vic's, the mid-century tiki-bar chain founded by Victor Bergeron. The drink appeared in Trader Vic's cocktail manual in 1946, and Bergeron put a "Mexican El Diablo" on his 1947 cocktail menu. Tiki scholar Jeff Berry speculates that Bergeron was riffing on a similarly structured rum drink called the Diablo. The drink vanished from the Trader Vic's menu in the 1950s, but then reemerged in the 1960s at Trader Vic's Mexican restaurant chain, called Señor Pico. However, not many other bars picked up on Vic's lead. The El Diablo is found in very few cocktail books published over the past century. It's not even in the annual Mr. Boston series of bar manuals. Julie Reiner was one of the first figures of the cocktail renaissance to give the cocktail some play in the current century. She sold the drink at the Flatiron Lounge, her trailblazing Manhattan cocktail bar that opened in 2003. It was also on the opening menu at PDT and an early menu at Milk & Honey in London. But it wasn't until

2022 that it became ubiquitous, becoming the cocktail bartender's suggestion to agave-thirsty customers after they have had already their Margarita, Paloma, and Oaxaca Old-Fashioned.

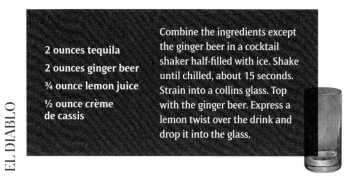

EL DIABLO

2 ounces tequila
2 ounces ginger beer
¾ ounce lemon juice
½ ounce crème de cassis

Combine the ingredients except the ginger beer in a cocktail shaker half-filled with ice. Shake until chilled, about 15 seconds. Strain into a collins glass. Top with the ginger beer. Express a lemon twist over the drink and drop it into the glass.

DON THE BEACHCOMBER

The tiki bar that started it all. The prototype upon which all other tiki bars were based for half a century. Don the Beachcomber was founded in Hollywood in 1934 by Ernest Raymond Gantt, who took on the name and persona of beachcomber Donn Beach, spelled with two "n"s just to keep you thinking. If you ever wonder why the owners of tiki bars all wear tropical shirts and straw hats, you can blame Donn. Beach invented the original Zombie cocktail, as well as dozens of other tropical cocktails, usually made with rum, which he called "rhum rhapsodies," including the Navy Grog, Three Dots and a Dash, Q.B. Cooler, Pearl Diver, Missionary's Downfall, and Cobra's Fang. He also invented the practice of layering multiple rums in one drink, and he created various mysterious syrups, such as Don's Mix and Don's Spices No. 2, whose contents he kept under wraps. Indeed, all Beachcomber drinks were house secrets he never shared or allowed to be printed. The bar was decorated in a vaguely tropical motif, with the various artifacts Beach had collected on his youthful travels. The overall formula was faux paradise, an escape for the weary American businessman. It worked, and not just with businessmen. Hollywood celebrities loved the place, which made everyone else want to go. Soon, Beach moved to roomier digs down the street.

Born in Texas in 1907, Ernest Raymond Gantt left home to travel the world and spend a good deal of time in the South Pacific. While he was serving during World War II, his first wife, Cora Irene "Sunny" Sund, took over the business and expanded it to sixteen locations. They divorced in 1940 and he eventually signed over the business to Sund. Legally forbidden from opening any Don the Beachcombers in the continental U.S., he then moved to the Hawaiian territory and opened Waikīkī Village, later the International Market Place. Beach engaged in a lifelong rivalry with Victor Bergernon, aka Trader Vic, his only real competition for the title of tiki bar king. While Beach was the genius who dreamed up the tiki aesthetic out of whole cloth, Vic, who stole most of his ideas from Beach, was the better businessman, blanketing the world with Trader Vic's restaurants and its various merchandise. Beach died in 1989 (by which time the tiki craze had subsided); he is buried in Honolulu. With the cocktail revival, and the subsequent tiki revival, however, Beach's legacy has been unearthed anew.

DORELLI, PETER

An Italian-born London bartender who ran the American Bar at the Savoy from 1984 to 2003. As such, he was a standard-bearer of his profession for all the brash young cocktail bartenders that came up in London in the 1990s. Dick Bradsell, the godfather of the UK cocktail revival, was himself influenced by Dorelli, though the two men couldn't have been less alike, Dorelli being suave and classical and president of the Bartenders Guild, while Bradsell was rough and iconoclastic and anything but a joiner. Born in Rome in 1940, he came to England when he was eighteen and in 1963 joined the Savoy Group at Stones Chop House in London as head barman of the Pebble Bar, where he stayed until 1981. When the company sold the restaurant he moved to the American Bar, becoming head barman and bar manager in 1984. After retiring, Dorelli embarked on a career as a roving bar authority, speaker, and cocktail competition judge. He often travels in tandem with Salvatore Calabrese, a fellow Italian bartender in London, with whom he developed a special bond. The two came to be a popular bar-world double act.

DORMAN, MEAGHAN

The bar director and face of a collection of Manhattan cocktail bars known for their intimacy and elegance, not to mention the quality of the cocktails. Raines Law Room, a well-upholstered subterranean speakeasy in the Flatiron District, equipped with curtains and call buttons, was the first to open in 2009. It was followed by a second Raines Law Room at the William hotel in midtown; Dear Irving in Gramercy Park, where each of four rooms evokes a different era in history; a second Dear Irving in midtown; and the short-lived The Bennett in Tribeca. As a mixologist, Dorman, who hails from Branford, Connecticut, has registered a modern classic in Wildest Redhead, a scotch sour riff, and is particularly known for her love of, and skill with, the Gibson.

DOWNEY, JONATHAN

A lawyer turned bar owner who, via his desire to duplicate in London what he viewed as the superior bar scene in his native Manchester, became a conduit between the leading cocktail bartenders of his time and the drinking public. Downey was the first defining force to emerge in the nascent London cocktail scene after Oliver Peyton and his Atlantic Bar & Grill. And he is the only bar owner to have employed both Dick Bradsell and Dale DeGroff, the godfathers of the English and American cocktail revivals, respectively, as well as Sasha Petraske, the founder of Milk & Honey, whose London branch of that speakeasy, opened with Downey, brought Petraske's philosophy and influence to the UK and Europe.

Downey began what would become an impressive, if short-lived bar empire in 1997, with Match, a West End bar that took cocktails seriously and paired them with food, a novel concept at the time. The bar was a surprise instant hit. He brought in Bradsell, then already a bartending legend, and showcased his original cocktails. The exposure Downey gave Bradsell's Vodka Espresso (later known as the Espresso Martini) set the cocktail off on its journey to global popularity that continues to this day. Within a few years, Downey opened another Match in London, as well as The Player, Sosho, Trailer Happiness, East Room, the London Milk & Honey (which was four times as big as the New York version as well as a members-only club), Match Bar & Grill in Melbourne, Match Bar in Spain, and many more. By hatching a deal with Petraske in 2001 to bring Milk & Honey to London, Downey likely saved the New York bar from bankruptcy and thus preserved the bar's long-term influence. Petraske, in turn, was influenced by the London scene and brought a couple of bartenders back with him to New York, including Vincenzo Errico. An outspoken, hard-charging type, Downey had a reputation for being difficult to work for. All of Downey's early bars eventually closed. Milk & Honey was the last to go, a victim of the Covid pandemic in 2020.

DRINK

A basement bar that, when it was opened by chef Barbara Lynch in 2008, became Boston's answer to Milk & Honey. Like the New York speakeasy, Drink had no menu, treated cocktails with the utmost seriousness, and was well versed in the classics. Fresh squeezed juice, exacting measurements, and custom carved ice were prominently deployed. Drink went Milk & Honey one better by removing the bottles from the back bar, thus circumventing customers' habits of falling back on their customary orders. John Gertsen ran the bar for many years, later to be succeeded by Ezra Star. The zigzagging, custom-made bar created three stages for the bartenders, around which the patrons gathered. Among the notable bartenders who worked there over the years are Misty Kalkofen and Josey Packard. Though not known for originals, Drink did produce a few notable modern drinks, including the Fort Point, a Manhattan variation that calls for rye whiskey, Punt e Mes, and Bénédictine; and Johann Goes to Mexico, a mezcal spin on the Trinidad Sour that calls for a full half-ounce of Angostura bitters. Gertsen also helped popularize certain New York cocktails, like the Red Hook and Trinidad Sour.

DRY SHAKE

A method used for emulsifying cocktails that contain egg or dairy. The dry shake requires two steps. First, a drink's elements are added to a tin and shaken without ice; then ice is added, and the cocktail is shaken once more to chill and dilute the drink. The technique is mentioned in the 1951 book *Bottoms Up* and was organically rediscovered in 2006 by Chad Solomon, a bartender at Pegu Club in New York who was looking for ways to alleviate his chronic back pain. The technique was quickly adopted by other bartenders in New York and then London. The method was later flipped on its head with the reverse dry shake, in which a drink is first shaken with ice, then again without ice.

DUKES BAR

A small, exclusive bar inside a small, exclusive hotel off St. James Place in London's Mayfair district. It has been overseen over the years by a series of Italian bartenders, including Gilberto Preti, Salvatore Calabrese, and Alessandro Palazzi. The bar's fame far outruns its size, primarily due to the renown of the Dukes Martini, a frozen, undiluted, lethally strong, and bitingly cold dry Martini served tableside

DUKES BAR

from a bar cart. The drink was devised by Calabrese as a way to attract attention to the bar and himself. It was made famous in 1987 when *San Francisco Chronicle* columnist Stanton Delaplane praised the Dukes Martini as the best in London. Fellow *Chronicle* columnist Herb Caen soon backed him up. Novelist Kingsley Amis was also a fan of the bar and sang its praises, and writer and James Bond creator Ian Fleming was an early habitué.

EASTERN STANDARD

A sprawling bar and restaurant on Boston's Kenmore Square, just a short walk from Fenway Park, that become one of the focal points of the city's cocktail boom in the late aughts and 2010s. The bar, which opened in 2005 under the guidance of bar manager Jackson Cannon, was one of the first in the nation to have success in putting out craft cocktails at high volume. It also succeeded in becoming an inclusive place, eschewing the snobbishness that marked many early cocktail bars of the era. The signature drink was the Jack Rose, a cocktail that Cannon mastered and that helped him win the job. The affiliated bar the Hawthorne, also located in the Hotel Commonwealth, had a more formal, serious-minded air. Both bars closed in 2020 during the Covid-19 pandemic.

EDMUNDS, LOWELL

A classics professor at Rutgers University who, in 1981, applied his academic rigor to a book-length study of the Martini entitled *The Silver Bullet: The Martini in American Civilization.* In the volume—the first serious book devoted to the Martini (many more would follow)—Edmunds tracked down the history of the famous drink and mused at length about its staying power as a cultural icon. The book was remarkable not only in its erudite treatment of a topic other writers might consider frivolous, but also in its timing, published at a time when the Martini was out of fashion and cocktail culture itself was at its nadir. "Its pleasure, which is not voluptuous but astringent," he wrote, "can only be expressed by oxymoron: sensuous coldness, opulent dryness, mysterious clarity, alluring purity." *The Silver Bullet* proved a potent reference tool years later when the cocktail revolution got underway. An updated version, called *Martini, Straight Up: The Classic American Cocktail,* came out in 1998.

EGGNOG

The ultimate Christmastime tipple, kept alive through the centuries as much by a sense of tradition as an actual liking of the drink. It rose to popularity in the early nineteenth century. A typical recipe called for eggs, milk, sugar, spirits (typically rum and brandy, but all sorts of booze are used), and baking spices such as nutmeg. It is traditionally served chilled in a punch bowl and ladled out into mugs or cups. Over time, nonalcoholic versions arose, delivering all the calories

EGGNOG

with none of the kick. During the holidays, commercially made versions pop up in the dairy aisle of the supermarket. The modern knock against the drink is that it is heavy, ponderous, and caloric. Epicureans of the twenty-first century have successfully experimented with aged eggnogs.

EGGS

A key ingredient in cocktails since there were cocktails. Typically found in sours, flips, and fizzes, but also as a component of dairy punches like eggnog and Tom and Jerry. When just the egg white is used, the adjective "silver" is typically affixed to the cocktail name; when just the yolk, "golden." As to the egg's contribution to a drink, here's William Schmidt in 1888: "Its effect is to oil and soften the drink as well as to flavor it. It lends richness to the flavor and a soft richness of color that enhances the drink greatly, for you must know that a large part of the pleasure of drinking lies in pleasure to the eye. From the physiological standpoint the egg in drinks is invaluable. It strengthens. It is meat. It softens the edge of the liquor also, and thus transforms a stomach-tearing liquid into an invigorating, healthful tonic." The mixologists of the twenty-first century took great pains to bring raw eggs back into the fold, often to the consternation of skittish guests and the local health department. At times, bartenders go overboard, adding egg to every sour, assured that an egg is an unquestioned improvement to any such drink.

EMBURY, DAVID A.

A Wall Street tax attorney who left an improbably indelible mark on cocktail history by penning the 1948 book *The Fine Art of Mixing Drinks.* The book was an exhaustive, opinionated, and prescriptive volume that delved into every aspect of home mixology and included recipes and dissections of hundreds of drinks. In a branch of literature then completely dominated by bar professionals and liquor companies, Embury was a rare layman, a skilled and knowledgeable enthusiast with plenty of axes to grind, but also with no strings attached. As far as the recipes go, he was a creature of his time, a heavy drinker and probably an alcoholic; the spirits portions for almost every cocktail are hefty, rendering many of the drinks too boozy and unbalanced. When the cocktail revival came into full swing at the turn of the twenty-first century, Embury's book, as one of the few still in print and easily obtainable, became newly influential. Robert Hess, in particular, an early voice of authority in the cocktail renaissance, found a mentor in Embury. In recent years, Embury's reputation has been tarnished by revelations that he was a bigot who vocally opposed desegregation. He died in 1960.

EMPLOYEES ONLY

A cocktail bar in New York that hit the middle point between the new fangled cocktail den and the formal European model of the past. The five founders were Jason Kosmas, Billy Gilroy, Henry LaFargue, Dushan Zaric, and Igor Hadzismajlovic. Most had worked at Keith McNally's high-volume Manhattan bars Pravda and Schiller's Liquor Bar before decamping to open EO on Hudson Street in the West Village. Like McNally, Zaric and company adhered to certain European traditions

(Zaric and Hadzismajlovic were from Serbia), including white bartender jackets, free pouring drinks (that is, eschewing jiggers), an all-male staff, and a hierarchical system in which bartenders worked their way up the ladder. The curtained, speakeasy-style entrance was borrowed from Milk & Honey, while the adoption of a food menu (the bar famously serves free chicken soup to patrons at the end of every evening) and the promotion of a party atmosphere appealing to the young crowd were entirely EO. A branch of EO opened in Singapore in 2016 and in Los Angeles in 2018. A location in Miami lasted little over a year.

ENRICO'S

An old San Francisco beatnik hangout from the 1950s, founded by Enrico Banducci, that, in its 1992 reboot, became a wellspring of modern cocktail culture. Paul Harrington worked there briefly but nonetheless had an outsized impact, helping to kick off the Mojito culture in the city. He served Bourbon & Branch for free to anyone who ordered it; the name stuck in the head of fellow staff member Todd Smith, who went on to open the famous bar Bourbon & Branch in 2005. Most significantly, Harrington hooked up with the editors of the new *Wired* magazine and began contributing cocktail content to their website. This eventually led to the book *Cocktail: The Drinks Bible for the 21st Century,* which had an impact on many bartenders around the world. David Nepove kept the Mojito train running at Enrico's after Harrington left. Other notable bartenders to work there include Marcovaldo Dionysos and Thomas Waugh. Enrico's closed in 2006.

ENSSLIN, HUGO

The bartender author of *Recipes for Mixed Drinks,* which, owing to its publication date—1917, on the brink of Prohibition—became a critical source of recipes and information for cocktail historians and bartenders of the twenty-first century. "The object of this book is to give a complete list of the standard mixed drinks that are in use at present in New York City," wrote Ensslin in the introduction. What follows are recipes and nothing but recipes, with simple instructions, printed in a clean style. Ensslin was born in Germany and moved to New York as a teenager to study the hotel business. He later took a job as maître d' at the grand Hotel Sterling in Wilkes-Barre, Pennsylvania. He died by suicide at his home in Kingston, Pennsylvania, at the age of fifty. Today, Ensslin's book is perhaps most famous for

HUGO ENSSLIN

containing the earliest recipe for the Aviation cocktail, proving the drink to be pre-Prohibition. However, it must be taken into account that the book's contents were plundered by authors Harry Craddock and Patrick Gavin Duffy, increasing the book's overall importance as a source.

ERRICO, VINCENZO

An Italian bartender who learned at the elbow of Dick Bradsell in London and Sasha Pestraske in New York. Errico moved from Naples to London in the late 1990s and got a job at Match, where Bradsell was consulting. It was there that Petraske, who was setting up the London branch of Milk & Honey, spotted him and convinced him to come to New York. Errico worked at Milk & Honey during its critical early years, a particularly creative period. There he invented the Manhattan/Brooklyn spin the Red Hook, which went on to inspire a dozen other cocktails. He also created the Enzoni, a Negroni–Gin Sour mash-up that would become popular twenty years later. In 2007 he moved back to Naples. He worked for a time at L'Antiquario in Naples before finally opening his own place, L'Artefatto, on the island of Ischia.

ESPRESSO MARTINI

The most famous invention of London bartender Dick Bradsell and simply one of the most popular and enduring drinks to arrive in the forty years spanning the turn of the twenty-first century. Though it was originally called, quite prosaically, Vodka Espresso, after its two defining ingredients, it is listed here under its more commonly accepted name. As legend has it, Bradsell created the first version of the drink one night in the mid-1980s at the Soho Brasserie, when a woman whom the bartender remembered as a model asked for a drink that would "wake me up and then fuck me up." This first version was an off-menu drink made of only vodka and espresso, tied together with a little simple syrup, and served on the rocks with a garnish of three espresso beans. The drink didn't appear on a menu until Jonathan Downey hired Bradsell at his bar Match EC1, which opened in 1997. By then, it was made with coffee liqueur and served up in a stemmed glass. In 1998, Bradsell renamed it the Pharmaceutical Stimulant and put it back on the rocks; this rendition was served at artist Damien Hirst's bar Pharmacy. In the aughts, the drink had made its way to coffee-loving Australia, where it proved phenomenally popular. Although still heavily associated with the 1990s, the drink made an unexpected comeback in the late 2010s. By 2020, it was ubiquitous and all but inescapable, more popular than it had ever been. The arrival on the market of high-quality coffee liqueurs like Mr. Black had something to do with this.

ESPRESSO MARTINI (aka vodka espresso)

2 ounces vodka

1 ounce fresh espresso

½ ounce coffee liqueur

¼ ounce simple syrup

Combine the ingredients in a cocktail shaker half-filled with ice. Shake until chilled, about 15 seconds. Strain into a coupe. Garnish with three espresso beans placed on the surface of the drink.

ESPRESSO MARTINI

EXPERIMENTAL COCKTAIL CLUB

The first bar in Paris to fully embody the world of craft cocktails in all its facets, and one of the first modern cocktail bars to forge a brand and franchise its business. The original Paris location was opened by Romee de Goriainoff, Olivier Bon, and Pierre-Charles Cros in 2007. It was inspired by New York bar models, particularly Flatiron Lounge, and, as the bar's name hints at, specialized in fussy, multi-ingredient libations. A London location opened in 2010 and a New York branch in 2012. (The latter did not last.) ECC alumni include Nico de Soto, who opened his own bars in New York and Paris.

FAT WASHING

A technique by which the flavors of a solid food are imparted to an alcoholic spirit, which is then incorporated into a cocktail. Typically, the fats from a food such as meat or nuts are blended with the spirit. The mixture is then frozen, after which the fat, which has risen to the top, is scraped away, leaving only its flavor and savory qualities behind. The process, while not a new one, became popular in the aughts after the success of PDT's Benton's Old-Fashioned by Don Lee, in which bourbon was fat-washed with bacon from Tennessee-made Benton's. Earlier experiments with fat-washed cocktails were conducted by bartender Eben Freeman at the restaurant WD-50 in New York, including blending brown butter with rum. He later served fat-washed drinks at the restaurant Tailor. Another famous example is the Honey-Nut Old-Fashioned, served at Varnish in Los Angeles, for which bourbon was fat-washed with peanuts.

FERNET

A subcategory of strongly flavored, intensely bitter amaro with a cultish reputation and a divisive personality. Its forbidding bitterness creates devoted fans on one side and avowed haters on the other. It is the ultimate scrunch-up-your-face spirit. Fernet is guided by no official regulations or criteria; it's more a you-know-it-when-you-taste-it kind of thing. It is closely associated with Italy, though fernets are made in other countries as well, including Germany, the Czech Republic, Argentina, and Mexico. The best-known brand by far is Fernet-Branca, based in Milan. There were once many brands, but the number dwindled as the twentieth century marched on. With the dawn of the cocktail renaissance—whose young bartenders loved Fernet-Branca not wisely, but too well—other brands came into wider circulation. Fernet is typically drunk neat after meals. However, it has occasionally been used in cocktails since the late nineteenth century. Its most famous host is Ada Coleman's Hanky Panky cocktail. The Old-Fashioned–like Toronto cocktail is also well known.

Argentina has a particular love of fernet. The amaro was introduced to the country by Italians who moved there in the late nineteenth century. The country consumes more fernet than any other, often in the form of a fernet and Coca-Cola highball (fernet con coca), and has the only Fernet-Branca distillery outside of Italy. In the U.S., most of the fernet consumption occurred within the Italian community in San Francisco. It was the bartenders of that city that embraced the liquor as a hip "bartender's handshake" in the early years of the current century and spread

FERNET

their love of it across the nation. Soon, bartenders around the country were mixing it. Damon Boelte of New York made it the base of the popular shot Hard Start. Toby Maloney in Chicago made it part of his Campari-based Eeyore's Requiem.

FIFTY-FIFTY MARTINI

A popular form of the classic Martini in which gin and dry vermouth sit in equal proportions, leading to a cocktail that is less alcoholic and lighter in body, affording each of the two main ingredients an equal voice. While equal-parts Martinis can be found in drink manuals of the late nineteenth century (albeit made with Old Tom gin and sweet vermouth), the style was never particularly dominant, and it achieved its zenith in popularity only in the twenty-first century, when it was championed by mixologists equally besotted with historical authenticity and vermouth. The first to proffer the style was Sasha Petraske of Milk & Honey fame. But widespread acceptance among the cocktail cognoscenti came with Pegu Club, where owner Audrey Saunders put her fifty-fifty Martini on the opening menu and left it there. The drink was soon adopted by fellow bartenders and the media who covered them. Preferring fifty-fiftys became accepted dogma and a badge of honor among those in the know. (Some have speculated that the style was popularized by liquor brand ambassadors looking to cut back on their alcohol intake.) The style remains popular among epicures, though it has never overtaken the dry Martini in terms of mass popularity. By the mid-2010s, many modern bartenders returned to drier styles of the cocktail with a renewed respect. A popular cheat on the recipe is to make it with Navy Proof gin, which increases the drink's punch but erases its initial purpose.

F

FIFTY-FIFTY MARTINI

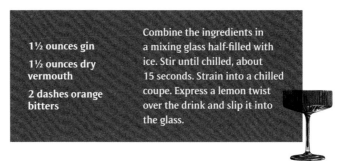

1½ ounces gin

1½ ounces dry vermouth

2 dashes orange bitters

Combine the ingredients in a mixing glass half-filled with ice. Stir until chilled, about 15 seconds. Strain into a chilled coupe. Express a lemon twist over the drink and slip it into the glass.

FITZGERALD

A gin sour with bitters, invented in the 1990s by Dale DeGroff at the Rainbow Room, who named it after the writer F. Scott Fitzgerald. Nowhere is it more loved than Minneapolis–St. Paul, where they appreciate the original Fitzgerald, too.

FITZGERALD

1½ ounces gin

1 ounce simple syrup

¾ ounce lemon juice

2 dashes Angostura bitters

Combine the ingredients in a mixing glass half-filled with ice. Stir until chilled, about 15 seconds. Strain into a rocks glass. Garnish with a lemon twist.

FIX

FIX

A genre of cocktail no different from a sour in that it features spirit, sugar, and citrus, except that the resultant mixture is served over shaved ice. That detail may not seem like much, but the experiential difference is significant. Fixes were regularly given their own section in cocktail books throughout the late nineteenth century, with common varieties being brandy, gin, rum, whiskey, and sherry. Sometimes bartenders tossed in a bit of this and a bit of that and adorned them with copious garnish—Harry Johnson was big on this—but usually they were pretty elemental. You didn't see them much in the twentieth century, though Harry MacElhone squeezed a couple into his books in the 1920s. Few genres of drink so completely disappeared after Prohibition as the Fix. The category was almost single-handedly resurrected by Sasha Petraske, who featured fixes at his bar and devoted a chapter to them in his posthumous book. If you step into a Petraske bar, or one owned by one of his protégés, you can still get one. Elsewhere, forget about it.

FIZZ

An old-school cocktail dating back to the mid-nineteenth century, made up of spirit, lemon juice, sugar, and soda water—the latter ingredient providing the fizz of the name. It is differentiated from the similar collins family in being served short and straight up. Various spirits were used, though gin was the most common. Nineteenth-century New York bartender William Schmidt was celebrated for his way with a gin fizz, which he shook for a full three minutes, delivering, in his own words, "a thick, creamy, puffy, soft and delicious liquid, beautiful to the eye, aromatic to the smell and delicious to the taste." Notable members of the family include the Silver Fizz, which contains an egg white; the Golden Fizz, which has an egg yolk; the Sloe Gin Fizz, pink and sweet, which enjoyed a heyday in the late twentieth century; the Southside Fizz, which adds mint; and, perhaps most famously, the creamy Ramos Gin Fizz, invented by bartender Henry Ramos of New Orleans. The Gunshop Fizz, which has a base of bitters, is a notable recent contribution to the genre. Although known to modern bartenders, it is rarely ordered or made, perhaps because, like the collins, it is considered too prosaic a choice. It is a drink that is of the moment, losing its spark quickly. As Harry Johnson wrote, "Bear in mind that all drinks called Fizz's must be [drunk] as soon as handed out, or the natural taste of the same is lost to the customer."

FLATIRON LOUNGE

The first New York craft cocktail bar of the modern era that offered well-honed drinks, both classic and original, in a high-volume setting. It was founded in 2003 in Manhattan's Flatiron District by Julie Reiner, who had earned attention as the bar director at the restaurant C3; Susan Fedroff, Reiner's life partner; Michelle Connolly; and Alex and Kristina Kossi, two New York siblings who had previously opened the Zinc Bar, a Jazz Age–flavored throwback bar with music. Flatiron's design, too, had a 1920s feel, with a long circular tunnel leading to an old art deco bar and the feeling you had passed into a bygone era. Reiner took the lead on the drinks, serving accessible and juicy vodka and gin drinks with just enough flair and ingenuity to stand out from the crowd. An early press of patrons led to speed-oriented innovations that were quickly adopted as industry standard, including "cheater bottles"—small vessels containing lesser-used but necessary spirits—and compounded blends that cut down on the number of bottles needed to complete each cocktail. As such, Flatiron's greater achievement was more in process and operation than cutting-edge cocktail creation. Reiner trained her bartenders in these new skill sets from the ground up, producing future industry leaders like Lynnette Marrero, Katie Stipe, Giuseppe González, Tonia Guffey, and Phil Ward. Much of the preparation for Pegu Club was done in Flatiron's basement, which Pegu leader Audrey Saunders used as an office. Flatiron was also a direct influence on the Experimental Cocktail Club, the first major modern cocktail bar to open in Paris. Flatiron Lounge closed in 2018, after fifteen years in business, because of a rent hike.

FLIP

The earliest flips were hot drinks involving warmed ale, to which spirits (brandy or rum, usually), sugar, eggs, and spices were added. The mixture was then heated up with a red-hot poker, causing the concoction to foam up. Over time, flips could be either hot or cold, as long as a whole egg was involved. Today, the name is conferred on cold cocktails using a whole egg. Given the public's general squeamishness about raw eggs, the genre has not experienced a robust revival, but it is not completely forgotten. The Death Flip (made of tequila, yellow Chartreuse, Jägermeister, simple syrup, and a whole egg) is a rare modern flip that has enjoyed renown.

FLOAT

A mixing technique in which an ingredient is gently layered on top of a cocktail by pouring it carefully over the back of a barspoon. Two popular drinks that feature floats are the New York Sour, in which red wine is floated atop a whiskey sour, and the Penicillin, which has a float of smoky scotch. Pousse cafés and shooters are two genres of drink that rely heavily on floating liquors on top of one another.

A BARTENDER AT EL FLORIDITA

EL FLORIDITA

A cocktail bar in Havana, Cuba. It is certainly the most famous bar in Cuba; and could be the most famous cocktail bar in the world; doubtless one of the most long-standing; and inarguably a standard-bearer in terms of technique, style, and quality. It calls itself "The Cradle of the Daiquiri" and indeed had much to do with the popularization of that rum sour. It mixed many of them for novelist Ernest Hemingway, the bar's most famous patron, memorialized with a life-size statue at the end of the bar. For said writer, the bar invented the Hemingway Daiquiri, which stands as the bar's second-most famous drink. Given its notoriety as a cocktail bar, visitors may be surprised to discover that much of Floridita's interior is devoted to a seafood restaurant. The place opened in 1816 on the corner of

Obispo and Monserrate streets as La Piña de Plata. The current name came a century later. Constantino Ribalaigua Vert began working there in 1914 and owned it from 1918. He left a lasting stamp on the bar and helped connect El Floridita and the daiquiri in the public's mind. The bar retains an air of glamour, with the bartenders in formal red jackets.

FRANCIS, RICHARD

One of the most prominent bartenders of his day in the Washington, DC, area. Born in 1827 to free Black parents in Virginia, from 1848 on Francis worked for four decades at Hancock's, a small bar on Pennsylvania Avenue near the White House. There he served and was friendly with the preeminent politicians of the day, including Senators Daniel Webster and Henry Clay, as well as die-hard slavery proponents like John C. Calhoun. In 1884, he was tapped to manage the restaurant and bar in the United States Senate. A paper in 1885 called him "the best fancy drink mixer in Washington." He died in 1888 at the age of sixty-two. His son, John, was a doctor whom Francis put through medical school.

FREEMAN, EBEN

A New York bartender known for a series of innovative, if short-lived, cocktail programs. He first gained fame in 2004 as the bar director at chef Wylie Dufresne's famous restaurant WD-50. There he experimented with the technique of fat washing cocktails. He then went on to Tailor, where he epitomized the school of molecular mixology through such offerings as absinthe gummy bears, bubble gum–flavored vodka, pumpernickel-infused scotch, and, most famous, a smoked whiskey-and-coke called the Waylon. He later worked for chef Michael White's Altamarea empire of restaurants, briefly running a supper club called Butterfly that showcased his cocktails; then AvroKO, for which he opened Genuine Liquorette, a basement bar that specialized in custom bulldog drinks.

FREE POURING

A widespread mixing technique by which a bartender relies only on his eyes, rather than a jigger, to measure out the ingredients in a cocktail. In the latter twentieth century, it was the only technique. Jiggers were rare sights in bars, and bartenders who used them were criticized by patrons as stingy misers. Joe Baum forbade Dale DeGroff to use jiggers at the Rainbow Room. But Sasha Petraske insisted on jiggers at Milk & Honey, convinced precise measurements led to more balanced cocktails. Advocates of either side of the argument are typically 100 percent convinced they are right.

FRENCH 75

A high-end sour royale of French origin composed of lemon juice, sugar, champagne, and—here's where things get interesting—either gin or cognac. The drink has its origins in the 1920s, and early recipes stipulate calvados and grenadine, but by the end of the decade they call for gin. Starting in the 1940s, however, some noted voices, such as David A. Embury, the opinionated lawyer-author of *The Fine Art of Mixing Drinks* (1948), began advocating for cognac. Dale DeGroff, the bartender godfather of the American cocktail revival, also liked cognac in the cocktail, and printed that version in his influential 2002 book *The Craft of the Cocktail.* But no one has done more to promote the cognac camp than New Orleans bartender Chris Hannah. And since Hannah was the head bartender of the French 75 Bar in New Orleans for more than a decade, his opinion went a long way. Over time, everyone agreed that both versions taste good. Still, given cognac's cost, gin remains the more common base.

FRENCH 75

1 ounce gin or cognac
½ ounce lemon juice
½ ounce simple syrup
2 ounces champagne

Combine all the ingredients except the champagne in a cocktail shaker half-filled with ice. Shake until chilled, about 15 seconds. Strain into a flute. Top with the champagne. Garnish with a lemon twist.

GARNISHES

Crowning touches to cocktails that serve either culinary or visual purposes—or both. Garnishes have been a part of cocktail making almost as long as cocktails have been made but really came into their own, and sometimes more so, in the mid- to late nineteenth century. Garnishes range widely in terms of produce. Fruits and herbs are predominant, but vegetables are far from unheard of. Many of the most famous cocktails are garnished, and often their garnish is very much a part of their public image. The Martini and the olive are inseparable in both the public mind and all imagery of the drink. A Manhattan without a cherry is not a Manhattan. A Gibson is completely defined by its unique garnish, a pickled onion. The flamboyant garnish of a Mint Julep is in the drink's very name. The Brandy Crusta, an early example of over-the-top garnishing, requires a long, snaking peel of lemon inside the glass. The Whiskey Sour is strongly associated with the double-barreled garnish of the orange slice–cherry "flag." A Bloody Mary would not be considered complete without a stalk of celery, and most drinkers demand much more beyond that, including olives, pickles, cubes of cheese and meat, peppers, and more. The Old-Fashioned has taken on a host of garnishes during different points in history, from a simple orange or lemon twist to an orange slice, cherry, and pineapple spear. In Wisconsin, olives, pickled mushrooms, and pickled Brussels sprouts are popular Old-Fashioned garnishes. Tiki drinks are perhaps the most garnished cocktails on the planet, calling on everything from pineapple fronds and orchids to upturned lime shells and bananas cut to look like dolphins. On the other end of the spectrum is the Sazerac, where the garnish is invisible: a lemon twist expressed over the drink and then discarded. The humble lemon twist is perhaps the most common of garnishes, an acceptable finale to a Martini and Manhattan and finishing off myriad other cocktails.

Citrus garnishes can take the form of a twist, a wedge, or a wheel. Garnishing was already a critical bartending art when Jerry Thomas came out with his famous bartending manual in 1862. Juleps and cobblers typically got the full treatment in that era, being topped with the "fruits of the season." "It is necessary to display taste in ornamenting the glass after the beverage is made," Thomas wrote of the cobbler. As the Gilded Age of the late nineteenth century arrived, garnishing got even more ornate. Bartender Harry Johnson was particularly garnish-happy, the drink illustrations in his cocktail book well ornamented. At the far end of Prohibition, drinks became more spare and elemental, and garnishes followed suit, though those drinks that did have garnishes became more rigidly tied to them. Some garnishes of olden days, such as whole eggs and pickled walnuts, have not survived into modern times. In the late twentieth century, people got creative with the dominant olive, stuffing the fruit with everything from almonds to anchovies to blue cheese, the latter becoming a lasting favorite among certain Martini drinkers.

Cherries suffered a sad fate for most of the twentieth century. The artificially colored, sugar-laden "maraschino" cherries dominated bars in the United States. Only with the cocktail revival were true maraschino cherries from Italy returned to use. Other bars chose to make their own cocktail cherries from scratch.

In the current century, bartenders began to take garnishes seriously again, insisting on fresh produce and playing around with ornately cut and shaped twists. The flamed orange twist came into vogue and remains so. The "rabbit ears" garnish, a pairing of lemon and orange twists, was popularized by Milk & Honey. Some modern classics came with unique garnishes of their own, such as the Espresso Martini, which is adorned with three coffee beans suspended on the surface, and the Penicillin, marked by a piece of candied ginger. Other bartenders went in the other direction, adamantly opposing garnishes and insisting the liquid drink speak for itself. Their arguments are respected, though their drinks aren't much fun.

GIBSON

Frequently described as a Martini with a cocktail onion, the Gibson has nonetheless held on to its own separate identity long enough to retain its specific name. The drink's defining garnish is actually a latecomer. Early recipes do not call for an onion at all. The famous allium first appears in the 1922 book *Cocktails—How to Mix Them* by Robert Vermeire. By the 1940s, drink and garnish were inseparable. The Gibson is also distinct from the Martini in terms of bitters; the Gibson has none. Various colorful and improbable stories circulate as to how the drink got its name, none of them true. After years shivering in the shadow of the Martini, this cocktail made a comeback in the 2010s, with many bars offering careful and imaginative takes on the Gibson, often using blanc vermouth instead of or in addition to dry, and their own house-pickled cocktail onions. Dear Irving in New York became particularly well known for its Gibson.

GIBSON

GIBSON

3 ounces gin

1 ounce dry
vermouth

Combine the ingredients in
a mixing glass half-filled with
ice. Stir until chilled, about
15 seconds. Strain into a
chilled coupe. Garnish with
a cocktail onion.

GIN

The preeminent cocktail darling of all time, the juniper-informed white spirit, in its various forms, has formed the base of hundreds of cocktails, among them dozens of classics, most significantly the almighty Martini. Other deathless gin cocktails include the gin and tonic, Tom Collins, Negroni, gin fizz, Ramos Gin Fizz, Corpse Reviver No. 2, Clover Club, Gimlet, French 75, Last Word, Southside, Singapore Sling, White Lady, Martinez, and Pegu Club. Modern drinks that have succeeded with gin include the Breakfast Martini, Bramble, Gin Basil Smash, Gin-Gin Mule, White Negroni, and Wibble. In the early years of cocktail culture, the gin that was used in American bars and called for in cocktail manuals was not the London dry style we are most familiar with today, but either the malty Dutch genever—often referred to as Hollands gin—or Old Tom gin, a sweetened version of the spirit. Thus the gin drinks of the nineteenth century were quite different in flavor and character from those of the twentieth. The Gin Cocktail was fairly akin to what would become known as the Old-Fashioned. Gin was amply applied to nearly all the popular cocktail forms of the time, including the fizz, fix, julep, sling, smash, sour, daisy, and toddy.

The spirit really came into its own in the 1880s with the creation of the Martini family of drinks, including the Turf Club, Martinez, and Tuxedo. The arrival of the Tom Collins in the 1870s also gave gin a boost. London dry gin, with its drier and more juniper- and citrus-forward flavor profile, began to assert itself at the turn of the twentieth century, never relinquishing its dominant position. Martinis became drier, as did the Tom Collins. Leading London dry brands included Beefeater, Tanqueray, Bombay, Gordon's, and Gilbey. Plymouth gin, made in the English coastal town, was considered a separate category unto itself, a distinction it held onto until 2015. It was often name-checked specifically in cocktail books of the early twentieth century. The United States had its own gins as well, including Fleischmann's and Seagram's, but they were generally considered not to be of comparable quality.

Beginning in the 1960s, gin began to lose market ground to vodka, which promised an anonymous experience as consumers veered toward flavorless drinks. Vodka Martinis, vodka and tonics, and Vodka Collins became widespread. By the turn of the twenty-first century, gin was in the dumps, ignored by bars and drinkers and very nearly forgotten in the United States. There were certain isolated brands that bucked this trend, mainly by aping the appeal and flash of vodka. Among these were the blue-bottled Bombay Sapphire, introduced in 1987, and Tanqueray No. Ten, in 2000. Hendrick's, a Scottish gin that came in an unusual black metal container and tasted of rose and cucumber, probably did the most to bring cachet back to the category. Young mixologists of the twenty-first century, recognizing an injustice when they saw one and wishing to return classic cocktails to their original glory, began to use and promote gin. Plymouth, brought back from the brink of death, was an early success story, becoming a favorite of bartenders and cocktail drinkers. Beefeater followed. Soon the gin market was rosy enough that new brands began to appear for the first time in ages, including many "craft" gins in America. Among such early brands were Aviation, Junipero, Leopold's, Bluecoat, and Death's Door.

In time, the gin boom in the United States was mirrored in other countries, including Australia, Spain, and Germany, which began to produce dozens of new gin brands. Spain's florid cult of the "Gin Tonic," basically a gin and tonic on steroids, started to become popular well beyond the country's borders. Bars dedicated to gin and gin drinks accompanied these booms, including Scofflaw in Chicago, Whitechapel in San Francisco, and Gin Joint in Charleston. Once gin as a category was resuscitated, disappeared styles like Old Tom, and neglected ones like genever, joined in on the revival. By the 2010s, however, a backsliding had begun, and category-compromising "flavored" gins and pink gins began to flood the market, rendering the gin shelf a confusing cacophony of expressions not unlike the flavored-vodka explosion of the 1980s and '90s.

GIN AND TONIC

A highball made of guess what? There's a squeeze of citrus in there, too, either lemon or lime, depending on where you live. A good drink if malaria is a constant threat for you, as it was for the British in India in the nineteenth century, who found a nifty way to temper their daily dose of quinine. Typically a simple, barely unadorned drink, but in Spain, where it is called Gin Tonic, it is the opposite: a colorful sideshow of herbs and fruits served in a goblet.

GIN AND TONIC

1½ ounces gin

3 ounces tonic water

Combine the ingredients in a collins glass filled with ice. Stir briefly. Squeeze a lime wedge over the drink and drop it into the glass.

GIN BASIL SMASH

The most famous modern classic cocktail to come out of Germany. It was the invention of Joerg Meyer, the owner of Le Lion in Hamburg. Meyer was influenced by the Whiskey Smash, which he experienced at Pegu Club during a trip to New York. Created in 2008, it is basically a gin Mojito, but with basil instead of mint as the muddled herb. Fantastically popular in Europe, it has never made the leap to North America. Le Lion sells three hundred to five hundred a night. In 2012, Meyer painted the words "Cradle of the Gin Basil Smash" on the outside of the bar.

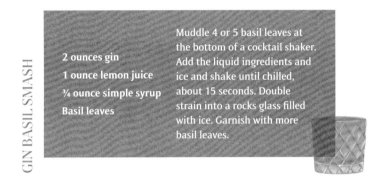

GIN BASIL SMASH

2 ounces gin
1 ounce lemon juice
¾ ounce simple syrup
Basil leaves

Muddle 4 or 5 basil leaves at the bottom of a cocktail shaker. Add the liquid ingredients and ice and shake until chilled, about 15 seconds. Double strain into a rocks glass filled with ice. Garnish with more basil leaves.

GIN-GIN MULE

A popular modern classic cocktail invented by Audrey Saunders in 2000 at Beacon restaurant in New York. It is basically a Mojito crossed with a Moscow Mule but made with gin and homemade ginger beer—a rarity at the time. It achieved wide popularity after being featured on the menu at Saunders's bar Pegu Club. Some have noted a similarity between it and the Ginger Rogers, a drink by Marcovaldo Dionysos, which was based on a 1914 drink by Jacques Straub called the Favorite Cocktail. The Ginger Rogers was the breakout cocktail at Absinthe, which opened in San Francisco in 1998.

1¾ ounces
Tanqueray Gin

¾ ounce lime juice

1 ounce simple syrup
(1:1)

2 mint sprigs
(1 for muddling;
1 for garnish)

1 ounce homemade
ginger beer*

Combine the lime juice, simple syrup, and one mint sprig at the bottom of a mixing glass. Muddle well. Add the gin and ginger beer and half-fill with ice. Shake until chilled, about 15 seconds. Strain into a highball glass filled with ice. Garnish with a mint sprig. Serve with a straw.

G

*GINGER BEER

1 quart filtered water

4 ounces ginger root

½ ounce fresh
lime juice

2 tablespoons
light brown sugar

Add the water to a saucepan and bring to a boil. Break up the ginger root into smaller pieces, and place in a food processor. Add a cup of the boiling water to make processing easier. Process till almost mulch-like. After the ginger is minced, add it back into the boiling water. Shut off the heat. Stir well, and cover for 1 hour. Strain through a fine chinois or cheesecloth, and add lime juice and light brown sugar. Let cool. Transfer into bottles or containers and store in the refrigerator. *Important:* When you are straining the ginger through the strainer, take a spoon or ladle and firmly press down on the ginger to extract the flavor. The strongest part of the ginger essence is still hiding in there and needs to be pressed out manually. Its appearance will be cloudy; this is natural.

GIN-GIN MULE

SHINGO GOKAN

GIN PALACE

An influential cocktail bar opened by Vernon Chalker on a narrow laneway in Melbourne in 1997. Chalker chose a gin focus for his bar in order to stand out from the vodka-soaked competition. In doing so, he unwittingly predicted the gin and gin-bar revival to come in the next two decades. He described the eclectic décor as an 1870s lounge bar in Budapest that was renovated in the 1950s and discovered intact decades later—which description is an apt window into the workings of Chalker's mind.

GOKAN, SHINGO

A Japan-born bartender who, after spending ten years working at Angel's Share, the Japanese-styled speakeasy in Manhattan, moved to Shanghai and became an important force in that city's cocktail scene. Gokan opened the speakeasy Speak Low in 2014, Sober Company in 2016, the SG Club in Tokyo in 2019, and The Odd Couple—a retro '80s bar he opened with Employees Only bartender Steve Schneider—in Shanghai in 2019. In 2020 he launched his own brand of shochu, a collaboration with three top distillers. In 2023, he opened his first American bar in New York.

GOLD RUSH

A Whiskey Sour variation using bourbon, lemon juice, and a rich honey syrup instead of sugar or simple syrup. It was created in 2001 at Milk & Honey, a collaboration of T. J. Siegel, who hatched the idea and ordered it, and owner Sasha Petraske, who created the honey syrup and stirred up the first specimen. It quickly became popular at the bar, suggested as a bartender's choice for customers interested in a new whiskey cocktail. From there, it leapt to other Petraske joints and other cocktail bars. The Gold Rush was Milk & Honey's first success in producing an original classic cocktail. It directly inspired the creation of the Penicillin, another Milk & Honey classic.

GOLD RUSH

2 ounces bourbon

¾ ounce lemon juice

¾ ounce rich honey syrup (3 parts honey to 1 part water)

Combine the ingredients in a cocktail shaker three-quarters filled with ice. Shake until chilled, about 15 seconds. Strain into an old-fashioned glass filled with one large ice cube.

GRASSHOPPER

One of the great dessert drinks of the twentieth century, a mixture of crème de cacao, crème de menthe, and cream. The cacao used is the clear sort; the menthe the green kind, which lends the drink its trademark color and its name. Its origins

GRASSHOPPER

are unclear. A popular story has it being invented in 1928 by Philip Guichet, the owner of the New Orleans institution Tujague's, but there is no evidence to back this up. Even if it was invented there and then, the Grasshopper did not take off. (The drink, however, continued to be served there for many years, and no bar is more associated with the cocktail.) It quickly rose to prominence in the post–World War II years, particularly in the Midwest, and for a few decades was ubiquitous, until it eventually faded from view as too old-fashioned, sweet, and caloric. In the 2020s, however, it made a comeback and was served at some of the best cocktail bars. This was due, in part, to the arrival on the market of quality, artisanal versions of cacao and menthe, liqueurs that had become tainted by coloring and chemicals over time. In the Midwest, a base of lingering popularity, the drink is often served as an ice cream drink, with vanilla ice cream replacing the cream, and the two liqueurs playing accenting roles. New

Orleans bartender Paul Gustings, who uses cognac in the drink, is considered a modern master of the Grasshopper.

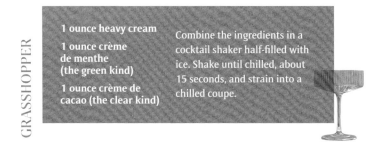

GRASSHOPPER

1 ounce heavy cream

1 ounce crème de menthe (the green kind)

1 ounce crème de cacao (the clear kind)

Combine the ingredients in a cocktail shaker half-filled with ice. Shake until chilled, about 15 seconds, and strain into a chilled coupe.

GREYHOUND

A highball made of gin and grapefruit juice or, later, vodka. There's a bar in Oakland, California, called Cafe Van Kleef that has made it their signature drink (with freshly squeezed grapefruit juice) simply because the owner liked them—the only way a bar is going to specialize in Greyhounds, if the boss insists.

GREYHOUND

1½ ounces vodka

4 ounces grapefruit juice

Combine the ingredients in a collins glass filled with ice. Stir briefly.

GRIMES, WILLIAM

A career *New York Times* journalist, born in 1950, who was among the first to note and report on the doings of bartender Dale DeGroff at the Rainbow Room, and thus penned a first draft of modern cocktail history. Grimes, known as "Biff," took up the subject at greater length when he published *Straight Up or on the Rocks: A Cultural History of American Drink* (1993), the first serious study of the history of the origins of American mixology. Though little noticed at the time, the book later became a critical text when bartenders and journalists of the craft cocktail movement were getting their sea legs. The book was republished in 2002. He also worked at the *Times* as a restaurant critic and obituary writer.

PAUL GUSTINGS

GUSTINGS, PAUL

A New Orleans bartender as renowned for his charmingly cantankerous personality as for his skill with classic drinks. Born in the Netherlands, he put in considerable time at two of the more fabled and ancient French Quarter bars, Napoleon House and Tujague's, where he served two terms, as well as Broussard's. He is celebrated for his way with libations of local pedigree, including the Sazerac, which he bitters heavily, and the Grasshopper, as well as various punches.

G

HAIGH, TED

The modern cocktail revival's first cocktail historian. A graphic designer in cinema by trade, he was bitten by the cocktail bug early on and would spend his on-location free time searching for out-of-print cocktail books and then combing through liquor stores to find the defunct ingredients he needed to recreate the drinks in the books. After working in New Orleans, he returned to L.A. with a trove of Peychaud's bitters. He browbeat Fee Brothers in Rochester, one of the last bitters makers in the United States, into recreating peach bitters. Haigh was host of the food and drink board in the early internet days of America Online (AOL) and launched the CocktailDB, an online database of drinks and ingredients. He eventually collected all his knowledge into a single book, *Vintage Spirits and Forgotten Cocktails,* published in 2004 and reissued, in much more elaborate form, in 2009. He was also an early columnist at *Imbibe* magazine. In 2005 he cofounded the Museum of the American Cocktail in New Orleans. The garrulous, yarn-spinning Haigh was also adept at fostering important early connections in the cocktail community, introducing future tiki historian Jeff Berry to important tiki bartenders in L.A., and bringing Dale DeGroff to Julie Reiner's first bar in New York. Early on, he gave himself the nickname Dr. Cocktail, after one of the forgotten drinks in his book. Appropriately, the cocktail featured a forgotten spirit, Swedish punsch.

HANKY PANKY

A cocktail invented in the 1920s by British bartender Ada Coleman, consisting of gin, sweet vermouth, and a small amount of Fernet-Branca. It was included in *The Savoy Cocktail Book,* though not attributed to Coleman. It is the most famous classic cocktail to call for fernet.

HANKY PANKY

1½ ounces gin

1½ ounces sweet vermouth

2 dashes Fernet-Branca

Combine the ingredients in a mixing glass half-filled with ice. Stir until chilled, about 15 seconds. Strain into a chilled coupe. Express an orange twist over the drink and drop it into the glass.

HANNAH, CHRIS

The child of a roving military family, Chris Hannah moved from Baltimore to New Orleans in 2004 and swiftly became one of the most important and influential bartenders in the city. Under his management, the French 75 Bar inside the historic Arnaud's restaurant in the French Quarter became a cocktail mecca and drinks destination for both locals and tourists. His championing of the cognac version of the French 75 stirred debate and won devotees of that expression. A student of cocktail history, he did much to bring back lost New Orleans drinks like the Roffignac and Creole cocktails. He also invented a fair share of well-known modern drinks while at the French 75 Bar, including the Bywater and Night Tripper. After spending fourteen years at the French 75, he left to cofound his own place, Jewel of the South, which took its name from a restaurant owned by the nineteenth-century New Orleans bartender Joseph Santini. The centerpiece of the menu was yet another old NOLA drink, Santini's most famous invention, the Brandy Crusta.

HARD SHAKE

A technique for shaking cocktails involving an intricate three-point combination of horizontal and vertical moves, invented by vaunted Japanese bartender Kazuo Uyeda, owner of the Tender bar in Tokyo. Though adopted and practiced by relatively few working bartenders, the style of shaking is renowned and one of the few with name recognition within the industry. The meaning of the name is often misconstrued. It does not mean the shake is more forceful than others; nor does it necessarily mean it is difficult to master. Rather, it means that the shake is individual to Uyeda and only he can execute it precisely. Whether there is anything of practical merit behind the shake is a matter of continued debate. Advocates say the complex path of the ice inside the shaker improves the texture, aeration, and chill of the cocktail. Detractors say the hard shake makes no difference whatsoever in the temperature or texture of a drink. Both agree that the hard shake is aesthetically pleasing, making for a balletic and entertaining show.

HARRINGTON, PAUL

A bartender from Washington State whose brief career in the San Francisco Bay Area had a lasting impression in the 1990s. He worked at the Townhouse, a renovated honky-tonk in Emeryville, and, for a shorter period, at Enrico's, an old beatnik hangout in San Francisco's North Beach neighborhood. He made Enrico's notorious for its Mojitos, made with fresh juice and mint. At the menuless Townhouse, he tailored cocktails to customer's preferences. One night, he invented a twist on the Pegu Club called the Jasmine; the drink would go on to become a standard. At Enrico's, he connected with editors of the new magazine *Wired* and later collaborated with them on an early internet cocktail site. Later, he collaborated with *Wired* editor Laura Moorhead on *Cocktail: The Drinks Bible for the 21st Century,* one of the first important, historically minded cocktail books of the dawning cocktail-revival era. The book, published in 1998, found its way into the hands of many up-and-coming young mixologists around the world. By then, Harrington had left bartending for architecture.

HARRY'S BAR (VENICE)

Giuseppe Cipriani, a Veronese who had bartended at the Hotel Europa, opened Harry's Bar in 1931 in a former warehouse at the end of Calle Vallaresso, a quiet street in Venice just steps from the Grand Canal. He named it after Harry Pickering, an American who gave him the seed money. At the time, if you wanted class and cocktails in Venice, you went to a hotel bar. Harry's was an anomaly, but it nonetheless became a destination watering hole for the cultural jet set: Noel Coward, Orson Welles, Barbara Hutton, Truman Capote (who, in his unfinished novel *Answered Prayers,* called it "Mr. Cipriani's microscopic fine-food-and-drink palace"), Peggy Guggenheim, and, most famously, Ernest Hemingway. Papa even set some scenes in his novel *Across the River and Into the Trees* in the bar. Its trademark drink, invented in the 1940s by Cipriani, is the Bellini, made of Prosecco and white peach puree. Harry's follows its own rules. Its Martini is nearly free of vermouth and served in a shot glass. The Daiquiris are made with lemon juice. Classic cocktails are exceedingly dry. Its back bar is sparsely stocked. The glassware is odd and atypical. Bartenders are formally dressed in white jackets. It remains today a tourist destination without being a tourist trap (though the prices are high). It is high in its standards but not snobbish, and is without question one of the great legacy cocktail bars in the world.

HARRY'S BAR (VENICE)

HARRY'S NEW YORK BAR (PARIS)

A Paris bar, in the American style, that, after several ownerships, was bought and renamed by Scottish bartender Harry MacElhone, who made it a magnet for American expatriates, including members of the press and several notable authors. In the 1920s, MacElhone jokingly founded the International Bar Flies (or I.B.F.), whose members included many of his famous regulars who had to abide by a list of joshing guidelines. Fernand Petiot, renowned as the creator of the Bloody Mary, worked there for a time before moving to New York, as did Bob Card, who had worked at the Bohemian Club in San Francisco. The German occupation of France caused the bar to close for much of World War II; it reopened in 1944. After Harry's death in 1958, his son Andy took over. The bar remains in family hands. According to the bar, it is the birthplace of such classics as the Sidecar and French 75, and, whether or not that is true, those drinks are devotedly honored here. Today, Harry's functions and looks much like it did in the 1920s.

HARVEY WALLBANGER

A simple highball made of vodka, orange juice, and a float of Galliano that burst into the American consciousness in the early '70s—so much so that it inspired Harvey Wallbanger mixes, cakes, parties, swag, and even a presidential campaign for its fictional mascot, a pained-looking cartoon surfer who quipped, "My name is Harvey Wallbanger, and I can be made." So popular was the drink that Galliano ranked as the best-selling liqueur in the United States through the decade. The drink's origins are murky, but they definitely involve a Los Angeles bartender named Donato "Duke" Antone and a marketing man named George Bednar. Bednar worked for McKesson Imports, who netted Galliano as a client in the late 1960s and went fishing around for an angle on how to increase sales. In California, he found the drink that would be marketed as the Harvey Wallbanger. Bednar did not connect with Antone at that time, but there is evidence that the bartender invented the drink as early as the 1950s, calling it the Duke Screwdriver and selling it at his L.A. bar Black Watch. How the new name came about is unknown. (There is nothing to the oft-repeated tale that it was named after a surfer who drank one too many and began banging on the wall.) Nonetheless, by the 1970s Antone was working for Galliano and Smirnoff vodka and was calling himself the inventor of the cocktail. The Harvey Wallbanger's greatest claim to fame is as the most successful corporate cocktail to have ever been launched until the Aperol Spritz came along. The cocktail's popularity had faded by the 1980s, and efforts by bartenders in the twenty-first century to bring it back or improve it have failed. Nonetheless, it retains a hold on the public imagination, primarily because of its catchy name, which, it must be admitted, is one of the best ever in cocktail history.

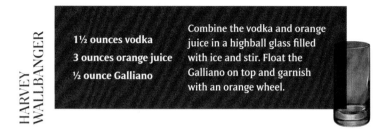

HARVEY WALLBANGER

1½ ounces vodka

3 ounces orange juice

½ ounce Galliano

Combine the vodka and orange juice in a highball glass filled with ice and stir. Float the Galliano on top and garnish with an orange wheel.

HEMINGWAY DAIQUIRI

A daiquiri variation made at El Floridita in Havana at the bidding of their best and most famous customer. As the oft-repeated story goes, diabetic Papa sampled a house daiquiri there and said, "That's good but I prefer it without sugar, and double rum." At some point, grapefruit juice and maraschino liqueur (the measurement usually being listed as a ludicrous "six drops") were added to the mix. The drink, sometimes called the Papa Doble, is still served at El Floridita. It is served at many other places besides, but the version you'll get is not exactly as prescribed by the novelist, but adapted; most bartenders believe the extra-boozy, sugar-free Daiquiri of Hemingway is all but undrinkable.

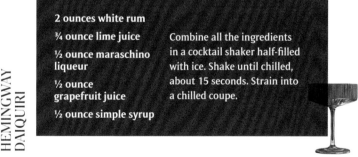

HEMINGWAY DAIQUIRI

2 ounces white rum

¾ ounce lime juice

½ ounce maraschino liqueur

½ ounce grapefruit juice

½ ounce simple syrup

Combine all the ingredients in a cocktail shaker half-filled with ice. Shake until chilled, about 15 seconds. Strain into a chilled coupe.

ERNEST HEMINGWAY

HEMINGWAY, ERNEST

The unavoidable literary barfly of all time. The novelist seems to have spent more time in famous bars than he did in front of a typewriter. He was such a fixture at El Floridita in Havana, where they concocted and serve a daiquiri named after him, that there is a life-size statue of the writer permanently stationed at the end of the bar. He is also well remembered at La Bodeguita del Medio in the same city. He is so associated with Sloppy Joe's in Key West that a Hemingway look-alike contest is held there every year. The Ritz Hotel in Paris, which Hemingway boasted of having liberated from the Nazis during World War II, named a bar after him in the '90s. He was a habitué of Harry's New York Bar in Paris and worked Harry's Bar in Venice into one of his novels. Bars named after Hemingway, meanwhile, are without number.

HIGHBALL

A category of drink so basic—a bit of this (alcoholic) with a bit more of that (not alcoholic)—that it encompasses multitudes. It's a big family, including the gin and tonic, Tom Collins, Paloma, Pimm's Cup, Screwdriver, Seven and Seven, Harvey Wallbanger, and Dark and Stormy. However, in general, when people think of the highball, they think of the simple whiskey and soda. At the turn of the twentieth century, the scotch and soda was all the rage. It was frequently mentioned and consumed in connection with golf, another Scottish tradition then recently introduced to the States. The whiskey and soda's popularity did not abate after Prohibition and World War II, when it was lapped up by legions of five o'clock–loving executives. Those postwar years were the highball's true heyday. While Americans were fairly loose about their whiskey highballs, in Japan the drink was elevated to a high art. By the 2010s, that art had reached the States. The origins of the name—which is also applied to the tall, thin glass the drinks are served in—are unknown and have long been disputed.

HOFFMAN HOUSE

The most stylish, opulent, and important New York hotel of the Gilded Age and, beginning in the 1880s, home to the city's most famous bar. The Hoffman House opened in 1864 on Broadway between 24th and 25th Streets, off Madison Square, then the epicenter of New York social life, and lasted until 1915. It was the watering hole of choice for countless famous actors, titans of business, and politicians, including presidents, usually of the Democratic Party, and various sporting men who traveled in the same circles. The mahogany bar was long, the mirrors tall, and the ceilings high. The large painting that dominated the room, which was fully lined with art, was William-Adolphe Bouguereau's *Nymphs and Satyrs,* which featured nudes and was the subject of delightful and continuous scandal. The liquors sold were of the very best, and sold at the best prices (for example, a fifty-year-old Hennessey that went for a dollar a drink), and the art of the cocktail was finely practiced by the seventeen bartenders who worked the bar. Its rival in hostelry and famous clientele was the neighborhood Fifth Avenue Hotel. Both hotels declined rapidly when New York society and theater migrated north to Herald Square. In 1905, the *Hoffman House Bartender's Guide* was published, leaving a written legacy of the glory years.

HOTEL NACIONAL SPECIAL

A drink of rum, lime juice, pineapple juice, and apricot liqueur named after, and associated with, the famed hotel in Havana. Credit, which is disputed, goes to either Wil P. Taylor or Eddie Woelke. It is not nearly as famous or popular as other cocktails with a Cuban pedigree, such as the daiquiri and Mojito. Indeed, it was all but forgotten when mixologists of the twenty-first century made efforts to reclaim it. Still, if you visit the Hotel Nacional today, you'll be hard-pressed to find a bartender who knows how to make one.

HOTEL NACIONAL SPECIAL

2 ounces rum

1 ounce pineapple juice

½ ounce lime juice

½ ounce simple syrup

½ ounce apricot liqueur

Combine the ingredients in a cocktail shaker half-filled with ice. Shake until chilled, about 15 seconds. Strain into a chilled cocktail glass.

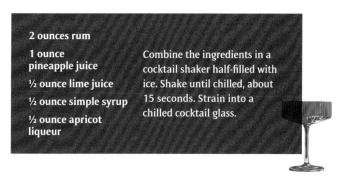

HUMMER

A popular Michigan cream drink invented by bartender Jerome Adams at the Bayview Yacht Club in Detroit in 1968. It is composed of white rum, coffee liqueur, and vanilla ice cream. Adams bartended at the club for more than fifty years and died in 2018.

HUMMER

1½ ounces white rum, preferably Bacardi

1½ ounces Kahlúa or another coffee liqueur

2 scoops vanilla ice cream

½ cup crushed ice

Combine the ingredients in a blender and blend until the ice is broken down. Serve in a chilled rocks glass.

HURRICANE

HURRICANE

A bright red, tropical, rum-citrus-and-passion-fruit drink served in its epony-mous glass, modeled after a hurricane lamp, and inextricably tied to its supposed birthplace, the sprawling French Quarter party bar Pat O'Brien's in New Orleans. O'Brien's story is that he invented the drink in the 1940s as a way to use up some excess rum. The bar has created a cottage industry around the drink, selling hur-ricane glasses and mixes, both bottled and powdered. It's doubtful anyone leaves Pat O'Brien's without consuming one.

H

ICE CREAM DRINKS

A genre of cocktail specific to the Midwest and other cold-weather states that emerged in the mid-twentieth century. More dessert than cocktail, the recipes call for traditional after-dinner drinks like the Grasshopper, Brandy Alexander, and Pink Squirrel to be projected onto ice cream, typically vanilla, and mixed up in a blender. There is not a lot of scholarship on the origins of the ice cream cocktail. But among those who have taken an interest in the subject, there is a general consensus that ice cream drinks are the result of a perfect storm of peculiarly Wisconsin phenomena. One: Wisconsinites like to drink. This has been well documented year after year. Two: Wisconsin produces a ton of dairy products and always has. Its nickname is America's Dairyland, after all. Three: The pioneering blender companies of the early twentieth century—including Hamilton Beach

AN ICE CREAM DRINK

and Oster—were based in Wisconsin, Racine specifically. Put those three things together and it's a very short road to ice cream drinks. Over time, a few bars have actually specialized in ice cream drinks, notably At Random and Bryant's Cocktail Lounge in Milwaukee and the Hobnob supper club, located between Racine and Kenosha.

INFUSIONS

A simple mixology technique by which a spirit is infused with a foodstuff such as herbs, fruits, or vegetables—that is, the food is rested inside a bottle of spirits—until the liquor takes on the flavor of the solid, either subtly or powerfully, depending on the length of the infusion. Some infusions are brief, taking anywhere from five to thirty minutes. Others last days. Liquor infusions are centuries old, but they were given a new lease on life in the cocktail revival, because they were, like homemade bitters, an easy way to create new and surprising flavors for a drink. In the early days of the movement, tea infusions were popular. Audrey Saunders's Earl Grey MarTEAni, which used Earl Grey–infused gin, was a prime example. With the rise of agave spirit cocktails, tequila infused with jalapeño peppers became a very common base liquor. Fat washing is another, more complex form of infusion. Other ingredients frequently used in infusions include hibiscus, vanilla beans, strawberries, pineapple, and coconut.

IRISH COFFEE

A hot blend of Irish whiskey, coffee, and sugar, topped with cream, that has reigned for more than half a century as one of the world's top hot drinks, daytime drinks, and coffee drinks simultaneously. The story goes that Stanton Delaplane, an influential columnist at the *San Francisco Chronicle* whose job it was to travel, discovered the drink during a layover at Shannon Airport in 1951. The man who handed it to him was Joe Sheridan, the chef there at the time. Invented by Sheridan in the 1940s and originally called the Gaelic Coffee, it caught on with Americans passing through the airport. Delaplane was in a position to take the cocktail beyond word of mouth. He brought the memory of the cocktail back to San Francisco and introduced it to Jack Koeppler, owner of the Buena Vista. After some experimentation, they nailed the drink's formula. The first Irish Coffee was reportedly sold there on November 10, 1952.

IRISH COFFEE

Delaplane, of course, couldn't help himself and wrote up his discovery. He wasn't the first American journalist to report on the drink; there were newspaper accounts as early as 1946. But Delaplane had a wider reach than his colleagues. In earlier accounts, the drink was still called Gaelic Coffee, but eventually the name Irish Coffee won out. By 1955, the Buena Vista was serving 700 of the things a day and the trend had jumped to New York and elsewhere. Ireland took note. In 1956, the deputy prime minister of Ireland himself, one William Norton, sampled an Irish Coffee at the Buena Vista and, knowing a winner when he saw one, encouraged Americans to buy more Irish whiskey. The Buena Vista continues to sell them hand over fist. The Dead Rabbit and Fort Defiance in New York also serve well-loved versions. But you can get one anywhere, although of widely varying quality.

4 ounces freshly brewed hot coffee

1 tablespoon brown sugar

1½ ounces Irish whiskey

Heavy cream, slightly whipped

Fill a footed mug or mug with hot water to preheat it, then empty. Pour hot coffee into the warmed mug. Add the brown sugar and stir until completely dissolved. Stir in the Irish whiskey. Top with whipped heavy cream by pouring gently over the back of a spoon.

IRISH WHISKEY COCKTAILS

Though Ireland and Scotland can battle it out till doomsday as to who invented one of world's great elixirs, neither can lay much of a claim to playing a major role in the cocktail world. Smoother and lighter than scotch, the number of classic Irish whiskey cocktails are, nonetheless, few, a painful reality that we are reminded of every St. Patrick's Day when dozens of trying-too-hard "Here's What to Drink on March 17" articles come out. The big Irish whiskey comeback, which began in the 1990s after a century of the spirit riding in the back seat of the whiskey wagon, hasn't improved the situation much. The Irish Coffee is the big gun. The Tipperary, a sort of Irish Manhattan laced with Chartreuse, has some standing. There's also the Emerald, which eliminated the Chartreuse; the Blackthorn, a Harry Johnson drink that brings in both sweet and dry vermouth as well as absinthe; and the Cameron's Kick, a 1920s drink that may be the best of the bunch, mixing Irish whiskey with scotch, lemon juice, and orgeat. The owners of Dead Rabbit, both Irish, went as far as publishing a book of Irish whiskey cocktails in 2022 to rectify the spirit's poor showing behind cocktail bars.

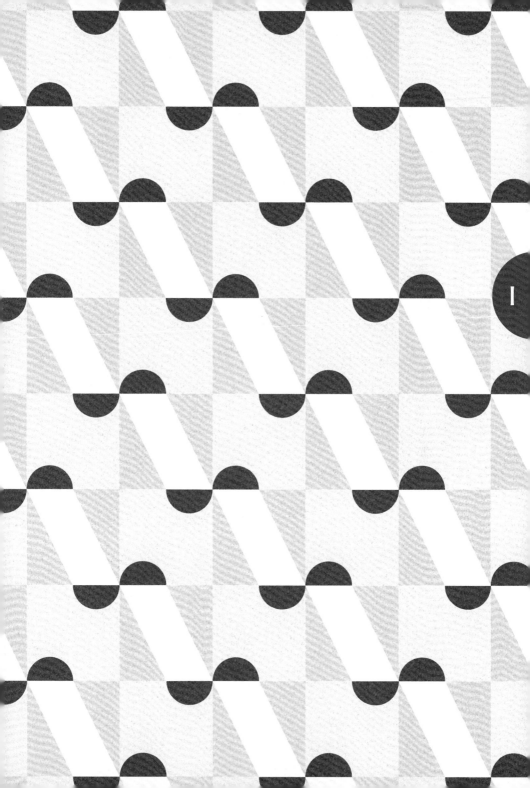

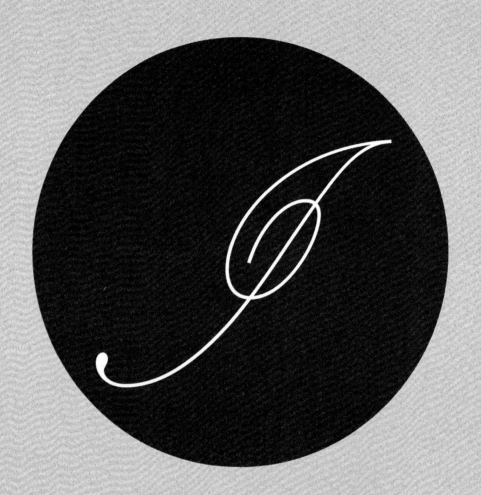

JACK ROSE

The premier apple brandy drink of the cocktail canon, it is a simple sour made of the spirit, grenadine, and either lemon or lime juice (recipes have varied over the years). The drink's origins are murky, and the stories behind the name are many, including that it was named after the 'Général Jacqueminot' rose, commonly known as the Jack Rose; though the fact that it is made with apple*jack* and has a *rose* color must be taken into account. It enjoyed a cameo in Ernest Hemingway's novel *The Sun Also Rises,* in which it is drunk by protagonist Jake Barnes. And, somewhat bizarrely, it is named as one of the six basic drinks by David A. Embury in his influential 1948 work *The Fine Art of Mixing Drinks.* Embury must have had a few too many Jack Roses when he wrote that chapter. The drink's popularity faded as the twentieth century came to a close, though it has retained a strong following in New Jersey, home of Laird's Applejack, the leading brand of apple brandy and the oldest licensed distillery in the United States. The twenty-first century brought it back, as Laird's bonded apple brandy was newly appreciated and more widely available. Bartender Jackson Cannon had a hit with the drink when he made it the centerpiece of his menu at Eastern Standard in Boston. Cannon was also a member of the Jack Rose Society, an elite club of Boston mixologists. Some, notably Thad Vogler, choose to make the drink with calvados.

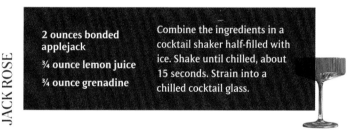

JACK ROSE

2 ounces bonded applejack
¾ ounce lemon juice
¾ ounce grenadine

Combine the ingredients in a cocktail shaker half-filled with ice. Shake until chilled, about 15 seconds. Strain into a chilled cocktail glass.

JAPANESE WHISKY

Japanese whisky has been produced commercially since the 1920s, when the Yamazaki distillery was built. For much of the twentieth century, Japanese distillers were perceived as little more than wannabe scotch makers. Masataka Taketsuru, Suntory's first master distiller and founder of Nikka Whisky Distilling, studied his art in Scotland and chose distillery sites that resembled its terrain and climate. Producers even spelled *whiskey* the Scottish way, without the "e." The juice was consumed almost entirely domestically. But after decades as an also-ran in the American whiskey market, Japanese whisky's fortunes changed dramatically in the twenty-first century. Suntory quietly introduced the Yamazaki 12-year in 1990, and that was the only option until 2005, when the 18-year arrived. By 2010, the United States had its first Japanese blended whisky, Suntory's Hibiki. The company's domination of the American market was challenged in the early aughts when its archrival, Nikka, arrived. Whiskey writers and experts began to reevaluate the spirit they had never given much thought to, and Japanese whisky makers racked up multiple plaudits and awards in short order. Soon enough, prices began to rise precipitously, and the best whiskys were being severely allocated. Suntory had achieved its goal of being viewed as a luxury product. Cocktail bars, which had employed Japanese whisky in cocktails when it was cheap, were priced out of the market. To combat the situation, Suntory introduced Toki, a younger, lesser whisky priced for easy consumer and bar use, and intended for highballs.

Japanese whisky is largely a blending art, and practices differ from the West. Unlike scotch makers, who swap liquid back and forth to build their blended whiskeys, the Japanese distillers do not trade with each other. Instead, they create countless in-house variations, using various yeasts, species of barley, and peat levels. They send the distillates through an array of stills of different shapes and sizes, then age them in a wide variety of barrels: virgin American oak, used American barrels from various suppliers, former sherry butts, and wine barrels. Adding a distinctive native flavor to some of the whiskys are barrels of expensive Japanese oak (called mizunara), which is thought to lend aromas of incense, and used plum-liqueur barrels. With all those treatments on hand, distillers can let their passion for blending run wild. And therein lies another difference: In Scotland, the single malts are the fair-haired tots, while the blends are the moneymakers, sometimes uninspired workhorses. The Japanese take their single malts seriously, too, but their blends never take a back seat.

JAPANESE WHISKY HIGHBALL

A whiskey and soda taken to artistic heights of precision, and one that stands in stark contrast to the sloppy number that goes by the name highball in the rest of the world. In the 1950s, just a few decades after Japan began to produce its own whisky, Japanese distillers seized upon this simple drink as a way to deliver their new, unfamiliar spirit to a skeptical population more accustomed to drinks with a lighter alcohol content. The effort was spearheaded by the distiller Suntory, which, in the 1980s, came up with the highball machine, which infused the whisky with carbonated water and dispensed it like a draft beer. In the 2010s, these machines began to appear in some American bars. Many were outfitted with Toki, a relatively low-priced whisky brand conceived by Suntory specifically for highballs and the American market. Those bars in Japan and the United States that do not employ a Toki machine for their highballs take great care in constructing their highballs, carefully selecting their whisky and water and delicately gauging the ratios, carbonation, and temperature.

JASMINE

A riff on the Pegu Club that includes gin, lemon juice, Cointreau, Campari, and a lemon twist. It was invented on the spot by bartender Paul Harrington one night in 1990 at the bar Townhouse, in Emeryville, California, when a regular customer asked for something new. The cocktail gained wider visibility when Harrington included it in his 1998 book *Cocktail: The Drinks Bible for the 21st Century*, which became a go-to handbook for 1990s mixologists looking for answers on cocktail history. By the mid-aughts, it was regarded as a modern classic. The drink was named after the man who ordered it—Matt Jasmin—but Harrington got the spelling wrong.

J

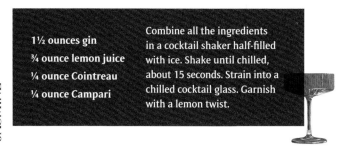

JASMINE

1 ½ ounces gin
¾ ounce lemon juice
¼ ounce Cointreau
¼ ounce Campari

Combine all the ingredients in a cocktail shaker half-filled with ice. Shake until chilled, about 15 seconds. Strain into a chilled cocktail glass. Garnish with a lemon twist.

JIGGER

A small tool, usually made of metal, with which the ingredients of cocktails are measured out. They can consist of a simple cup of anywhere from one to several ounces or, more commonly, be double-sided and hourglass-shaped, with differing measurements on either end. Of the latter, typical configurations include 1 ounce on one side and ½ ounce on the other or 1½ ounces and ¾ ounce. In Europe and elsewhere, the measurements are in milliliters. Some jiggers are angular, some

JIGGER

are rounded; some are tall and slender, some short and stout. Most are utilitarian, but, as with shakers and spoons, there's plenty of room for style and aesthetics. Jiggers began appearing at bars in the 1870s; before that, various glasses were used for measurements. Following the repeal of Prohibition, jiggers fell into disuse, and they eventually fell in disfavor in the eye of the customer, who viewed a bartender who jiggered as a chiseler who was ungenerous with customers. This perception was tough to fight against, but fight twenty-first-century mixologists did, convinced that a properly measured cocktail was a better cocktail. The jigger was one of the many weapons wielded on the battleground of the cocktail renaissance. Dale DeGroff, the godfather of the American cocktail revival, was forbidden to use jiggers at the Rainbow Room by his boss, restaurateur Joe Baum. But Sasha

Petraske, founder of the pioneering Milk & Honey, was his own boss and insisted on jiggers. Many of the bars who followed his example—and there were scores—did the same. A few modern cocktail bars insisted on free pouring, but they were outliers and usually harkening to a European ideal, as was Employees Only. A jigger is also a specific measurement, equaling one and a half ounces.

JOHNSON, HARRY

A prominent bartender of the late nineteenth century who is arguably Jerry Thomas's only rival in terms of fame and influence. His 1882 book, *Bartender's Manual,* is one of the most lasting and important tomes of the profession. Its

HARRY JOHNSON

primary distinction through its several editions, setting it apart from other volumes of the time, is that Johnson not only features the recipes for many cocktails but devotes more than half of the book to advice and instruction on how to properly run a bar, be a bartender, deal with the public, handle equipment and liquors, and anything else that might possibly come up in the professional life of a mixer of drinks. He claimed to have published an earlier version of his book in 1860 and sold ten thousand copies, but if he did, no evidence of the work has ever been found. He was born in Prussia and reached San Francisco in 1861. Johnson first worked at the Union Hotel, before moving to Chicago to open his own bar. In New York, he bought and ran the bar Little Jumbo and opened and ran other bars. Johnson's drinks were illustrative of his time, lavishly adorned and piled high with fruit and other garnishes. Inside the glass, simple drinks sported numerous final touches and flourishes. A four-ingredient drink becomes a seven-ingredient symphony in Johnson's hands. The 1888 edition of his book contains one of the two first recipes for the Martini. Johnson died in 1930 in Berlin.

JUNGLE BIRD

A very simple and once-obscure tiki drink made of rum, pineapple juice, lime juice, simple syrup, and Campari. It was invented in 1978 at the Kuala Lumpur Hilton and rediscovered by tiki historian Jeff Berry in a 1989 paperback called *The New American Bartender's Guide.* Berry then reprinted the recipe in his 2002 book *Intoxica!* The New York bar Painkiller took the recipe and tweaked it, replacing the prescribed dark Jamaica rum with the more intense blackstrap rum. It was this version that caught the bartending community's fancy, primarily owing to the unexpected presence of the bitter Campari, making the drink something of a unicorn in the tiki canon. By the mid-2010s, the Jungle Bird was being served in bars across the United States and was widely popular with the public. Several bars have named themselves after the cocktail. Today, the Jungle Bird ranks among the most familiar of all tiki cocktails.

JUNGLE BIRD

1½ ounces blackstrap rum, preferably Cruzan

¾ ounce Campari

1½ ounces pineapple juice

½ ounce lime juice

½ ounce simple syrup

Combine all the ingredients in a mixing glass half-filled with ice. Stir until chilled, about 15 seconds. Strain into a rocks glass over one large piece of ice. Garnish with a pineapple wedge.

KALKOFEN, MISTY

A Boston bartender who became one of the leading lights of that city's cocktail revival in the aughts and later an ardent advocate of mezcal. Kalkofen, a native of Green Bay, Wisconsin, and former divinity student, was taken under the wing of Brother Cleve, Boston's resident cocktail guru, at Lizard Lounge. She later helped to open B-Side in Somerville, a critical early craft cocktail bar in the area. For a time, Kalkofen shared the same Somerville house with Cleve, his wife, and Jackson Cannon, another important Boston bartender. It was there that the Jack Rose Society, an informal group of like-minded cocktail geeks, was formed. She subsequently worked at Green Street, Brick & Mortar, and Drink. After becoming enamored of mezcal, Kalkofen eventually won a post as brand ambassador for Del Maguey.

MISTY KALKOFEN

KAPPELER, GEORGE J.

A German-American bartender whose legacy is *Modern American Drinks,* the book he published in 1895. It is primarily a cocktail book, with the recipes written out in prose and with no advice or instructions on how to be a bartender. But it is highly regarded nonetheless and received a number of printings. It notably includes the Widow's Kiss, a minor classic Kappeler is thought to have created. Little is known about Kappeler otherwise, though one account states he worked at the Holland House in New York.

KING COLE BAR

A bar inside the St. Regis Hotel in New York that is recognized as the place where the modern Bloody Mary was introduced to the American public by the French bartender Fernand Petiot, who claimed he had invented it in Paris in the 1920s. At the King Cole it was offered as the Red Snapper, as the Bloody Mary was considered too vulgar a name. It remains the bar's signature drink. The bar's other significant feature is the large Maxfield Parrish mural *Old King Cole* that hangs behind the bar. It originally hung in the bar at the Knickerbocker Hotel on 42nd

KING COLE BAR

Street and Broadway, a commission of John Jacob Astor IV. When that short-lived hotel closed, the mural eventually made its way to the St. Regis, which was also owned by the Astors. The bar, which opened in 1937, was named after the painting, perhaps the only occasion where the bar art came first, the bar second.

KÜMMEL

An aromatic liqueur flavored by cumin and caraway, common to northern Europe and going back centuries, kümmel has never been a major player in the cocktail world, not having a single classic cocktail to its credit. It made appearances in drinks often enough beginning in the 1890s, typically doled out in small amounts of dashes and often paired with gin. It has not yet found a place on the back bar in the cocktail revival.

K

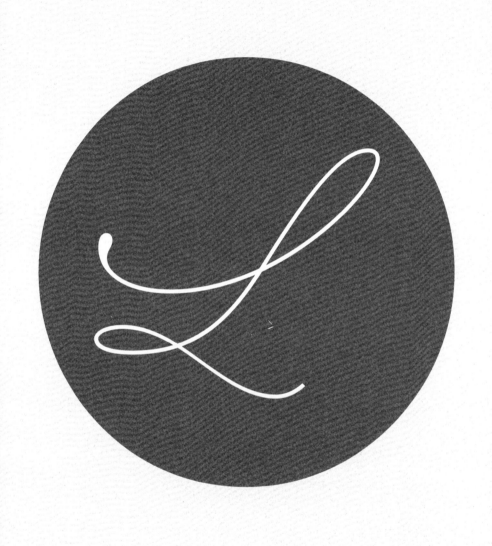

LAB

An acronym for London Academy of Bartenders—a name nobody uttered, preferring the shortened version. LAB began as a bartending school in the modern mixological style and morphed into an influential Soho bar. The former, founded by bartenders Douglas Ankrah, Richard Hargroves, and Alex Turner, opened its doors in 1996 and never really made a go of it. The school was chronically underfunded and always in danger of closing, so in 1999 the partners decided to open a bar of the same name in a two-story space on Old Compton Street, as a sort of living advertisement for the skills being taught at the school. The bar was an instant roaring success that smacked of anything but the classroom. It was a party bar, high-volume and high-energy. The mood was raucous, but the bartenders were working at a high level, molding fresh produce and mountains of crushed ice and elaborate garnishes into exotic cocktail creations from a menu littered with

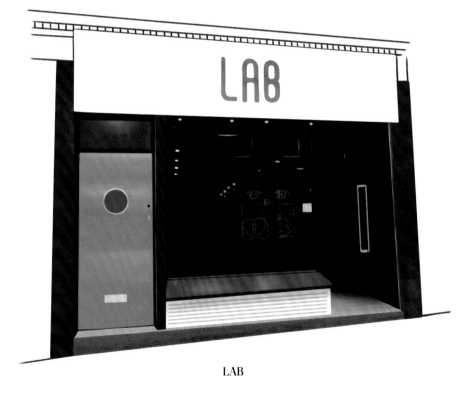

LAB

dozens of original drinks sporting risqué names. The bar produced few modern classic cocktails (though it helped to popularize the Porn Star Martini, created by Ankrah), but it helped forge the idea of bartenders as not working-class grunts but celebrities. The staff was largely composed of ex–Atlantic Bar & Grill bartenders, including Jamie Terrell, who came in after Turner left, and Dré Masso. LAB was soon eclipsed by other London bars, and its star players left and went on to success elsewhere. The bar limped along until 2016, when it finally closed.

LAST WORD

A lost, pre-Prohibition cocktail made of gin, maraschino liqueur, Chartreuse, and lime juice, rediscovered by veteran Seattle bartender Murray Stenson in the pages of Ted Saucier's 1951 cocktail book *Bottoms Up!,* where it was credited to the Detroit Athletic Club. Stenson began to serve the drink in 2004 at the Zig Zag Café, where he worked. Word of the Last Word quickly spread through the internet and bartender grapevine, and soon it was being served at Pegu Club in New York and elsewhere. The drink's equal-parts construction and use of products then being championed in mixology circles (gin, Chartreuse, maraschino liqueur) made it popular among cocktail bartenders and enthusiasts. The drink has inspired dozens of variations, including the Final Ward, Paper Plane, Naked and Famous, Division Bell, and Green Eyes.

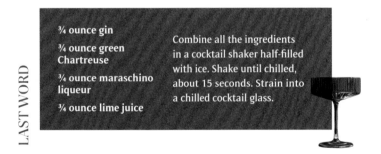

LAST WORD

¾ ounce gin

¾ ounce green Chartreuse

¾ ounce maraschino liqueur

¾ ounce lime juice

Combine all the ingredients in a cocktail shaker half-filled with ice. Shake until chilled, about 15 seconds. Strain into a chilled cocktail glass.

LATITUDE 29

A tiki bar opened by Jeff "Beachbum" Berry and his wife, Annene Kaye, inside the Bienville House hotel in New Orleans in 2014. Berry's groundbreaking research into the history of tiki culture and drinks had led to a rash of new tiki bars in the early 2010s, most opened by bartenders who had honed their tiki chops by reading Berry's many books on the subject. (One bar, Three Dots and a Dash in Chicago, was actually named after a lost drink Berry discovered.) Thus Berry became the rare cocktail writer to wade into the practical and bruising world of bar ownership. Latitude 29 was, however, a critical and popular success from the beginning.

LEE, DON

This New Yorker is perhaps the most prominent example in the cocktail renaissance era of a layman transforming themselves into a player in the cocktail community. Lee, an IT professional, latched onto the budding New York cocktail

DON LEE

renaissance of the early aughts as a devoted barfly, haunting bars like Pegu Club in the company of fellow cocktail nerd John Deragon, and holding elaborate home cocktail parties, which bartenders often attended. A fluke invitation for Lee and Deragon to man the bar at Death & Co. for one night led Jim Meehan to hire the duo for his opening staff at PDT. There, Lee distinguished himself through many innovations, the most prominent of which was the creation of the Benton's Old-Fashioned, a bacon-fat-washed Old-Fashioned that became PDT's most popular drink. Deragon and Lee were also influential through their many years of managing the Cocktail Apprentice Program at the Tales of the Cocktail convention. Lee left PDT to pilot the drinks programs at David Chang's Momofuku restaurant empire. While there, he created such notable cocktails as the Sawyer and Seven-Spice Sour. Lee then moved on to the bar-equipment company Cocktail Kingdom, where he worked on product development. In 2018 he returned to the bar world, opening the highly innovative Existing Conditions with Dave Arnold, but sadly the bar was extinguished by Covid two years later. In 2022 he was put in charge of the cocktail program at David Geffen Hall in Lincoln Center.

LEWIS BAG

A thick, medium-sized canvas bag, usually accompanied by a large wooden mallet, used by bartenders to crush ice for use in cocktails, particularly the Mint Julep. These were embraced in the twenty-first century, as bartenders returned to handmade large-format ice and the old ways of making drinks. Canvas ice bags have been around for a long time. However, the name Lewis is a new development, being the brand of a canvas ice bag that first appeared in the late 1990s. It has stuck.

LEYENDA

A Brooklyn bar opened in 2015 by Julie Reiner and Ivy Mix, and run by Mix, that specializes in cocktails made with Latin American spirits, including tequila, mezcal, pisco, rum, and cachaça. The bar's draft versions of the Margarita and Paloma are considered standard bearers for those drinks.

LILLET

A citrus-flavored, fortified French aperitif wine that is typically drunk on its own over ice with a slice of orange or other citrus. It has, however, found its way into a few important cocktails over the years. Lillet is called for in the Vesper, 20th Century Cocktail, and Corpse Reviver No. 2, drinks that enjoyed new popularity in the twenty-first century. Using Lillet blanc to recreate these old cocktails has been problematic, in that the modern formula is generally considered a weakened version of the original aromatized wine, which used quinine and was called Kina Lillet. The White Negroni by Wayne Collins is a modern classic that can be made with confidence, as it has always used the modern version of Lillet.

LE LION–BAR DE PARIS

A tiny, second-story, originally illegal, speakeasy-style bar in Hamburg, Germany, opened in 2007 by Joerg Meyer and Rainer Wendt. The primary inspiration was New York's Milk & Honey, which Meyer learned about and studied on the internet. The success of the new bar forced it to move to a legit larger space. Meyer, a formal man who favors a retro style of slicked-back hair and Winchester shirts, quickly became a leading voice in the German cocktail community. Le Lion's reputation was secured when Meyer, inspired by Dale DeGroff's Whiskey Smash, which he had sampled at Pegu Club in New York, created the Gin Basil Smash. The drink was an instant sensation, quickly spreading across Germany and Europe. A sign was later painted on the outside of the bar reading "The Cradle of the Gin Basil Smash."

LIQUEURS

A category of spirit encompassing a wide variety of elixirs of innumerable flavors, all tied together only by their inclusion of sugar and booze. Most have been drunk by themselves for many years and still are today. They have a second life, however, as the binders and enhancers—"modifiers," as bar lingo goes—of a wide host of cocktails. The list of liqueurs that are important to any good cocktail back bar is nearly endless, but among the most vital are curaçao/triple sec (used in the Margarita, Pegu Club, Corpse Reviver No. 2, and Sidecar), Chartreuse (Last Word, Bijou), yellow Chartreuse (Widow's Kiss), maraschino liqueur (Red Hook, Martinez), Bénédictine (Bobby Burns), Cherry Heering (Singapore Sling),

LE LION

crème de cacao (Grasshopper, 20th Century), crème de menthe (Grasshopper, Stinger), crème de cassis (Kir Royale), crème de mure (Bramble), crème de violette (Aviation), sloe gin (Sloe Gin Fizz), coffee liqueur (Espresso Martini), St. Germain (Elder Fashioned), Midori (Midori Sour), absinthe (Sazerac), and Drambuie (Rusty Nail). Most amari and red bitters are also part of the liqueur family. Very occasionally, liqueurs are the star of the drink, as in the Sloe Gin Fizz, Amaretto Sour, Grasshopper, and Chartreuse Swizzle. But most of the time they play a supporting role. Still, like all good supporting actors, they frequently steal the show.

LITTLE ITALY

A twist on the Manhattan, created by Audrey Saunders, which debuted at her New York cocktail bar Pegu Club when it opened in 2005. The drink has the requisite rye and sweet vermouth found in a Manhattan, but the Angostura bitters is replaced by a half ounce of Cynar, the Italian artichoke liqueur. It was one of many Manhattan and Brooklyn cocktail riffs to follow in the wake of the creation of the Red Hook cocktail by Vincenzo Errico. Very easy to assemble, the drink was quickly adopted by other bars and home bartenders.

LITTLE ITALY

L

2 ounces Rittenhouse bonded rye

¾ ounce Martini & Rossi red vermouth

½ ounce Cynar

Combine the ingredients in a mixing glass half-filled with ice. Stir until chilled, about 15 seconds. Strain into a chilled coupe. Garnish with a brandied cherry.

LOW-ABV DRINKS

Cocktails whose ingredients, when their various alcohol levels are added up, have a less powerful kick than your average mixed drinks. For the most part, this is due to the inclusion of a large portion of juice or soda water, as with many highballs. However, a low-ABV (alcohol by volume) cocktail can result from the use of ingredients that are already low in alcohol, like sherry and vermouth. Low-ABV drinks became a popular trend in bars during the late 2010s and early 2020s.

MACELHONE, HARRY

A Scottish bartender who, by dint of running an American-style cocktail bar in Paris during Prohibition and publishing two cocktail books during the 1920s, became a figure of influence in the cocktail world stretching into the twenty-first century. Born in Dundee in 1890, he bartended before World War I at the Plaza Hotel in New York and after the war at the popular Ciro's Club in London. In 1923 he bought a Paris bar once owned by celebrity American jockey Tod Sloan, where he had formerly worked as a bartender, and renamed it Harry's New York Bar. The name and the heavily advertised address (5, Rue Daunou, translated phonetically to "Sank Roo Doe Noo") worked magic on Yankee tourists. Harry's became a popular spot for American expatriates and roving celebrities, including F. Scott Fitzgerald, Ernest Hemingway, Sinclair Lewis, Brendan Behan, and Humphrey Bogart. In 1922, MacElhone published *Harry's ABC of Mixing Cocktails,* a book that had several editions. It was followed by *Barflies and Cocktails* in 1927. Together, the volumes are a window into cocktail styles in Europe during the Prohibition era, and they remain relevant owing to the general soundness and simplicity of the recipes. MacElhone has been credited, rightly or wrongly, with the invention of such drinks as the Sidecar, White Lady, Monkey Gland, Three Mile Limit, and French 75. *Barflies* contains the formula for the Boulevardier, which would become popular a century later. Once Prohibition ended, Harry's continued to be a popular tourist destination. MacElhone died in 1958. The bar still stands.

MADEIRA

A fortified wine made on the Portuguese islands of Madeira. Because the wine traveled well and was long-lived, it was a great favorite of the likes of Thomas Jefferson in the early days of the United States. As such, it found its way into popular punches of the era. Madeira's popularity in America faded precipitously over time. The Prince of Wales is a notable cocktail that calls for Madeira.

MAIBOWLE

A punch traditionally drunk at Maifest, a festival held to greet the arrival of spring in northern European countries, particularly Germany. It is composed of German white wine, champagne, sugar, sometimes brandy, strawberries, and, critically, woodruff, which is steeped in the wine. Woodruff is one of the earliest plants to sprout following winter and therefore considered a harbinger of spring. It lends a fresh, grassy, clover-like fragrance to the punch. Maibowle was once a common sight at German restaurants across the United States but has declined in popularity in recent decades.

MAI-KAI

A sprawling restaurant and bar in Fort Lauderdale that, as one of the last of its once numerous breed, acts as a veritable campus for tiki culture and history. Founded in 1956 by Chicagoans Bob and Jack Thornton, the six-hundred-seat complex has a striking A-frame silhouette and an interior complete with waterfalls, thatched roofs, a stage that is home to nightly time-warp floor shows (fire dancers and the like), and a backyard garden. It hosts the annual Hukilau festival, during which every Hawaiian-shirt wearing, orchid-bearing, coconut-sipping tiki nut descends on the place. The food and drinks have remained largely unchanged over the decades. Mariano Licudine, who spent sixteen years at Don the Beachcomber in Chicago, worked at Mai-Kai as the head bartender and drink creator from its opening until 1980.

MAI TAI

One of the two most iconic tiki cocktails, and the more popular, given the forbidding nature of its sibling, the Zombie. Most histories say the Mai Tai was born in 1944 at Trader Vic's in Oakland, where Victor Bergeron, aka Trader Vic himself, invented the drink on the spur of the moment for two friends visiting from Tahiti. In tiki terms, it is a relatively simple drink, made up of two rums, lime juice, curaçao, mint, and orgeat.

The drink was not an instantaneous hit. Little was written about it until the mid-1950s. When it did eventually catch on, the true recipe was difficult to extract from the countless imitators, as Vic kept his formula a secret. When Bergeron took the drink to Hawaii, things became more confused. In 1953, he taught the genuine article to bartenders at the Royal Hawaiian Hotel in Honolulu, but that recipe did not hold for long. Cheap rum and premade mixes came into play, and most recipes substituted softer and more place-appropriate pineapple juice for the original lime juice. Most of the drinks served under the name Mai Tai were fruity and frothy, as well as various strange colors, and bore no resemblance to the original. The Mai Tai didn't right itself until around 2010, when the serious bartending approaches

MAI-KAI

of the cocktail renaissance were finally applied to the tiki canon of cocktails. The arrival of various artisanal orgeats also aided the fortunes of the drink.

MAI TAI

1 ounce dark
Jamaican rum

1 ounce aged
Martinique rum

1 ounce lime juice

½ ounce curaçao

¼ ounce orgeat

¼ ounce simple syrup

Combine all the ingredients in a cocktail shaker half-filled with ice. Shake until chilled, about 15 seconds. Strain into a double old-fashioned glass. Garnish with a spent lime shell and a mint sprig.

MALONEY, TOBY

A career service worker born in Colorado, Maloney began bartending in Chicago in the 1990s. After moving to New York in 1995, he played a key role in a series of bars important to the early evolution of the New York cocktail scene. He first worked with bartender Del Pedro at Grange Hall, a Greenwich Village restaurant with an advanced cocktail philosophy. He was then the first bartender hired by Sasha Petraske at Milk & Honey, a bar he frequented and admired. In 2005, he was the opening head bartender at Audrey Saunders's Pegu Club. He left after less than a year. In 2007, he drew on the influences of Milk & Honey and Pegu Club, as well as Flatiron Lounge, to open the Violet Hour, the first important craft cocktail bar in Chicago. He later headed the bar program at the Patterson House in Nashville, bringing craft cocktails to that city. He is also associated with the bar Mother's Ruin in Chicago.

MANHATTAN

The first in a creatively momentous wave of new cocktails in the late nineteenth century that combined spirits with vermouth, and one of the indisputably great and most enduring cocktails ever invented. The formula is as 1-2-3 simple as the Martini, which quickly followed it: whiskey, sweet vermouth, aromatic bitters. It burst onto the scene in the early 1880s. The first recipes, which appeared in books in 1884, called for equal parts whiskey and vermouth. Some formulas actually called for more vermouth than whiskey. Either way, it was a sweeter drink than we know today. Whether it was made with bourbon or rye was a matter of choice, a debate that still goes on. It can be made with Canadian whisky or Tennessee whiskey. But not scotch; there you have a Rob Roy. The equal-parts formula continued for some decades until it settled resolutely into the 2 parts whiskey to 1 part vermouth setup that is the accepted norm now. Early versions, if they had a garnish, went with the lemon twist. After repeal, however, a cocktail cherry was the accepted final flourish. In the late nineteenth century, some bartenders enhanced the drink with a dash of absinthe or curaçao or whatnot, but those touches did not survive. In its early days, it was often confused with the Martini, which would have had a similar appearance, whiskey being lighter in color at the time, and dry vermouth being darker.

A story that the Manhattan was invented at an event at the Manhattan Club in honor of presidential candidate Samuel J. Tilden, hosted by Jennie Jerome, future mother of Winston Churchill, has been thoroughly debunked, but it persists nonetheless. The Manhattan was always a popular drink. Banker J. P. Morgan had one at the end of every business day. Unlike the Martini, important variations on the Manhattan have been few over the years. The drink was a steady, reliable customer. There was the perfect Manhattan, which split the difference between sweet and dry vermouth, and the rarer dry Manhattan, which went all in on dry vermouth. The Boothby, named after San Francisco bartender Bill Boothby, was basically a Manhattan Royale—that is, topped with champagne. With the 1960s, the Manhattan-on-the-Rocks became a popular choice and remains so today in certain segments of society and parts of the country.

Because of its notoriety and ease of preparation, the Manhattan survived the cocktail dark ages at the end of the twentieth century. With the arrival of the cocktail renaissance, the drink rose in stature through a few simple, commonsense changes: Fresh vermouth was used, as was quality whiskey; bitters were always included (they were often forgotten by late-twentieth-century bartenders); and nonfraudulent cherries came into play. The main shift, however, was in the preference for rye over bourbon among the cocktail smart set. Bartender Vincenzo Errico's Red Hook cocktail, created in 2003, was perhaps the first important twist on the Manhattan formula in decades (though he was equally inspired by the Brooklyn cocktail). It inspired a deluge of Manhattan variations in the aughts—including the Greenpoint, Slope, and Carroll Gardens—and gave the Manhattan new relevance. The Black Manhattan, in which Averna takes the place of the vermouth, has been a popular twenty-first-century order. In Wisconsin, meanwhile, locals often prefer to use domestic brandy instead of whiskey. The Manhattan remains one of the few classic cocktails you can order in most any bar with confidence that they will have the necessary ingredients on hand and the know-how to put together a decent one. It is a remarkably forgiving drink, the simple ironclad recipe a seeming bulwark against the lowliest whiskey or inept bartending.

MANHATTAN

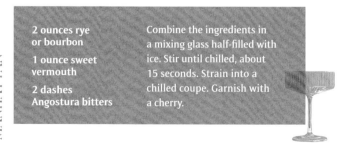

2 ounces rye
or bourbon

1 ounce sweet
vermouth

2 dashes
Angostura bitters

Combine the ingredients in a mixing glass half-filled with ice. Stir until chilled, about 15 seconds. Strain into a chilled coupe. Garnish with a cherry.

MARASCHINO LIQUEUR

A liqueur derived from the distillation of whole marasca cherries. It has been produced in Croatia since the late eighteenth century. It has played an important role in cocktails since the 1870s, being a part of such classic drinks as the Martinez, Turf Club, Tuxedo, Brooklyn, Aviation, Mary Pickford, Fancy Free, Last Word, and Hemingway Daiquiri. It was also an intrinsic layer in the once-popular Pousse Café and was one of the bottles commonly reached for by late-nineteenth-century bartenders when they wanted to "improve" a cocktail. In that era, it was not unusual to encounter Old-Fashioneds and Manhattans with a dash of the stuff in them. After many years of languishing in obscurity and being unavailable in the United States, maraschino was brought back into use in the twenty-first century by bartenders who used it to recreate old drinks as well as to invent significant new cocktails, such as the Division Bell, Final Ward, Red Hook, Ritz, and Laphroaig Project. Because of its intensity of flavor and cloying sweetness, the liqueur is typically used sparingly in cocktails, rarely accounting for more than a quarter or half an ounce. Leading brands include Maraska and Luxardo, the latter the clear leader, instantly recognizable with its green bottle, red cap, and straw casing, known as a "fiasco."

MARGARITA

A tequila daisy (tequila, sugar, lime, curaçao) that ranks as one of the most popular cocktails in the world, year in and year out, and the main way most people experience tequila. The origins of the drink are unclear. There are many improbable and unprovable stories, none of which hold water, and they won't be given any further oxygen in these pages. Very likely it is, like many simple cocktails, one of those inevitable drinks that was bound to happen, and probably happened simultaneously in various places. (A drink that looks very much like a Margarita appears in 1937 London book *Café Royal Cocktail Book* under the name of Picador.) As to the name, Margarita is the Spanish word for daisy. It's that simple. Many of the early mentions of Margarita-like drinks call the cocktail a Tequila Daisy. Over time, the two appeared to separate, the Tequila Daisy being made with grenadine and the Margarita with curaçao. A 1961 article in the *El Paso Herald-Post* tried to clear up the confusion, saying, "First is the Margarita, composed of one jigger tequila, a half jigger each of Cointreau and lime juice, one tsp of sugar and chipped ice. Place this briefly in a blender and serve in a glass, the lip of which has been wetted with lemon juice and then dipped in salt. . . . Next is the tequila daisy. This drink is one jigger tequila, one teaspoon grenadine, juice of one lime, one tsp sugar and chipped ice, blended and served in a clear glass, without lime or salt." The earliest newspaper mentions of the Margarita come from California and the Southwest. In the 1950s Jose Cuervo began including the drink in its advertising. But it was in the 1970s that the drink really took hold. This was also when the first frozen Margarita machine was introduced, in Dallas in 1971. With the popularity of the cocktail, tequila sales soared in the U.S. Not long after achieving widespread visibility, the great and simple drink was bastardized in a million ways, served in various colors and flavors, and often with cheap mixto tequila (a mix of agave spirit and whatever) and sour mix instead of fresh juice. With the arrival of the cocktail revolution, bartenders began to make the drink properly again, with 100 percent agave tequila, fresh lime juice, and Cointreau or some other reputable orange liqueur. The drink can be served up or on the rocks and typically features a salt rim.

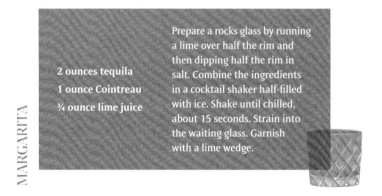

MARGARITA

2 ounces tequila
1 ounce Cointreau
¾ ounce lime juice

Prepare a rocks glass by running a lime over half the rim and then dipping half the rim in salt. Combine the ingredients in a cocktail shaker half-filled with ice. Shake until chilled, about 15 seconds. Strain into the waiting glass. Garnish with a lime wedge.

M

MARRERO, LYNNETTE

A leading bartender and educator in the U.S. cocktail revival, Marrero got her start at Julie Reiner's Flatiron Lounge in the aughts. She teamed with Brian Miller to do some brief, but influential, early work in the tiki drink field at Elettaria, also in Manhattan. She also worked at Freeman's and Rye House and had a lengthy stint as beverage director at Llama Inn in Brooklyn and Llama San in Manhattan. But she is best known as the cofounder, with Ivy Mix, of Speed Rack, the roving bartending competition that features the talents of female bartenders while raising money for breast cancer research.

MARTINEZ

A cocktail from the 1880s that is closely associated with the Martini, given the similarity of their names and the relative simultaneity of their debuts. Like early Martinis, and early Turf Clubs for that matter, the first recipes for the Martinez called for Old Tom gin or genever, combined with sweet vermouth. The drink had mainly faded from view by the mid-twentieth century, not to be revived again until the early twenty-first century, when history-minded young mixologists became obsessed with old, forgotten cocktails. The return of Old Tom gin secured the drink's rebirth, though it remains an unusual order. As with the Martini, none of the various origin stories surrounding the drink are verifiable.

1½ ounces
Old Tom gin

1½ ounces sweet
vermouth

¼ ounce
maraschino liqueur

2 dashes
Angostura bitters

Combine the ingredients in a mixing glass half-filled with ice. Stir until chilled, about 15 seconds. Strain into a chilled coupe. Express an orange twist over the drink and drop it into the glass.

MARTINI

The big dog of the cocktail world. The flashing neon silhouette at your corner bar. Nearly a synonym for "cocktail," it is so universally known and drunk. The only cocktail that has gripped the imagination of the public for the entirety of its existence and the only one to have a body of literature devoted to it—and to have inspired enough accompanying tools, gadgetry, and accessories to fill a small museum. This king of cocktails was a latecomer to the party, showing up in the 1880s, when vermouth-and-anything was a hot idea in barrooms. Its arrival followed hot on the heels of the Manhattan, with which it was often confused in its early days. A recipe first appeared in print in 1888 in books by both Harry Johnson and Theophile Proulx. No one has ever determined the identity of the inventor of the drink; very likely multiple bartenders combined gin and vermouth—then new to the American market—at the same time.

As to the name, that is also a mystery, though the fact that the leading vermouth at the time was called Martini is a whopping indicator. The early Martini was a sweet drink, made of Old Tom gin and sweet vermouth. The drink's slow but steady march toward dryness was twofold. The portion of vermouth, which was sometimes equal to that of gin, decreased over time. And the gin and vermouth used in the drink switched from Old Tom to London dry, and sweet vermouth to dry vermouth. Still, the sweet Martini and "medium" Martini (equal parts sweet and dry vermouth) were popular enough that they continued to be served and appear in cocktail books as late as the 1940s. So confused, for so long, was the persona of the Martini that some books offered multiple recipes.

By the 1940s, the dry ideal had begun to take hold of the American imagination. The vermouth quotient grew smaller and smaller, and the drink grew stiffer and stronger, to the point of fetishism. Much of this likely had to do with the mishandling of vermouth in those days, causing it to be held in disdain. Many were the techniques and devices introduced to the bar to ensure that a Martini would be as dry as the Sahara. At around the same time, in direct contrast to the dry Martini, the Martini-on-the-Rocks appeared. Served in a rocks glass over ice, this swift-and-sloppy version proved popular for decades with those who wanted no fuss and didn't want to get plastered quite so quickly.

During these post-repeal years, the Martini became a cultural icon in a way no cocktail ever had been, hoisted up by writers, painters, poets, songwriters, and filmmakers as something as mysteriously American as baseball and apple pie. Among those to rhapsodize and theorize about the drink were Ernest Hemingway, Robert Benchley, Ogden Nash, Luis Buñuel, Winston Churchill, H. L. Mencken, James Thurber, Noel Coward, William Faulkner, Bernard DeVoto, and Ian Fleming, who caused no end of mischief and debate by having his fictional creation James Bond order a Vodka Martini "shaken, not stirred." The drink found regular work as a supporting player in the movies as well, showing up in *The Thin Man, Sabrina, Father of the Bride,* and *The Apartment,* to name a few.

Beginning in the 1960s, vodka began to creep into the picture, and soon the Vodka Martini was the preferred choice of the sophisticated businessman. Olives were the preferred garnish, the lemon twist of pre-Prohibition time fading from view. With the counterculture upheaval of the late 1960s and 1970s, the Martini grew unfashionable, the drinking choice of another generation. When cocktails made a comeback in the 1990s, however, the Martini returned as the 'tini—that is, anything the customer or bartender wished to pour into the by-then-iconic conical Martini glass. Hundreds of bars featured "Martini lists," with

MARTINI

nary a true Martini on them. Most of these concoctions were colorful and overly sweet; almost none contained either gin or vermouth. The Martini's reputation as a serious drink suffered greatly during this time, a period that nonetheless produced a few modern classics that traded off the drink's notoriety, including the Dukes Martini, Breakfast Martini, and Espresso Martini.

When the cocktail revival came along in the 2000s, few young mixologists paid much attention to the Martini, considering it part of the bad-drinks problem they were fighting to resolve. By the late 2010s, however, serious, classic Martinis made a comeback, among them the trendy Fifty-Fifty Martini, which returned vermouth to the glass with a vengeance. Also restored to its former place was orange bitters, an original ingredient that had been abandoned after repeal. With the

Covid-19 pandemic, and people quarantined at home in dire need of a belt, the age-old, ever-ready Martini answered the call of the thirsty once more, while also serving as a reminder of a more carefree past.

MARTINI

3 ounces gin

1 ounce dry vermouth

2 dashes orange bitters

Combine the ingredients in a mixing glass half-filled with ice. Stir until chilled, about 15 seconds. Strain into a chilled coupe. Garnish with an olive or lemon twist.

MARTINI GLASS

A long-stemmed cocktail glass with a conical bowl. The style of glass the Martini was served in during the first several decades of the cocktail's life included everything from coupes to tumblers. But by the 1970s, for reasons that remain cloudy, the cocktail and its namesake glass, often of enormous dimensions, became irrevocably linked. Mixologists in the early twenty-first century attempted to return the drink to a more modest-sized coupe, but the ubiquity and popularity of the martini glass held firm.

MATUTINAL COCKTAIL

The term applied in the nineteenth century to cocktails that were typically enjoyed in the early part of the day. The Whiskey Cocktail, which would evolve into the Old-Fashioned, began life as a matutinal cocktail. The Bloody Mary has single-handedly kept the habit of the "matutinal" cocktail alive, though today we just call that day-drinking.

MAYAHUEL

An agave spirit-focused bar opened by bartender Phil Ward in 2009. Not the first of its kind, it was the most important and influential of what would become a tidal wave of agave bars opening in the ensuing decade. The *New York Times* called it "the world's first tequila bar with a hypothesis, not a theme." Ward offered dozens of tequilas and mezcals, and just as many cocktails using the spirits. Among them were a few drinks with staying power, including the Division Bell and Spicy Paloma. An unhappy partnership and an uncooperative landlord led to the closure of the bar in 2017.

MCMILLIAN, CHRIS

A large, shambling, garrulous Louisiana resident, McMillian was born into a family of bartenders, but came to bartending himself late in life in New Orleans. He quickly made an impact, immersing himself in the history of his profession and its drinks, bringing his knowledge to the people, and becoming a mentor figure to younger bartenders. He plied his trade at the Clock Bar in the Royal Sonesta, the Richelieu Bar in Arnaud's restaurant, the Ritz-Carlton's Library Lounge, and Kingfish. A well of bar-world information, he is known for telling the story of a cocktail while preparing it. He is particularly famous for the line of 1890s doggerel he recites while preparing Mint Juleps with a Lewis bag and an enormous wooden mallet. In 2019 he opened his own bar, Revel, with his wife, Laura.

MEEHAN, JIM

One of the biggest names in bartending in the twenty-first century. Meehan, an Illinois native, cut his teeth at New York's Gramercy Tavern and Pegu Club, but he made his name as the shaping force and public face of PDT, a miniscule, hidden cocktail bar in the East Village that, as much as Milk & Honey, defined the speakeasy era in New York and well beyond. He amplified his and the bar's impact tenfold with the 2011 publication of *The PDT Cocktail Book,* the first important modern volume to canonize the drinks of one particular bar. He followed it up in 2017 with the comprehensive *Meehan's Bartender Manual,* which won a James Beard Award. His association with PDT ended in 2019. His next project, Prairie School, an ambitious, Frank Lloyd Wright–themed bar in Chicago, was short-lived. In 2021, Meehan—who moved to Portland, Oregon, in 2014—launched the bar program at Takibi, a Japanese restaurant in Portland.

MEIER, FRANK

The bartender who ran the bar at the Ritz hotel in Paris from 1921 until after World War II. Born in Austria, he studied at a waiters' school in Berlin, and as a young man worked in London, Egypt, and the Hoffman House in New York. During World War I, he served in the French Foreign Legion. After the war, he began his long tenure at the Ritz. Given his gaudy perch and the time period, he had a celebrated clientele, including many American expatriates seeking refuge from Prohibition. Meier possessed a fame all his own. One paper called him as "famous as Napoleon." Cole Porter, a regular, created a character based on Meier for his 1929 musical *Fifty Million Frenchmen,* which is set in Paris. In 1936, Meier authored the handsome book *The Artistry of Mixing Drinks,* which included cocktail recipes as well as various almanac-like guides and tables, sandwich recipes, and cleaning tips. He is credited with the recipe for the Bee's Knees, which is in the book. The print run was small, and many copies were earmarked for Meier's well-heeled clientele. When the Germans invaded during World War II, Meier retreated. But he soon returned and reopened the bar. It has been speculated that during the war he acted as a secret agent, aiding the French Resistance in various ways. He died in 1947.

MEZCAL

The worldwide golden cocktail child of the 2010s, this agave spirit from Mexico mainly stayed in Mexico for most of its existence, which goes back centuries. There it was almost exclusively drunk neat, and within earshot of the local mezcaleros who made it generation after generation in the villages where they lived. Unlike tequila—which is a location-specific and agave-varietal–specific expression of the larger agave spirit category—it was seen in few mixed drinks until the twenty-first century. It was then that agave evangelists like Ron Cooper and Steve Olson made young bartenders aware of the many expressions and possibilities of good mezcal. The Del Maguey line of "single-village" mezcals imported by Cooper were the first quality mezcals most mixologists encountered. By the late aughts, mezcal was being taken seriously as a mixing spirit, with bartenders embracing the complex, smoky flavors it brought to a cocktail, and agave-centric bars like Mayahuel in New York and The Pastry War in Houston began to open. The Oaxaca Old-Fashioned by Phil Ward and Mezcal Mule by Jim Meehan were two early examples of mezcal cocktails. They were followed by hundreds more,

MILK & HONEY

including the Naked and Famous, Barbacoa, and Division Bell. The world market was flooded with newly exported mezcals. That supply was met with demand, as the public picked up on mezcal with surprising rapidity, eager to learn about it and consume it, while asking for it as a substitute spirit in every classic cocktail, from the Margarita and Manhattan to the Negroni and Old-Fashioned. Mezcal rose to this challenge, proving itself to be the most versatile cocktail spirit to come along since gin. Most of these cocktails were made with mezcal derived from the widely planted espadin agave (*Agave angustifolia*), which constitutes most of the mezcal that travels beyond Mexico.

MILK & HONEY

The most influential cocktail bar of the twenty-first century, and one of the most important in history. It didn't seem like much on the outside; it looked like a long-abandoned Lower East Side tailor shop. That was intentional. You entered through a gray metal door, then a heavy velvet curtain. It didn't look like much on the inside, either, though it certainly looked better than anyone on the sidewalk outside might expect. It was opened by New Yorker Sasha Petraske on December 31, 1999, appropriately enough the start of a new era. Jazz music played. The lighting was dim. There was no menu. You came to your order by way of a conversation with the bartender, who knew how to make hundreds of cocktails. Ice was hand carved. For the first year, Petraske made all the drinks. Then he finally hired someone. The bartenders were well dressed. The drinks arrived on trays with candles and thick napkins. The check was a figure written on a small piece of paper. There was a mural of the Cynar label painted on the wall. The bar had five stools. There was no sign outside. There was no phone number. There was no website. It was not listed anywhere. People found it anyway. There was no food. The water had a slice of cucumber in it. There were rules of etiquette posted in the bathroom. They were enforced. It was the first neo-speakeasy. Petraske hated speakeasies. He just wanted a quiet bar. Petraske didn't care about inventing new cocktails, but Milk & Honey created more important new cocktails than anybody. It never made money. Everyone copied it. The space is still there, but it's called Attaboy now and run by two former Milk & Honey bartenders. Milk & Honey moved to 23rd Street but closed two years later. A London Milk & Honey closed in 2020.

MINT JULEP

MINT JULEP

One of the oldest and most romanticized of cocktails, whose simple working parts consist of a good slug of bourbon, a bit of sugar, a mound of crushed ice, a silver cup, and an ample tuft of mint. Made correctly, it tastes as close to pure nectar as any mixed drink. Inextricably associated with the southern United States, it likely began as an aristocratic drink enjoyed by the landed gentry of eighteenth- and nineteenth-century Virginia, and typically was made with rum or brandy. By the twentieth century, however, it was forever a bourbon drink most closely linked to Kentucky, where, every Derby Day in Louisville, thousands are consumed under wide-brimmed hats. And while the Kentucky Derby has most certainly kept the drink alive, it has also burdened it with a somewhat cartoonish image. Until recently, bartenders would tell you it was a drink you could sell hundreds of on one day, and none the other 364. That has changed a bit, as cocktail bars have put the original, and many variations, on their menus any warm month they choose. In the nineteenth century, the julep was a full genre of drink, and you could buy ones made with gin, brandy and, most famously, champagne. The Prescription Julep, which enjoyed a comeback in the 2000s, called for both cognac and whiskey. New Orleans bartender Chris McMillian did quite a lot to restore the drink's fortunes in the aughts. The drink is also the chief modern reason for anyone to own a Lewis bag.

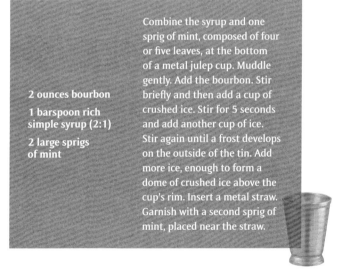

MINT JULEP

2 ounces bourbon

1 barspoon rich simple syrup (2:1)

2 large sprigs of mint

Combine the syrup and one sprig of mint, composed of four or five leaves, at the bottom of a metal julep cup. Muddle gently. Add the bourbon. Stir briefly and then add a cup of crushed ice. Stir for 5 seconds and add another cup of ice. Stir again until a frost develops on the outside of the tin. Add more ice, enough to form a dome of crushed ice above the cup's rim. Insert a metal straw. Garnish with a second sprig of mint, placed near the straw.

M

MIX, IVY

One of the prominent cocktail bartenders of the 2010s, both a cofounder, with Lynnette Marrero, of the charity-oriented, female-focused roving bar competition Speed Rack, and an owner of Leyenda, a Brooklyn bar that champions, and makes cocktails with, the spirits of Latin and South America. Mix also published a book with this same focus in 2021, *Spirits of Latin America.* The following year, she opened a wine and spirits store in Brooklyn called Fiasco. Her interest in Latin spirits was first ignited by a long stay in Guatemala. In New York, she got her start in cocktails at Phil Ward's agave bar Mayahuel. She went on to work at Fort Defiance, Lani Kai, and Clover Club. With Julie Reiner, the owner of the latter two, she opened Leyenda in 2015.

MIXING GLASS

A glass of decent height, ranging anywhere from five inches to more than a foot, in which cocktails are stirred over ice. These can be as simple and utilitarian as a pint glass, which makes up half of a Boston Shaker unit, or fabulously ornate, made of etched glass and crystal. The latter are primarily designed for home use, where ornamental barware is more in order, rather than in a bar, where they might be broken. Yet during the cocktail renaissance, bars got in the habit of stocking fancy mixing glasses to lend a certain flash and dignity to the creative process. Dedicated mixing glasses did not appear in bars until the late nineteenth century. Before that, the mixing of a drink occurred in the glassware where the drink ended up, with the liquid often tossed back and forth between two vessels. By the 1880s, mentions of bartenders using mixing glasses were common. By the 1900s, mixing glasses were sold in stores, and liquor companies were giving mixing glasses away as promotional items. With the repeal of Prohibition and the ascent of home bartending, the variety of mixing glasses available on the market grew wide and varied. During the mid- and late twentieth century, the use of mixing glasses to make cocktails fell out of use, as most bartenders simply shook every drink they made. With the advent of the twenty-first century, the elegant practice of stirring cocktails that contained only spirits returned and, with it, the use and proliferation of mixing glasses.

MOJITO

A rum highball made with lime juice, sugar, mint, and soda water. It became known outside of its native Cuba when thirsty Americans began to visit the island during Prohibition. Those tourists later took the drink back home with them. The bar La Bodeguita del Medio, in particular, became known for the drink and serves hundreds of them every day to tourists. The drink didn't really break out in the United States until the 1990s, in Miami, with its large Cuban population, and in San Francisco, when the bar Enrico's began making them using fresh mint, kicking off a craze. By the early 2000s, everyone was drinking Mojitos. The cocktail demanded fresh juice and herbs before such practices became trendy. Being featured in the Bond film *Die Another Day* gave the drink another boost. You can order one anywhere now, or at least any place that carries fresh mint, though you'll earn the whispered curses of muddle-hating bartenders. In Cuba, it remains the most popular cocktail by a long shot, far outdistancing the daiquiri. As with other wildly popular cocktails, most versions are indifferent in quality, and top-notch examples are rare. The Mojito has partly inspired some modern classics, including the Gin-Gin Mule and Old Cuban.

M

2 ounces rum

¾ ounce simple syrup

¾ ounce lime juice

Mint leaves

Soda water

Combine the simple syrup and mint leaves in a cocktail shaker and gently muddle. Add the rum, lime juice, and ice and shake until chilled, about 15 seconds. Fine strain into a collins glass filled with ice. Top with soda water. Garnish with a mint sprig.

MOJITO

MOJITO

MORGENTHALER, JEFFREY

A Portland, Oregon, bartender who, despite his less-than-central perch in the Pacific Northwest, managed to become one of the leading voices in the cocktail renaissance through a combination of bartending, cocktail creation, blogging, and books. Beginning his bartending career in Eugene, Oregon, Morgenthaler rose to prominence as the bar director of Clyde Common inside the Ace Hotel in Portland, a post he held until the restaurant was felled by the Covid-19 pandemic. He also opened and ran Pépé le Moko, a smaller bar underneath the hotel. In 2022, he returned to running a bar, opening Pacific Standard in Portland. His website, jeffreymorgenthaler.com, was one of the more prominent and opinionated voices around during the late-aughts heyday of the cocktail blog, as well as being one of the few written by a bartender. In 2014, he published *The Bar Book,* a best-selling volume on bar technique. In terms of influence on cocktail trends, his impact has been chiefly two-pronged. In 2009, he developed the technique for barrel-aging cocktails, drawing inspiration from the experiments of Tony Conigliaro in London, beginning with barrel-aged Negronis. The simple and quick technique was soon adopted by bars worldwide. He is also the patron saint of lost causes, devoting himself to bringing back cocktails he felt were unjustly maligned by the mixology world. His primary success in this realm is his whiskey-fortified take on the Amaretto Sour, a recipe that has become the industry norm.

MOSES, CEDD

The preeminent cocktail bar baron of Los Angeles in the aughts and teens, he opened more than twenty properties in a short period of time, utterly transforming the scene in once-decrepit downtown L.A. His most significant venture by far was The Varnish, a collaboration with cocktail godfather Sasha Petraske and bartender Eric Alperin. Tucked in a room behind Cole's, an iconic French Dip purveyor, it ignited the city's cocktail revival overnight, effectively becoming Milk & Honey West. That his life would be colorful seemed preordained, since he was a son of noted artist Ed Moses and was surrounded by artists and musicians from an early age. He showed a youthful talent for gambling and played the horses. He drank with poet Charles Bukowski and dated his daughter. He made a pile as a hotshot hedge-fund dude in the 1990s. Then he quit and used his money to pick up bargains in L.A.'s gritty downtown. His journey began with the saving of the Golden Gopher, a storied downtown watering hole that had descended into a crack haven when he bought it in 2001. Since then, he opened Seven Grand, workplace of many bartenders who would become cocktail leaders in L.A.; Bar Jackalope, a Japanese-style speakeasy in back of Seven Grand; Las Perlas; the Slipper Clutch; the Normandie Club; Honeycut; and Bar Clacson, as well as bars in Austin, San Diego, and Denver.

MR. BOSTON OFFICIAL BARTENDER GUIDES

A ubiquitous cocktail compendium issued annually as a marketing tool by the Mr. Boston spirits company from 1935 until 2012. First called Old Mr. Boston, after the Boston distillery's original name, the manuals, which sported an eye-catching bright red cover, contained recipes for hundreds of drinks and were used by professional and home bartenders alike. For much of its existence, it was the only cocktail guide most bars carried. The initial guide was reportedly put together with the aid of "four old-time Boston bartenders whose background and experience make them the authorities." The guides were compiled and edited by Leo Cotton, a purchasing agent for Mr. Boston, until 1970. While not always the most accurate account of cocktail formulas, the books were, in retrospect, a reliable window into the drinking habits of the time. More recent editions of the book were edited by bartenders Jim Meehan and Jonathan Pogash. The manual now exists only in digital form.

MR. POTATO HEAD

A theory of mixology, generally credited to New York bartender Phil Ward, in which a new cocktail is created by removing one or more ingredients from an already proven cocktail template—Manhattan, Martini, Old-Fashioned, what have you—and substituting a similar ingredient. Example: Ward's own Final Ward cocktail, which takes the Last Word cocktail and replaces the usual gin with rye. The method, while simple and not necessarily new (the Martini of the 1880s was nothing more than a Mr. Potato Head version of the Manhattan), is remarkably sound, and has led to literally hundreds of new cocktails in the current century.

MUDDLER

A bar tool of ancient provenance and endless utility, not much different in shape and function from a pestle. Though traditionally made of wood, metal and plastic versions have cropped up in modern times. Muddlers can be of varying lengths, from a few inches to nearly a foot, and are used to do everything from pulverizing to gently bruising various sugars, fruits, and herbs that go into drinks. Muddlers play a pivotal role in the history and creation of numerous classic cocktails. In the late nineteenth century, they were used to crush the lump sugar used in an Old-Fashioned and Sazerac, as well as to tenderly coax the aromatics out of mint in a Mint Julep. In the years following the repeal of Prohibition, they played a new part in the Old-Fashioned, smashing up the orange slice, cherry, and sugar at the bottom of the muddled version of the drink. In Brazil, it is used to muddle the lime wedges and sugar in a Caipirinha. The tool made a big comeback in the 1990s when the Mojito became a nationwide fad.

MUDDLER

Modern classic cocktails that called for a muddler include the French Pearl, Ellison, Gordon's Cup, Juniperotivo, Old Cuban, Whiskey Smash, Basil Gimlet, and Gin Basil Smash.

MUSTIPHER, SHANNON

A New York–based bartender who first made her name at Gladys Caribbean, a Brooklyn rum bar and restaurant. She became a rare female voice in the tiki world with the 2019 publication of her book, *Tiki: Modern Tropical Cocktails,* while also being the first Black American bartender since Julian Anderson in 1919 to publish a major cocktail book.

NAPOLEON HOUSE

A long-standing corner bar and restaurant in the French Quarter of New Orleans, treasured for its timeworn atmosphere, long connections to the city's past, classical music soundtrack, and role as the most significant seller of the Pimm's Cup in the United States. The bar goes through a case of Pimm's No. 1 a day. It's also known for its Sazeracs. The name is derived from an offer of safe harbor made to Napoleon by the building's first occupant, Nicholas Girod, then mayor of New Orleans. It was owned and operated by the Impastato family since 1914 and Ralph Brennan since 2015. The house drink came about because owner Peter Impastato didn't want his clientele getting drunk quickly, and he

NAPOLEON HOUSE

thought Pimm's Cups and Sazeracs made for nice, slow sipping drinks. The bar makes other drinks, but it's doubtful many of its customers know about them.

NAVY GROG

One of the better known and best-loved of all tiki drinks, surpassed in fame only by the Zombie and Mai Tai. Created by Donn Beach of Don the Beachcomber fame, it is a mixture of three kinds of rum, honey syrup, grapefruit, and lime juice, and traditionally served in a double rocks glass with an ice cone—that is, ice in the form of a cone, through which the drink is sipped. Beach rival Trader Vic's did good business with their own version, enough to inspire them to sell a commercially bottled product called Navy Grog Mix.

NEGRONI

Italy's crowning contribution to the cocktail canon, a strong and sweetly bitter aperitivo composition made of equal parts of dry gin, sweet red vermouth, and a red bitters, typically Campari. It is a direct descendent of the Milano-Torino and the Americano, the former a mix of vermouth and red bitters, the latter the same with the addition of soda water. Neither of those drinks were stiff enough for Count Camillo Negroni (1868–1934), an adventurer, gambler, and bon vivant who in 1919 asked the bartender at Caffe Casoni in Florence to replace the soda water with gin. The success of the drink was minimal for a good long time, a relatively obscure epicurean delight adopted by the *La Dolce Vita* types of the 1950s and '60s, such as Tennessee Williams, Rudolf Nureyev, and Orson Welles. It received regular mentions in the press beginning in the 1950s, but it hardly gave the Martini or Old-Fashioned a run for their money. During that era, the drink was routinely served up, without ice. The Negroni's true heyday came with the turn of the twenty-first century, when it was embraced by the mixologists of the cocktail revival as something true, pure, and challenging. It didn't hurt that it was made of three things they loved and were trying to get others to love: gin, vermouth, and Campari. By the 2010s, it was one of the most consumed cocktails in the world. Variations were legion. The gin was swapped out for bourbon, tequila, mezcal, aquavit, you name it. Every kind of vermouth got its turn, as did all sorts of red bitters, as well as other

NAVY GROG

liquors from the wide amaro family. A few twists, such as the White Negroni and Kingston Negroni, became classics in their own right. The Boulevardier and Old Pal, once completely unknown, owe their lives to the rebirth of the Negroni. And the Negroni Sbagliato, once a specialty enjoyed only in Milan, is drunk internationally. Finally, Campari went from Italian icon to global liquor monolith on the back of this cocktail. By the time it reached its hundredth birthday, the Negroni, a onetime also-ran curiosity, had secured its place as one of the handful of indisputable classic cocktails of all time.

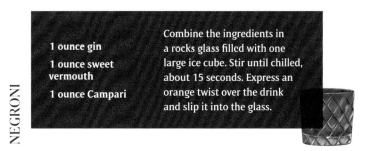

NEGRONI

1 ounce gin

1 ounce sweet vermouth

1 ounce Campari

Combine the ingredients in a rocks glass filled with one large ice cube. Stir until chilled, about 15 seconds. Express an orange twist over the drink and slip it into the glass.

NEW YORK SOUR

A Whiskey Sour made classy and visually pleasing by a picturesque float of dry red wine. It gained steady visibility through constant inclusion in the annual Mr. Boston bar guides beginning in the 1930s, but never really rated much as a classic or popular order until the cocktail renaissance, when historians and young bartenders in search of sacred causes hauled it back into use. By 2010 it was a common sight and, like the modern Gold Rush and Penicillin, an easy way to make the Whiskey Sour a bit more exciting, as well as a way to show off bartenders' newfound skill at floating ingredients. Julie Reiner was a particularly ardent early advocate of the drink, which she served at Flatiron Lounge.

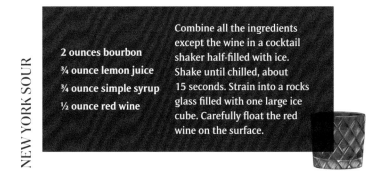

NEW YORK SOUR

2 ounces bourbon

¾ ounce lemon juice

¾ ounce simple syrup

½ ounce red wine

Combine all the ingredients except the wine in a cocktail shaker half-filled with ice. Shake until chilled, about 15 seconds. Strain into a rocks glass filled with one large ice cube. Carefully float the red wine on the surface.

NEW YORK SOUR

NIGHTCAP

The final drink of the night, taken before retiring. It caps the night and comforts like the nightcaps sleepers wore back in the nineteenth century when the custom took hold. A nightcap is typically of the "simple, but significant" variety, composed of warming, serious spirits that invite meditation and the settling of the stomach. Whiskey, brandy, and amari are made for nightcaps. Sours are not.

OAXACA OLD-FASHIONED

The founding creation of the mezcal cocktail boom that enveloped the American bar world in the 2010s. Invented by bartender Phil Ward at Death & Co. in 2007, it is simply an Old-Fashioned riff with a spirit base split between reposado tequila and mezcal, with Angostura bitters, agave syrup, and a flamed orange twist completing the picture. It directly inspired other bartenders to toy around with mezcal as a cocktail mixer and is the most famous original cocktail to come out of Death & Co.—a fact the bar memorialized by putting the drink on a T-shirt in 2020.

1½ ounces reposado tequila, preferably El Tesoro

½ ounce mezcal, preferably Del Maguey San Luis Del Rio

2 dashes Angostura bitters

1 barspoon agave nectar

Combine the ingredients in a rocks glass filled with one large piece of ice. Stir until chilled, about 15 seconds. Make a flamed orange twist by cutting a piece of orange zest about the size of a silver dollar. Hold the orange zest, skin side down, several inches above the drink. Light a match and use it to warm the skin side of the peel. Quickly squeeze the zest in the direction of the match. The oil from the zest will briefly burst into flame, showering its essence over the drink's surface.

OHIO

A cocktail named after an American state, but with a rich history in Germany and, mysteriously, almost nowhere else. The cognac version first appeared in German cocktail books in the 1910s. Two rival recipes persisted for much of the Ohio's mid-twentieth-century reign: one with cognac, curaçao, and bitters, topped with champagne; and one, resembling a Manhattan, using whiskey (sometimes American, sometimes Canadian) and sweet vermouth, again finished with champagne, and sometimes including curaçao, too. By the 1980s, the Ohio's popularity had faded, and the drink drifted into obscurity, though it is still served at some cutting-edge cocktail bars such as Buck and Breck in Berlin.

1 ounce rye whiskey

½ ounce sweet vermouth

1 dash Bigallet China-China Amer

1 dash curaçao

2 dashes Angostura bitters

2 ounces champagne

Combine all the ingredients except the champagne in a mixing glass half-filled with ice. Stir until chilled, about 15 seconds. Strain into a silver cup filled with ice. Top with the champagne. Express an orange twist over the drink and discard.

(There are many versions of this cocktail. This recipe is just one, currently served at the Berlin bar Buck and Breck.)

OJEN

An anise-flavored liqueur favored in New Orleans for decades before it completely disappeared, only to be revived soon after. Ojen has a history almost as romantic as absinthe's. First produced in the mid-1800s by a Spanish distiller in the small town of Ojen, it developed a rather cultured reputation. Picasso painted a bottle into his *Spanish Still Life* (1912). Hemingway wrote about it in *To Have and Have Not.* And it was lapped up in New Orleans, where it was strongly associated with Mardi Gras. The liqueur was popular enough that it had its own namesake drink, the Ojen Cocktail (Ojen, Peychaud's bitters, and seltzer). When the Spanish source decided to shut down production in the early 1990s, Martin Wine Cellar, a well-known New Orleans shop, panicked. It pleaded for one more run of the juice and got it: six thousand bottles' worth. But the last was sold in 2009. In 2016, a formula was reverse-engineered by the Sazerac Company.

OJEN

OLD CUBAN

A Mojito riff using aged rum, Angostura bitters, and, most critically, champagne. It is, in essence, a Mojito Royale. It was created in 2001 by Audrey Saunders when she was bar director of Bemelmans Bar, the classic cocktail lounge tucked inside Manhattan's Carlyle Hotel. Saunders subsequently introduced the drink to Europe through a Bemelmans pop-up at the Ritz in London in 2002. It thereafter appeared on menus in several European capitals and won a permanent home in 2005 when Saunders put it on the menu at her New York bar Pegu Club.

1½ ounces aged rum (Bacardi 8 recommended)

1 ounce simple syrup

¾ ounce lime juice

Two dashes Angostura bitters

6 whole mint leaves

2 ounces champagne

Muddle the mint leaves, lime juice, and simple syrup at the bottom of a cocktail shaker. Add the rum and bitters. Fill the shaker with ice and shake until chilled, about 15 seconds. Strain into a chilled cocktail glass. Top with the champagne.

OLD-FASHIONED

The original cocktail, such as it was originally defined as spirits, sugar, water, and bitters, and, in its whiskey form, one of the most globally popular and enduring of all mixed drinks. It has never fully fallen off the drinking radar in two centuries and can safely be ordered at nearly any bar that serves spirits. Originally called, simply, the Whiskey Cocktail, it was just one of many standard cocktails following the same formula, made of various spirits. It was first served up, sans ice, in a footed glass, and often taken as a matutinal drink. By the 1870s, bartenders began to offer "improved" versions of the Whiskey Cocktail, dashing in touches of curaçao, Chartreuse, absinthe, and whatnot, leading to a patron rebellion of traditionalists who demanded an "old-fashioned whiskey cocktail." This name, over the decades, led to the abbreviated name the cocktail bears today, sometimes rendered "old fashion" or "old fashioned" without the hyphen. Variations like the old-fashioned gin cocktail and old-fashioned rum cocktail held on for a while, appearing in bar manuals before eventually dropping off the map, leaving the whiskey version of the drink as the sole claimant to the title Old-Fashioned. During the late nineteenth century the cocktail converted from an ice-less up drink to one built in a stubby, heavy-bottomed rocks glass that eventually came to be named after the drink. This rendition of the Old-Fashioned featured muddled sugar and bitters, a good slug of bourbon or rye served over a large piece of ice, and an orange or lemon twist. Sometimes the customer was trusted to pour in the whiskey themselves. The drink was typically served with a small metal spoon, used to stir the drink and scoop up the residual sugar at the bottom.

OLD-FASHIONED

Recipes for the drink under the name Old-Fashioned began to appear in cocktail books in 1888. Before the arrival of Prohibition, the Old-Fashioned became more ornate, with fruit like orange, cherry, and pineapple piled on top. After repeal, the fruit had fallen to the bottom of the glass and was often muddled. This preparation, with the muddled fruit—which detractors called "the garbage"—became the predominant one for the remainder of the twentieth century. The drinks of this period, what with all the garnishing, grew in size, leading to the development and domination of a larger glass, called the double old-fashioned glass. The Old-Fashioned remained a popular choice through the 1960s, when it began to decline in favor, left behind in the wake of Disco Drinks and vodka, until the Old-Fashioned was truly old-fashioned, a drink your parents or grandparents enjoyed.

Widely misunderstood by mixologists during the early years of the cocktail revolution, the cocktail's code was eventually cracked, and late-nineteenth-century expressions of the drink began to appear on cocktail menus in the late aughts. This new presentation, which showcased the whiskey, coupled with the rise of interest in bourbon and rye in general, led to a rebirth for the Old-Fashioned. By the 2010s, it was one of the most called-for drinks in bars around the world, and a favorite of younger people for the first time in generations. The arrival of the 1960s-set television show *Mad Men,* in which the lead character Don Draper drinks Old-Fashioneds, contributed to the drink's new trendy status. The new interest led to the creation of thousands of Old-Fashioned variations, returning the drink to its versatile origins. A few of these attained their own reputations, including the Benton's Old-Fashioned, Elder Fashioned, Conference, and Oaxaca Old-Fashioned. The drink's history and popularity has been so long-lived that it has led to persistent regional expressions. In Wisconsin and other parts of the Midwest, the drink is commonly made with domestic brandy and muddled fruit, topped with citrus soda or soda water, and garnished with everything from orange and cherry to mushrooms and Brussels sprouts. In Buenos Aires, the sugar and bitters are mixed and made to coat the entire inside of the glass, in the form of a Crusta. In London during the late twentieth century, the cocktail was an elaborately built affair, made and stirred down with ice over the course of five to ten minutes.

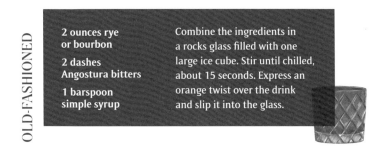

OLD-FASHIONED

2 ounces rye
or bourbon

2 dashes
Angostura bitters

1 barspoon
simple syrup

Combine the ingredients in a rocks glass filled with one large ice cube. Stir until chilled, about 15 seconds. Express an orange twist over the drink and slip it into the glass.

OLD PAL

An equal-parts mix of whiskey (historically Canadian), dry vermouth, and Campari that earned new favor in the aughts when bartenders and drinkers were latching onto anything that had a remotely Negroni-esque profile. It was attributed to Paris-based American sportswriter William H. "Sparrow" Robertson in Paris bartender Harry MacElhone's 1927 cocktail book *Barflies and Cocktails.* But in that book, the recipe calls for sweet vermouth, which doesn't distinguish it much from the Boulevardier in the same volume. In later editions of the book, and by the time it landed in *The Savoy Cocktail Book* in 1930, the drink had the dry vermouth it's come to be known for. But Mr. Boston listed it with sweet vermouth a few years later, in 1935, as well as with rye or bourbon and, uh, grenadine; and some 1930s recipes replace the Campari with crème de menthe, another ghastly idea. The modern version is strictly rye, dry vermouth, and Campari; while it has fans, it has ever dwelled in the shadow of the heartier Boulevardier. Robertson reportedly called all friends and acquaintances "old pal."

OLD PAL

1 ounce rye
1 ounce dry vermouth
1 ounce Campari

Combine the ingredients in a rocks glass filled with one large ice cube. Stir until chilled, about 15 seconds. Express an orange twist over the drink and slip it into the glass.

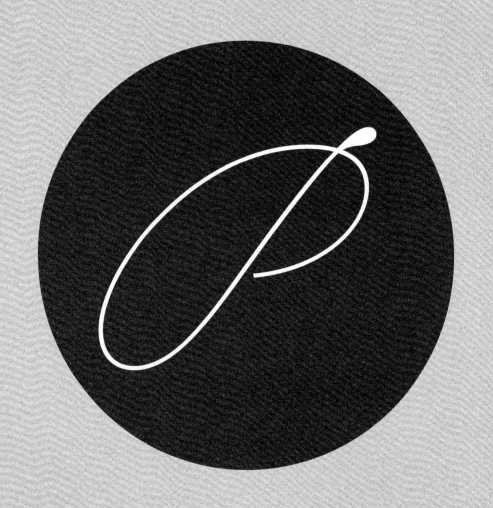

PALOMA

A refreshing mixture of tequila, grapefruit soda, and lime juice, with an optional salt rim, usually served as a highball. Popular in Mexico since the 1960s, it was largely unknown in the United States until the 2010s, when agave-loving American bartenders began offering it as an alternative to the ubiquitous Margarita. In the 2020s the drink is nearly as common in U.S. bars as the Margarita. Its creation was partly sparked by the introduction of the grapefruit soda Squirt to the Mexican market in 1955. In the 1970s, Squirt began promoting it in its advertising. Craft mixologists often replaced the commercial soda with various combinations of fresh grapefruit juice, sugar, simple syrup, agave syrup, and sparkling water. At Mayahuel, the influential New York agave bar, the Spicy Paloma used jalapeño-infused tequila as its base.

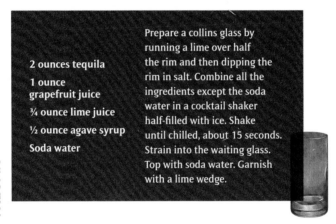

PALOMA

2 ounces tequila

1 ounce grapefruit juice

¾ ounce lime juice

½ ounce agave syrup

Soda water

Prepare a collins glass by running a lime over half the rim and then dipping the rim in salt. Combine all the ingredients except the soda water in a cocktail shaker half-filled with ice. Shake until chilled, about 15 seconds. Strain into the waiting glass. Top with soda water. Garnish with a lime wedge.

PAPER PLANE

An equal-parts twist on the Last Word, made of bourbon, Aperol, Amaro Nonino, and lemon juice, this Sam Ross cocktail was created in 2007 for the opening menu at the Violet Hour in Chicago at the request of founder Toby Maloney. The initial version featured Campari instead of Aperol, but Ross quickly adjusted the formula, and the Aperol version began to be sold at Milk & Honey and Little Branch, where he worked. Because of the ease of the build and the broad appeal of the ingredients, the drink quickly caught fire, particularly in Canada. In 2014, a bar in San Jose named themselves after the cocktail. The drink was named after the M.I.A. song "Paper Planes."

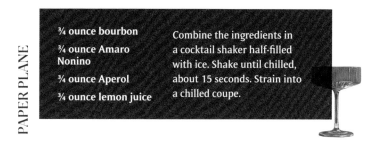

PAPER PLANE

¾ ounce bourbon

¾ ounce Amaro Nonino

¾ ounce Aperol

¾ ounce lemon juice

Combine the ingredients in a cocktail shaker half-filled with ice. Shake until chilled, about 15 seconds. Strain into a chilled coupe.

PASSERBY

A bar that opened in 1999 in the Chelsea neighborhood of Manhattan, inside an art gallery owned by Gavin Brown. It was run by Toby Cecchini, the epicurean veteran of the Odeon and Kin Khao who invented the Cosmopolitan. With that split personality, Passerby fittingly operated as a cultural hybrid: part club, part bar, part art salon, catering to art world elites, Chelsea's gay community, bridge-and-tunnel thrill seekers, and downtown hipsters. Its tongue-in-cheek, *Saturday Night Fever*-ish illuminated floor design was copied by bars such as Glass in Paris and Honeycut in Los Angeles. Passerby closed in 2008. While never a player in New York's cocktail revival, seen in retrospect it proved influential.

PDT

One of the most famous and successful of the cocktail bars of the modern cocktail era, and the epitome of the speakeasy model. (The acronym name stands for Please Don't Tell. Everyone did, though.) It was opened by Brian Shebairo in a tiny basement space next to Crif Dogs, his hot dog business in the East Village neighborhood of New York. One entered through an old wooden phone booth (Shebairo's idea), which immediately became the most notorious bar entrance in the world. Inside was a low-ceiling, wooden-panel-and-brick space, which seated no more than a couple dozen people. Shebairo hired noted New York mixologist Jim Meehan (Pegu Club, Gramercy Tavern) as a consultant to take charge of the place. Meehan would quickly become the face and soul of the bar and, through PDT and the copious press it garnered, one of the best-known bartenders in the

THE OUTSIDE ENTRANCE TO PDT

world. Meehan hired layman novices Don Lee and John Deragon for his early team, and although they worked only one day a week, they became part of the early legend of the place. Other bartenders who worked there over the years include Michael Madrusan, John deBary, David Slape, and Jeff Bell, who eventually assumed control of the bar after Meehan had relocated to Portland, Oregon, and later bought the bar from Shebairo. Famous and influential drinks that emerged from PDT include the Benton's Old-Fashioned, which popularized the fat-washing technique; the Paddington; the Mezcal Mule, one of the first big mezcal cocktails; The Shark, an early craft cocktail that toyed with the color blue; and the Staggerac, a strong Sazerac riff that used overproof George T. Stagg bourbon. Food came from Crif Dogs and consisted of high-end interpretations of low-brow staples like tater tots and hot dogs, often named after the celebrity chefs that haunted the bar. In 2011, PDT and Meehan added a further layer of global influence by publishing *The PDT Cocktail Book,* one of the first such bar-branded cocktail books of the era. A PDT branch opened in Hong Kong in 2018.

PEGU CLUB

A New York cocktail bar that, during its existence (2005–2020), was among the important world centers of mixology; one of the most influential of the modern cocktail revival and, arguably, of all time. It was named after a favorite early-twentieth-century cocktail created at a British officers' club in Rangoon (now Yangon). From its second-floor perch on Houston Street in Manhattan came a flood of cocktails, techniques, and personnel that would be adopted and embraced by the bar world at large. It was opened by the same team behind Flatiron Lounge, but run by the newest member of that group, Audrey Saunders. A Long Islander, she came up quickly in cocktail circles under the wing of Dale DeGroff and had previously run the bar programs at Bemelmans Bar, Beacon, and Tonic. Saunders's methods were meticulous and exacting. She would test dozens of versions of the same drink before settling on the recipe that would go on the Pegu menu. That menu was largely filled with classic cocktails and original drinks of Saunders's creation that would become classics, such as the Old Cuban, Gin-Gin Mule, and Little Italy. For her opening bartending crew, Saunders assembled the best mixers in the city, including Toby Maloney, Phil Ward, Chad Solomon, Brian Miller, and Jim Meehan. Each would eventually go on to open their own cocktail bar.

The bar's opening coincided with the press's sudden realization that the cocktail renaissance was something worth covering. Journalists were among the bar's original habitués, ensuring that Pegu and Saunders and her innovations would stay in the public eye. Many advances in the field occurred within the bar's walls. Saunders secured then-hard-to-get spirits such as Rittenhouse rye, Laird's bonded applejack, and Suze. The Last Word cocktail first found its way to New York drinkers at Pegu, as did the White Negroni. Solomon invented the dry shake technique while at Pegu. The Fifity-Fifty Martini was championed and popularized there. Every December, Saunders served Tom and Jerrys, leading to a renewed appreciation of that hot holiday drink.

Other more controversial aspects of the cocktail revival were largely born there, including the eschewing of vodka; formalized bartender attire; bar talk

PEGU CLUB

that consisted of nothing but dissecting the minutiae of cocktails and cocktail history; and a certain adversarial relationship between the all-knowing bartender and needing-to-be-schooled customers. But Saunders stuck to her guns, wanting to elevate the cocktail to the same level of respect enjoyed by cuisine. Within two years, much of the original bar staff had departed for Death & Co. and PDT. Notable bartenders who took their place over the years included Del Pedro, St. John Frizell, Sam Ross, Kenta Goto, and Giuseppe González. Over time, the bar's preeminence faded, as newer and trendier cocktail bars opened. Though it was one of the first in Manhattan to become a victim of the Covid pandemic, there were already plans for the bar to shutter in fall 2020 when its lease ended.

PENICILLIN

One of the most prominent successes of the modern cocktail era, this drink was invented by New York–based Australian bartender Sam Ross at Milk & Honey in 2005. Drawing inspiration from the Gold Rush, invented at the same bar, Ross combined blended scotch, lemon juice, and honey-ginger syrup with a float of smoky Islay single-malt scotch and a garnish of candied ginger. The cocktail, first offered at Milk & Honey's sister bar Little Branch as a bartender's choice, became enormously popular very quickly and has since been served in bars all over the world. It is also frequently riffed upon. Ross himself has created both a frozen and a hot version of the Penicillin. The name is a joking reference to the ingredient list, as honey, lemon, and whiskey are all good for what ails you.

2 ounces blended scotch

¾ ounce honey-ginger syrup*

¾ ounce lemon juice

¼ ounce Islay single-malt Scotch, preferably Laphroaig 10YO

Combine the blended scotch, syrup, and lemon juice in a cocktail shaker half-filled with ice. Shake until chilled, about 15 seconds. Strain into a rocks glass filled with one large ice cube. Float Islay scotch on the surface of the drink. Garnish with candied ginger.

*HONEY-GINGER SYRUP

8 ounces honey

1 six-inch piece of ginger root, peeled and sliced

8 ounces water

Combine the ingredients in a pot. Bring to a boil, lower the heat, and simmer for 5 minutes. Let cool. Refrigerate overnight, then strain, discarding the solids.

PENICILLIN

PETRASKE, SASHA

As founder and owner of Milk & Honey, Petraske is the single most influential figure in the global cocktail renaissance of the twenty-first century and the movement's one true visionary. Petraske was born in Manhattan in 1973 in a Communist household, which instilled in him a respect for workers that would eventually be extended to the bartenders he employed. An iconoclast contemptuous of conventional schooling, he left high school early, took a cross-country bicycle trip, lived in San Francisco for a while, and joined the Army, serving for three years. Back in New York, he worked at Von, a bar in the East Village, and began to dream of opening a bar that would reflect his love of jazz, vintage clothing, and old-fashioned decorum. Responding to an ad in the *Village Voice* for a narrow commercial space at 134 Eldridge Street at $800 a month, he learned that the landlord had been a friend of his in elementary school. Promising to run a quiet bar, he began renovating the space. Soon broke, he borrowed money from friends and, with little fanfare, opened Milk & Honey on December 31, 1999. He borrowed many stylistic aspects—rules of etiquette, quiet atmosphere, large ice cubes, no large groups—from Angel's Share, a bar he admired in the East Village.

The bar had no phone number and did not advertise; Petraske was allergic to press and wanted to avoid creating the sort of "hot" bar that made the pages of *Time Out New York* and its ilk. At first, few visited, and Petraske covered all shifts, learning as he went. After a year, regular Toby Maloney, a bartender at Grange Hall, convinced Petraske to hire him. Milk & Honey might have died on the vine had celebrity bartender Dale DeGroff not known a friend on the same street, who took him to the bar. DeGroff befriended Petraske and lent him a few old cocktail books. He also brought in Jonathan Downey, a London bar owner, who proposed a London version of Milk & Honey. The collaboration likely saved the New York location from certain closure. From London, Petraske brought back two Italian bartenders, Vincenzo Errico and Laura Zanella, as well as new-old approaches to drinks like the Old-Fashioned and Martini.

The bar was a composition of many small but important brushstrokes. Drinks at Milk & Honey were always served on a tray with a lit candle and accompanied by a thick napkin and a glass of water with a slice of cucumber in it, all to a backdrop of jazz music. Many of Milk & Honey's bartending innovations were stopgap fixes in disguise. The hidden entrance and lack of a sign—both later hallmarks of the neo-speakeasy movement—were in keeping with Petraske's promise to the landlord to not run a noisy bar. When lines quickly formed outside, he was forced

P

SASHA PETRASKE

to adopt a reservation policy. There was no menu because he didn't know how to run a laser printer. He froze and carved up his own ice because there was no space for an ice machine behind the tiny, five-stool bar.

Petraske's emphasis was always on reviving and perfecting the classics. Nonetheless, a number of modern classics emerged from the bar over the years, including the Gold Rush, Penicillin, Red Hook, Greenpoint, Paper Plane, and, to a lesser extent, American Trilogy, Gordon's Cup, Gordon's Breakfast, and Silver Lining. He also championed and helped popularize old drinks such as the Queen's Park Swizzle and the Fix genre of sours. Ever interested in advancing the careers of his bartenders, he quickly began opening additional bars with them, including Little Branch with Joseph Schwartz; Dutch Kills with Richard Boccato; Middle Branch with Lucinda Sterling; The Varnish in Los Angeles with Eric Alperin;

and Adelaide in Melbourne, Australia, with Michael Madrusan. All of these bars became landmarks in their own right. He also consulted on many other bars, including Weather Up in Brooklyn; the Lamb's Club, Double Seven, and John Dory Oyster Bar in Manhattan; and Bonahan's in San Antonio. Two long-standing Milk & Honey bartenders, Australian Sam Ross and Irishman Michael McIlroy, eventually took over Milk & Honey, renaming it Attaboy but retaining much of the original spirit. Petraske then moved his bar to bigger digs on West 23rd Street. The new location did not last long. The building was sold, and a demolition clause in the lease forced him to vacate. (The London Milk & Honey closed in 2020, a victim of the Covid-19 pandemic.) Petraske was admittedly not much of a businessman: Many of his ventures were quick failures, including the East Side Company, meant to be a more casual Milk & Honey, and White Star, one of the first neo-absinthe bars. Idealistic, Petraske did not travel the cocktail circuit as did many of his colleagues, avoiding conventions and competitions, lecturing seldomly, and eschewing brand work. That said, in 2012, he was a founder of the San Antonio Cocktail Conference, an annual convention.

Petraske was found dead in August 2015 in a hotel room in Hudson, New York, where he was working on a consulting project. A book he had been working on, *Regarding Cocktails,* was published posthumously. A planned bar in Red Hook, Brooklyn, called Seaborne, was opened by Sterling. Years after his death, Pestraske's influence is still felt in many bars across the world, and in the quality and care behind the cocktails drunk every night by millions.

PICKLEBACK

P

A lowbrow, two-step shot, in which a dram of whiskey is chased by a shot of straight pickle brine. Created at the Bushwick Social Club in 2006 to satisfy a request of a regular, it was first served by bartender Reggie Cunningham and named by bar owner John Roberts. It was made using Old Crow and brine from McClure's pickles, then a start-up brand whose owner lived above the Bushwick Social Club and stored some of his product in the bar's basement. The shot quickly spread throughout New York. A score of articles written around 2009 rocketed the trend into the stratosphere. By 2010, the Pickleback was inescapable. Jameson co-opted the shot early on, promoting its whiskey as a Pickleback go-to. The drink is remarkably egalitarian, served in restaurant bars, sports bars, pubs, and haughty cocktail bars.

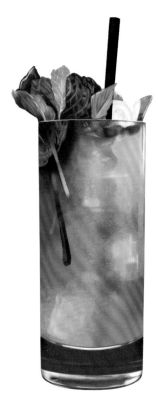

PIMM'S CUP

PIMM'S CUP

A refreshing highball that uses the spicy-sweet British liqueur Pimm's No. 1 as its bedrock. Pimm's No. 1, a gin-based liqueur, is named after James Pimm, the bar owner who created it in the mid-1800s. By the 1860s, it was bottled. It is No. 1 because at one point there were other "cups," numbered 2 through 6, based on brandy, rum, and other spirits. But the No. 1, a reddish tonic with citrusy and bitter notes, has always been the star, and it is not quite like anything else on the shelf. Over the years, it has developed a reputation as a quintessentially British refresher, consumed in ungodly amounts every year at Wimbledon. The popularity of the Pimm's Cup in the United States has ebbed and flowed over the last half-century or so; until the current century, it was associated mainly with

New Orleans, and specifically with the French Quarter bar the Napoleon House, which sells hundreds a day. The Pimm's Cup there is simplicity itself: Pimm's, lemonade, and 7-Up, crowned with the singular garnish of a cucumber slice. Indeed, the drink is the cucumber's raison d'être behind any bar. Beginning in the 2010s, the cocktail became more common in the United States, and more open to interpretation. Maison Premiere in Brooklyn, in particular, has debuted dozens of different Pimm's Cups over the years.

PIMM'S CUP

| 2 ounces Pimm's No. 1 | Combine the ingredients in a highball glass filled with ice. Stir briefly. Garnish with a cucumber slice. |
| 4 ounces ginger ale or lemonade | |

PIÑA COLADA

Rupert Holmes's 1980 number one hit "Escape (The Piña Colada Song)" has made sure we will never escape this holiday-in-a-glass rum drink. But it was massively popular well before that, a dessert-like magnet that one drinks historian declared "fails as a balanced cocktail, [but] succeeds brilliantly as a pineapple-coconut milkshake." It made its debut at the Caribe Hilton hotel in 1954 and quickly became a sensation. The name means "strained pineapple," which, prior to the Caribe cocktail, is just what the drink was (with coconut sometimes added, and occasionally rum) throughout the Caribbean, particularly in Cuba. This early nonalcoholic version also found its way to certain parts of the United States. The popularity of the Caribe version, which included Coco Lopez coconut cream, led to all sorts of commercial offshoots, including piña colada mixes, liqueurs, ice cream, cake, and bottled piña coladas. The drink is a popular punching bag among drinks writers, epicures, and aesthetes. Novelist Kingsley Amis listed it in the index of his book *Everyday Drinking* as "Piña Colada, as threat to civilization." So far, the drinking public have paid no mind.

P

2 ounces white rum

1 ounce Coco Lopez coconut cream

1 ounce heavy cream

6 ounces pineapple juice

4 ounces crushed ice

Put the ingredients in a blender. Blend for 15 seconds. Pour unstrained into a large goblet. Garnish with a pineapple wedge.

PINK SQUIRREL

A sweet after-dinner drink made of crème de noyaux, crème de cacao, and cream or, alternatively, ice cream. It became a popular drink in the early 1950s after a stunt in which singer Betty Reed, accompanied by a squirrel painted pink, requested the drink at a New York club—an event that was picked up by the press. The cocktail's most loyal audience resides in the Midwest. There is an enduring origin story that the drink was invented at Bryant's Cocktail Lounge in Milwaukee in the 1940s, but there is no evidence to back up the claim. Because 1951 articles described it as "the new Bols drink," it was likely a potion invented and marketed by that liqueur company. However, no bar in the world is more associated with the drink than Bryant's, which serves many of the pink things every week. The Bryant's version is an ice cream drink.

PINK SQUIRREL (ice cream version)

2 ounces crème de noyaux

1 ounce crème de cacao

2 six-ounce scoops of vanilla ice cream

Put the ingredients in a blender and blend until smooth and creamy. Serve in a chilled glass topped with whipped cream (preferably homemade with a little sugar and vanilla to taste) and a maraschino cherry.

PISCO

A grape brandy over which Peru and Chile continually fight for bragging rights. Its role in cocktail history basically boils down to two drinks, the Pisco Punch and the Pisco Sour. The Pisco Punch was a sensation in late-nineteenth-century San Francisco, which received regular shipments of the spirit via ship from South America. It was made famous and popular by Duncan Nicol at the Bank Exchange Saloon. The concoction was made of pisco, pineapple, lime juice, sugar, gum syrup, and water. It had quite a reputation and caused many a writer to lapse into hyperbole. "I have a theory it is compounded of cherub's wings," wrote Rudyard Kipling, "the glory of a tropical dawn, the red clouds of sunset, and the fragments of lost epics by dead masters."

Nicol was a fine marketer. He would allow a customer only two glasses of punch, a gimmick later copied at Don the Beachcomber with its Zombie, and many other bars besides. But because Nicol never shared his recipe, the drink's heyday died with Nicol in 1926, seven years after Prohibition killed his bar. Many bartenders and historians have since tried to duplicate the punch's magic, but their potions, while often delicious, must always be enjoyed with a touch of skepticism. The Pisco Sour came later and was much easier to duplicate, being simply a sour made with pisco, egg white, lemon or lime juice, sugar, sometimes bitters, and no secret ingredients. It is widely credited to Victor Morris, an American bartender working in Peru. It is wildly popular in Peru and Chile, but in the United States the drink is not overly common. Joe Baum's La Fonda del Sol served it in the 1960s. But the Pisco Sour's spiritual home is San Francisco, and you will still see the drink there more often than anywhere else. Bartender Duggan McDonnell was a prominent pisco evangelist back in the aughts, and he served a fine Pisco Sour at his bar, Cantina. McDonnell went on to produce his own line of piscos. And yet, his and other bartender's efforts weren't quite enough to bestow upon the Pisco Sour the mass popularity the Pisco Punch enjoyed in San Francisco in the late nineteenth century. Modern bartenders have tried to fold pisco more fully into the cocktail repertoire, but with limited success, making the spirit truly a two-hit wonder. However, when the hits are that big, you don't really need any others.

P

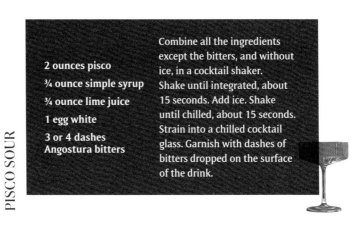

2 ounces pisco
¾ ounce simple syrup
¾ ounce lime juice
1 egg white
3 or 4 dashes
Angostura bitters

Combine all the ingredients except the bitters, and without ice, in a cocktail shaker. Shake until integrated, about 15 seconds. Add ice. Shake until chilled, about 15 seconds. Strain into a chilled cocktail glass. Garnish with dashes of bitters dropped on the surface of the drink.

POLICASTRO, SANTIAGO

The leading figure in the Argentina bartending world from the 1930s to the 1950s and author of the 1955 cocktail book *Tragos Mágicos.* The son of Italian immigrants, he was born in Buenos Aires in 1912. At his peak, he owned three bars, had a radio show, and won international cocktail competitions. Such was his fame that he earned not one but two nicknames: Pichin and El Barman Gallant. His most famous creation was the Clarito, a Martini variation with a sugar rim. Invented in 1935, it all but disappeared after he left the country, but came roaring back in the twenty-first century through the efforts of local young mixologists. In 1954, Policastro was drafted by President Juan Perón as a cultural ambassador, promoting Argentine products in a variety of countries. This association came to haunt him in 1955 when Perón was overthrown. Seen as an intimate of the ousted leader, Policastro became an exile for the rest of his life and his eminence as a bartender effectively ceased. He died in Miami in 2010.

PORN STAR MARTINI

A creation of bartender Douglas Ankrah that, by virtue of a host of likable flavors (passion fruit, vanilla, more passion fruit, more vanilla, side of bubbly) and a naughty name, became a drinking sensation in early-aughts London. Ankrah hatched the idea while traveling in South Africa. He first named it the Maverick Martini, after a strip club he patronized in Cape Town. It got its new name when he brought it back to London and put it on the menu at Townhouse. It was also a popular order at LAB, which Ankrah cofounded, becoming, it could be argued, the bar's signature drink. Twenty years on, when most cocktails of its era had faded away, the Porn Star Martini had not only endured but grown in popularity. There are bottled and canned versions, though corporate UK shies away from the X-rated name.

PORN STAR MARTINI

1 ⅓ ounces vanilla-flavored vodka

1 ⅔ ounces passion fruit puree

½ ounce passion fruit liqueur, preferably Passoã

2 barspoons vanilla syrup*

1 ounce Prosecco

Combine all the ingredients except the Prosecco in a cocktail shaker half-filled with ice. Shake until chilled, about 15 seconds. Strain into a chilled cocktail glass. Serve with a shot of Prosecco on the side.

*VANILLA SYRUP

Put a split vanilla bean in a saucepan with 8 ounces of water and 8 ounces of sugar. Heat to a boil, stirring, until the sugar dissolves. Let cool. Strain out the vanilla bean.

P

PORT

Port is a fortified wine made in Portugal that comes in several styles, including the common ruby port, which is red, fruity, sweet, and full-bodied. It has long enjoyed a role in cocktails, though primarily in pre-Prohibition times, when the wine was more generally popular with Americans. In the nineteenth century, port could be found in punches, cobblers, flips, and sangarees. One of the most famous port cocktails of this time went by the misleading name of Coffee Cocktail (made of port, brandy, egg, and sugar). The cocktail got its name from its appearance, which resembled coffee. The use of port generally diminished after repeal, as cocktails veered toward more simple and less opulent constructions.

Since cobblers, flips, and punches were no longer being made much, port lost its perch at the bar. As the century wore on, port developed a reputation as an old-fashioned, fuddy-duddy beverage. In the current century, there was an effort among port producers and some bartenders to bring port back in the fold, but with minimal success.

POUSSE CAFÉ

A stunt, after-dinner cocktail in which multiple liqueurs—as many as ten and as few as three—of varying weight, and preferably different colors, are carefully layered in a small, narrow glass. Once a staple drink at every pre-Prohibition fancy cocktail bar, its appeal was largely visual. Typically utilized were curaçao, crème de menthe, yellow and green Chartreuse, raspberry syrup, and maraschino liqueur, among other elixirs. The Pousse Café declined precipitously in popularity after World War II as tastes skewed simple and the desire for sweet drinks declined. No doubt, busy bartenders also lost the urge to build the time-consuming drink. It didn't help that some of the necessary ingredients, such as crème de violette, disappeared from the market. When the cocktail revival came along in the twenty-first century, it was one of the few old drinks to be issued a do-not-resuscitate order.

PRIDE, LINDEN

Born in Sydney, Pride became a leading cocktail bartender in the aughts. As the son of a food writer and cookbook author, he grew up going to restaurants with his mother. He spent time in London as bartender at Hakkasan, a Chinese restaurant with a cocktail list by London cocktail godfather Dick Bradsell. At China Doll in Sydney, he dabbled in molecular mixology and made enough of a name for himself to be included in a molecular-mixology summit in Paris in 2005. Pride's biggest impact on cocktails, however, was Dante, a temple of aperitivo-style drinking that he and his wife opened in Manhattan in 2015. The bar inspired a new worldwide interest in that European style of lighter drinks and day drinking.

POUSSE CAFÉ

PROULX, THEOPHILE

A French-Canadian bartender, born in Montreal in 1861, who in the 1880s worked at Chapin & Gore, one of the most acclaimed saloons in Chicago. While there, in 1888 he self-published *The Bartender's Manual,* a volume notable for containing the first known recipe for the Old-Fashioned in a cocktail book, and—in a tie with Harry Johnson's own *Bartender's Manual*—the first recipe for a Martini. Proulx's recipes for cocktails are written out in prose, and his notes on how to be a good bartender are thoughtful and as applicable today as they were then. Copies of the book are exceedingly rare, and it has never been republished. Proulx, who sometimes went by the name Theodore, later

THEOPHILE PROULX

left bartending, became a lawyer, and was active in politics and in the Chicago French-Canadian community. He died in 1918.

PUNCH

A big cocktail, suitable for sharing. Or, if you prefer, the large-format communal beverage, made of spirit, citrus, sugar, water, and sometimes spices, that is the direct ancestor of the modern, solo-sized American mixed drink. After being largely ignored by the mixology crowd of the twentieth century, punch came roaring back in the late aughts. Early advocates included the Hawksmoor in London and Death & Co. in New York. By 2010, many hip new bars had a daily punch on the menu. The format's popularity was aided by the 2010 publication of *Punch* by David Wondrich, a serious historical treatment of the subject, with recipes.

QUARANTINI

A cocktail-hour coinage that took hold in the early days of the Covid-19 pandemic, when everyone was quarantining in their home, relearning their bar skills, and in dire need of a stiff drink. As the name indicates, this drink was often a Martini, but, as the pandemic dragged on, the term was applied to whatever cocktail you happened to mix up around 5 p.m. while waiting for the world to reopen.

QUEEN'S PARK SWIZZLE

One of the most famous members of the swizzle family, this drink is made of demerara rum, Angostura bitters, lime juice, sugar, mint, and crushed ice. It first appeared in print in 1946, in *Trader Vic's Book of Food & Drink.* It is named for the

QUEEN'S PARK SWIZZLE

Queen's Park Hotel in Trinidad, where it was first concocted. The drink was fairly obscure when it found an unlikely champion in Milk & Honey founder Sasha Petraske, who began to serve it in highly theatrical form at his bars, with the muddled mint kept at the bottom by crushed ice, and copious bitters sprinkled on top, making for a tricolor, striped visual effect.

2 ounces demerara rum

1 ounce lime juice

¾ ounce simple syrup

1 sugar cube

6 dashes Angostura bitters

4 mint sprigs, leaves stripped, plus one whole sprig for garnish

Put the mint leaves in a cocktail shaker with the sugar cube, lime juice, and syrup. Using a muddler or wooden spoon, gently bruise the mint. Pour in the rum, swirl the shaker, and pour the contents into a 10- or 12-ounce tall glass. Add crushed ice until the glass is three-quarters full, then add the bitters. Insert a genuine swizzle stick or a barspoon into the glass, stopping just above the mint leaves, and hold its handle between your palms. Slide your hands back and forth against each other, gently spinning the spoon or swizzle stick. Ideally, liquid and ice will swirl together, while the top layer of bitters and bottom layer of mint stay undisturbed. Top with more ice and garnish with a mint sprig.

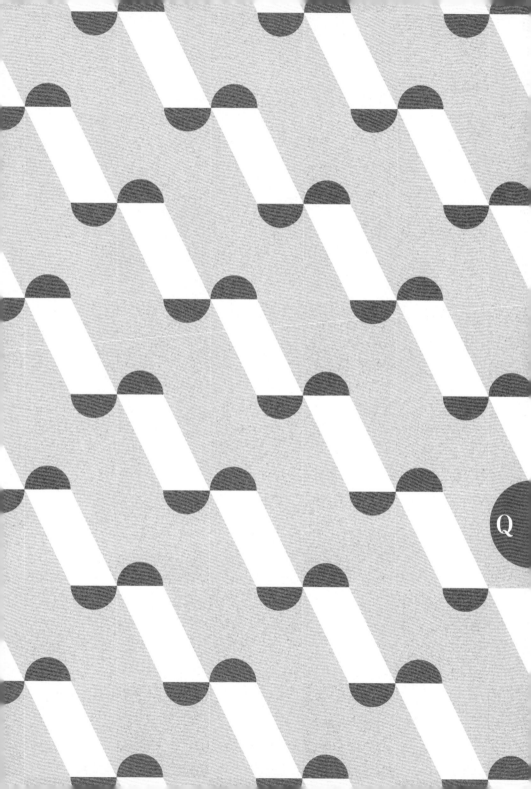

RAFFLES HOTEL

A hotel in Singapore that opened in 1887 and has long held a claim as the birthplace of the Singapore Sling, making it a drinking destination. The bar sells thousands of the things every day. The bar was frequented by many literary types in the early twentieth century, including Somerset Maugham, Hermann Hesse, James Michener, Günter Grass, Noel Coward, Joseph Conrad, Rudyard Kipling, and the inevitable Ernest Hemingway. The hotel was named for Sir Thomas Stamford Bingley Raffles, which is apparently the actual name of a real person.

RAINBOW ROOM

A 1930s-era Manhattan restaurant and club that, when it was reopened by restaurateur Joe Baum in 1987, became a showcase for the classic cocktails of a bygone era and helped kick off the cocktail revival in the United States. Rainbow's many bars were placed under the leadership of bartender Dale DeGroff, whom Baum groomed. Baum first tested DeGroff's mixological prowess at Baum's restaurant Aurora, which acted as a workshop for Rainbow. Lazy shortcuts that had become commonplace in bars in the preceding decades were discarded. There were no soda guns. A fresh juice program was instituted. DeGroff refused to carry shoddy liquor brands, and he foraged for forgotten and rare spirits to complete his cocktails, such as maraschino liqueur, falernum, and Peychaud's bitters. Old drinks like the Sazerac and Ramos Gin Fizz were put back in rotation. He also, over time, invented a few notable originals at the Rainbow Room—including the Fitzgerald, Ritz, and Whiskey Smash—and played a part in popularizing the Cosmopolitan. He differentiated between stirred and shaken cocktails, instead of shaking everything, which was the norm then. DeGroff reintroduced the flamed orange twist as a theatrical garnish, a move that became his signature and is now commonplace. He located needed tools, like the julep strainer, which had fallen out of use. Customers responded enthusiastically, crowding around the smartly dressed bartenders every night. So did the media, which slowly began to write about cocktails in a serious way, often calling upon DeGroff for a quote. DeGroff left the Rainbow Room in 1999.

RAMOS GIN FIZZ

RAMOS GIN FIZZ

The gin fizz to rule them all, and the main reason we still remember and order this category of cocktail at all. The drink is composed of gin, lemon juice, lime juice, cream, sugar, egg white, a few critical drops of orange flower water, and sparkling water. It looks as white as snow and is delivered in a long, slim glass. The result is light, fragrant, and frothy with a dessert-like quality that disguises its alcoholic potency. Everything about the drink is semi-legendary. It is regarded as gospel in New Orleans drinking circles as a drink that all citizens love and all local bartenders must know, and the only equal in fame and prestige to the beloved Sazerac. It is the rare classic cocktail to which the bartender, Henry C. Ramos (1856–1928), managed to affix his name for all eternity. The process of making one is near mythological, with stories of lines of "shaker boys" shaking the drink for anywhere from five to fifteen minutes. The tales were likely apocryphal, but nevertheless deathless. By 1895, Ramos's bar, The Imperial Cabinet, which he had opened in 1886, was already famous as the "gin fizz place," according to a local paper. The same paper called Ramos the "prince of New Orleans bartenders." Following the repeal of Prohibition, the drink was made famous all over again by Louisiana demagogue Huey P. Long, who brought a bartender up from the Roosevelt Hotel in New Orleans to demonstrate to the New York press how to make a proper Ramos Gin Fizz. Even in the modern days of the cocktail renaissance, it was considered de rigueur to master the difficult libation and achieve a creamy head that rose far above the rim of the glass. The Sazerac Bar inside the Roosevelt Hotel in New Orleans is renowned for its version. In the 2020s, some bartenders broke from orthodoxy and began to make Ramos Gin Fizzes in a blender.

RAMOS GIN FIZZ

2 ounces gin
1 ounce heavy cream
½ ounce lemon juice
½ ounce lime juice
½ ounce simple syrup
1 egg white
2 dashes orange flower water
1 ounce soda water

Combine all the ingredients except the soda water in a cocktail shaker. Dry shake for about 15 seconds. Add ice to the shaker. Shake further, about 30 seconds. Pour soda water into a collins glass. Slowly strain the mixture in the shaker into the glass, so that a head rises above the rim.

RED HOOK

A modern classic cocktail by Italian bartender Vincenzo Errico that landed somewhere between a Manhattan and a Brooklyn, and spawned a mid-aught explosion on Manhattan/Brooklyn riffs. Errico, who was working at Milk & Honey at the time, was looking for a way to showcase the Italian vermouth Punt e Mes, then getting some fresh attention from American mixologists. His mix of rye, maraschino liqueur, and Punt e Mes opened fellow bartenders' eyes to the possibility of creating new drinks by simply riffing off the already proven recipes of old classics. The Red Hook quickly led to a host of new creations, which came to be known as the "neighborhood cocktails"—so-called because they took their names from various Manhattan and Brooklyn neighborhoods—including the Carroll Gardens, Greenpoint, Cobble Hill, and Bushwick.

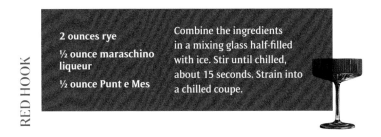

RED HOOK

2 ounces rye

½ ounce maraschino liqueur

½ ounce Punt e Mes

Combine the ingredients in a mixing glass half-filled with ice. Stir until chilled, about 15 seconds. Strain into a chilled coupe.

REGAL SHAKE

A technique credited to Milk & Honey bartender Theo Lieberman, who developed it in 2010. It involved dropping a bit of citrus peel in a drink, typically lime or grapefruit, before shaking. The method is thought to make the drink brighter, drier, and less sweet. It is typically used in making a daiquiri or other sours. Early on, Lieberman applied it to the Gold Rush at Milk & Honey.

REINER, JULIE

One of the enduring early leaders of the cocktail renaissance, as well as one of the few to remain in the actual bar business. She founded or cofounded more important cocktail bars in New York than anyone besides Sasha Petraske. Unlike Petraske's, Reiner's bars were high-volume and popular, offering the public access to high-quality cocktails in a nonspeakeasy atmosphere at both Flatiron Lounge and Pegu Club. She was also a pioneer of the cocktail scene in Brooklyn, opening Clover Club in 2009 and Leyenda in 2015. Reiner's first bar work was in Hawaii, where she was born and raised, but she earned her stripes as a bartender in San Francisco, working at such places as the Red Room Cocktail Lounge. Moving to New York in 1998, Reiner garnered the attention of the city's small cocktail clique, as well as the press, when working the small bar at C3, a peculiar restaurant on the northern edge of Washington Square. Her infusions, creativity, and enthusiasm were something new to the city. Realizing there was a vacancy to be filled in Manhattan, she opened Flatiron Lounge in 2003 with her partner

JULIE REINER

Susan Fedroff and three other partners. It was an immediate hit and New York's first egalitarian cocktail den, a direct contrast to the elite aerie that was Rainbow Room and the secretive hideout that was Milk & Honey. Two years later, the same team opened up Pegu Club, an even bigger success, with Dale DeGroff protégé Audrey Saunders as its figurehead.

A resident of Brooklyn, Reiner brought cocktails to her home borough with the classically oriented Clover Club. She later teamed with her bartender Ivy Mix to open Leyenda, a bar focused on Latin spirits, across the street from Clover Club. A Manhattan venture into tiki drinks, Lani Kai, was less successful, lasting only from 2010 to 2012. In 2022, after both Flatiron and Pegu had closed, Reiner returned to Manhattan, opening Milady's in SoHo.

R

The number of notable bartenders Reiner has mentored is long. Her most notable alumni include Phil Ward, Brian Miller, Katie Stipe, Giuseppe González, Tonia Guffey, Lynnette Marrero, and Tom Macy (eventually a partner in Clover Club). She is particularly known for fostering the careers of female bartenders.

REMEMBER THE MAINE

A Manhattan laced with Cherry Heering and absinthe, this mid-twentieth-century cocktail from Charles H. Baker Jr. was revived in the aughts, largely through the efforts of bartender and Baker historian St. John Frizell. It has remained in barroom circulation ever since.

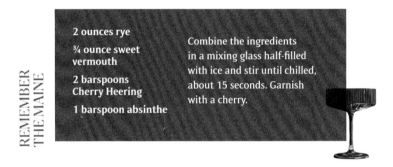

REMEMBER
THE MAINE

2 ounces rye

¾ ounce sweet vermouth

2 barspoons Cherry Heering

1 barspoon absinthe

Combine the ingredients in a mixing glass half-filled with ice and stir until chilled, about 15 seconds. Garnish with a cherry.

RHUM AGRICOLE

A style of rum distilled from sugar cane juice, as opposed to molasses, and produced primarily in the French Caribbean islands, particularly Martinique, which enjoys an AOC (appellation d'origine contrôlée) for the product. Rhum agricole is known for its grassy, vegetal, complex flavor profiles. It is the base spirit of the Ti' Punch and has played a fairly sizable role in tiki cocktail culture. It is one of the rums called for in the Mai Tai, tiki's most famous drink, as well as the Three Dots and a Dash. Still, it was rare to see a bottle of the stuff in a bar outside of the Caribbean. Rhum agricole got much more exposure in the twenty-first century when mixologists of the cocktail revival began taking it up and mixing with it. Thad Vogler went so far as to name his place, Bar Agricole, after the spirit.

RIBALAIGUA VERT, CONSTANTINO

First a bartender, and later the owner of the El Floridita bar in Havana, Cuba, the bar that would become world-renowned under his stewardship. He was born near Barcelona in 1888; his family, including his bartender father, emigrated to Cuba around 1900. While he did not invent the daiquiri, he mastered the drink, perfecting various versions of the cocktail and rendering it in frozen form via a blender. He also helped to popularize it with both locals and visiting Americans. The cocktail booklet he published in the 1930s contained five different recipes for daiquiris, all varying slightly in ingredients and preparation. "The Daiquiri was born near Santiago at the opposite end of the island from Havana," wrote cocktail expert David A. Embury in 1949. "At the Floridita, however, it has really attained the stature and vigor of full manhood." Constante, as he was known to all, was widely regarded as the dean of Cuban bartenders. A laconic, saturnine man of diminutive stature and immaculate dress who rarely drank himself, he was admired for his innate efficiency, skill with ratios, and ability to create original drinks. He was known to squeeze by hand all of the many limes he used in drinks. His most famous patron was novelist Ernest Hemingway, who fell under the spell of his daiquiris and for whom he invented the Hemingway Daiquiri—which, per the writer's request, has less sugar and more rum. Constante was a great influence on Victor Bergeron, who studied his drinks and techniques and applied them to his own restaurant, Trader Vic's. He died in 1952.

THE RITZ BAR (PARIS)

An enclave where the rich, famous, and powerful have wet their whistles for more than a century. It was strictly a men's bar at first. Located inside the rarefied Ritz hotel, it is small, with just twenty-five seats, and has the aura of a private club. Frank Meier ran the bar for many years, beginning in 1921. F. Scott Fitzgerald was a regular. His famous short story "Babylon Revisited" opens at the Ritz bar. Ernest Hemingway frequently bragged of having "liberated" the bar after the Germans were chased out of Paris in 1944. The bar catered almost exclusively to Americans. A 1928 newspaper account joked, "I don't believe anyone ever spoke French in the Ritz Bar." As to the clientele, a 1937 account related, "As in 1928–29, the bar is packed all day long with New York debutantes, brokers, social-climbing jewelry salesmen from Fifth Avenue, South American gigolos, Newport dowagers, bad women who walk good dogs on Park Avenue,

R

chic divorcees, and college boys on toots." Since 1994, Englishman Colin Peter Field has been head bartender.

ROB ROY

The crown prince of scotch cocktails and, aside from highballs, the main way scotch is used in most cocktail bars. It was one of the many vermouth-informed cocktails that followed in the wake of the immensely popular Manhattan and Martini cocktails of the late nineteenth century. Early recipes were equal parts scotch and vermouth. Sometimes Angostura bitters was called for, other times orange bitters, and often both, before Angostura became the accepted accent. More often than in a Manhattan, you'll see a lemon twist as a garnish instead of the usual cherry. The drink has not the smoothness you'll get with a fine Manhattan, but the slightly rough smokiness makes for its own attraction.

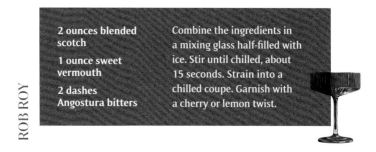

ROB ROY

2 ounces blended scotch

1 ounce sweet vermouth

2 dashes Angostura bitters

Combine the ingredients in a mixing glass half-filled with ice. Stir until chilled, about 15 seconds. Strain into a chilled coupe. Garnish with a cherry or lemon twist.

ROCKS/OLD-FASHIONED GLASS

A short, stout, heavy-bottomed glass commonly used to house its eponymous cocktail, as well as other typically strong-spirited drinks that—as the glass's alternate name indicates—are served on the rocks. Historically, there are slight cosmetic differences between the two types of glassware. A rocks glass may take many forms, as long as it remains short and low to the ground. The traditional old-fashioned glass, meanwhile, was relatively small and tapers slightly at the foot, which is typically dimpled and has a sturdy base anywhere from one-quarter to one-half inch thick. The base was necessary to absorb the punishing muddling of sugar and bitters that was once a needed step in making an Old-Fashioned. References to the old-fashioned glass began to appear in cocktail books at the turn of the twentieth century. Old-fashioned glasses began to be marketed to consumers after Prohibition. Soon after, the larger double old-fashioned glasses, holding between twelve and sixteen ounces, became the norm and stayed so. This may well have happened to hold the muddled fruit and soda water that became part of the typical Old-Fashioned formula after Prohibition.

ROLLING

A bar technique, used primarily for preparing Bloody Marys, in which the liquid ingredients are mixed by languidly pouring them from one mixing tin or glass to another. Though the process is often compared to throwing, it is considerably less theatrical.

ROSITA

A tequila version of the Negroni, of unknown provenance. It was first seen in the 1974 version of the "Mr. Boston Official Bartender's Guide." With the advent of the cocktail renaissance, and its affinity for lost cocktails and bitter ingredients, the Rosita was embraced anew in the 2000s.

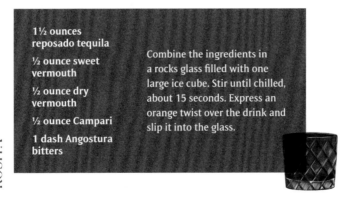

ROSITA

1½ ounces
reposado tequila

½ ounce sweet
vermouth

½ ounce dry
vermouth

½ ounce Campari

1 dash Angostura
bitters

Combine the ingredients in a rocks glass filled with one large ice cube. Stir until chilled, about 15 seconds. Express an orange twist over the drink and slip it into the glass.

R

ROSS, SAM

A prominent Australian bartender of the twenty-first century who, after making his name in his home city of Melbourne, moved to New York, where he eventually became a student of Sasha Petraske and inherited, with Michael McIlroy, the original location of the iconic bar Milk & Honey. Before that, in 2001, Ross, along

SAM ROSS

with his brother Toby and sister Alex, opened Ginger in Melbourne, a cocktail bar that combined serious experimentation with light-hearted, fun-loving tomfoolery. In 2004, seeking greener pastures, he bought a one-way ticket to New York. Impressed with Milk & Honey, he landed a position at Sasha Petraske's sister bar, Little Branch. He also won a job at Pegu Club, thus positioning himself at two of the most important cocktail bars of the era. In time, he established a presence at Milk & Honey alongside McIlroy, who was from Belfast. When Petraske decided to move Milk & Honey uptown to 23rd Street in 2014, he bequeathed the bar's original space on Eldridge Street to Ross and McIlroy. They rechristened it Attaboy, added additional stools, and adopted a more laid-back attitude. The two opened a second Attaboy in Nashville in 2017. Over the years, Ross earned a reputation as a deft drink creator, inventing two of the enduring modern classic cocktails of modern times, the Penicillin and Paper Plane, as well as minor classics like the Left Hand and Cobble Hill.

RUM

A variegated and little-regulated spirit, distilled from molasses, sugar cane, or cane syrup, depending on the country of origin and distiller. It is produced in dozens of countries but is primarily and historically associated with Central America and the Caribbean. As a cocktail spirit, it has shown many faces to the world and is the base of many famous cocktails, a few of them amounting to national drinks. The most famous is the daiquiri, which emerged from Cuba in the early twentieth century and soon conquered the world. The daiquiri mixture of rum, lime juice, and sugar was duplicated in other drinks from other places, but always in a reassembled form. The Ti' Punch of Martinique used the grassy rhum agricole, distilled from sugar cane juice, a spirit native to the French Caribbean isles, and only a small disc of lime. The caipirinha, Brazil's national drink, employs the country's native spirit cachaça, distilled from sugar cane juice. The Dark and Stormy highball of Bermuda calls for Gosling's Black Seal, a dark rum, lime, and ginger beer. The Mojito, also from Cuba, takes the three elements and adds muddled mint to them. The Cuba Libra, another Cuban rum icon, pairs rum with Coca-Cola and a squeeze of lime. The Mai Tai, which calls for two rums, was the most famous drink of the tiki era, which began in the 1930s, lasted half a century, and represented the pinnacle of rum as a cocktail mixer. Consumption of rum in the United States has soared and flagged over the country's history, but never ceased. As Wayne Curtis wrote in his history of rum as a cocktail beverage, "rum is the history of America in a glass"—including the repellent parts of that history, as the spirit was inextricably tied up in the slave trade from the sixteenth to nineteenth centuries. New England developed an early reputation as a producer of rum, distilled from sugar and molasses from the Caribbean. Medford, Massachusetts, in particular, was closely linked with rum production. This led to the drink's popularity among the colonists. Rum was very much in evidence during the early years of American cocktail consumption, forming the basis of many punches, toddies, nogs, fixes, and juleps. (Drinks of this time were made from rum styles that are understood to be extinct today.) Rum received a renewed burst of popularity during Prohibition, courtesy of the "rum runners" smuggling booze into America. It got another boost from the tiki fad, becoming the bedrock of most tropical

R

drinks of the period, mainly because rum was cheap and plentiful at the time. In the 2010s, with the resurgence of tiki bars, rum was treated with a more discerning eye by many bartenders and returned to a more active role behind the bar. These bartenders encouraged rum to be treated with respect and promoted the idea of sipping rum, in the style of whiskeys and brandies. However, rum remains primarily a mixing spirit. Rums come in a wide variety of age expressions and alcohol levels, not to mention the popular and crowded spiced rum subcategory. It can therefore be a fairly dizzying liquor category to sort out for the layman. Or even the booze professional.

RUM COLLINS

A simple twist on a Tom Collins, using rum instead of gin or Old Tom gin, which became one of the most popular cocktails in the United States in the decades following repeal. Very likely, Americans discovered the drink while vacationing their Prohibition thirsts in Havana, where booze was still legal. Many made a beeline straight to Sloppy Joe's, the celebrated drinking joint on the island. Sloppy Joe's produced, throughout the 1930s, a giveaway cocktail booklet that featured the Rum Collins prominently. When Yanks retreated to the States after repeal, rum companies followed them, heavily promoting the Rum Collins in their ads. An easy way to enjoy rum, it was popular until it was eventually supplanted by the Rum and Coke, the daiquiri, and, later on, the Mojito craze of the 1990s. It was memorably featured in the Christmas Eve bar scene in the 1960 film *The Apartment*.

RUM COLLINS

2 ounces dark rum
1 ounce simple syrup
¾ ounce lemon juice
1 ounce soda water

Combine the first three ingredients in a cocktail shaker half-filled with ice and shake until chilled, about 15 seconds. Strain into a collins glass filled with ice. Top with the soda water. Garnish with a cherry and lemon wedge "flag."

RYE WHISKEY

A whiskey as old as the United States, and one of the great beneficiaries of the cocktail renaissance, whose participants rescued this poor, disused, and debased spirit from the dustbin of history and returned it to barroom favor. Rye is distilled from a mash bill made predominantly of rye. During the century that led up to Prohibition, it was, along with bourbon, the go-to whiskey type used in most cocktails, including benchmark classics like the Whiskey Cocktail (which would become the Old-Fashioned), Manhattan, Whiskey Sour, and Sazerac. Often rye and bourbon were interchangeable; in early cocktail books, recipes that called for whiskey often stated "bourbon or rye."

After repeal, rye began a slow decline in production and popularity. The robust rye industry that historically existed in Maryland and Pennsylvania vanished. What few ryes survived, including Jim Beam Rye, Old Overholt, and Wild Turkey Rye, were made in bourbon country for a dwindling audience. The spirit developed a negative reputation as the drink of choice of rummies, such as the protagonist of the movie *The Lost Weekend*. Only the historical leanings of twenty-first century mixologists saved rye from oblivion. Many bartenders believed, rightly or wrongly, that rye—with its drier, spicier flavor profile—was the historically accurate spirit choice for many classic whiskey cocktails. The first forgotten rye brand to be championed was the bonded Rittenhouse rye, made and ignored by Heaven Hill for years. People like bar owner Audrey Saunders, historian David Wondrich, and liquor merchant LeNell Smothers coaxed it back onto the New York market. Bulleit rye, introduced in San Francisco, was one of the first new ryes to make an impact in the aughts. By the 2010s, thirst for rye was so strong among cocktail bartenders and enthusiasts alike that every distiller of bourbon felt compelled to add a rye whiskey to their catalogue. Sales for the category grew every year, as did consumer choices at the liquor store. Multiple modern classic cocktails had a rye base, including the Black Manhattan, Red Hook, Little Italy, and Greenpoint; and forgotten cocktails like the Vieux Carré and De La Louisiane came roaring back because of rye's fashionable status. Some bars advertised their allegiance by naming themselves after the spirit, including Rye in San Francisco, Rye in Brooklyn, Rye in Baltimore, and Rye House in Manhattan.

SAKE

A Japanese alcoholic beverage made from fermented rice and usually drunk neat, which has increasingly found a place in cocktails, particularly at the Japanese-style cocktail bars that became popular in the United States in the 2010s and '20s. Often it joins gin or vodka, or both, in modern Martini variations. (The house Martinis at Long Island Bar, Bar Goto, and Katana Kitten, three famous cocktail bars in New York, all contain sake.) The Saketini, made of sake and vodka, is the best-known sake cocktail, as well as one of the oldest, having emerged in the 1960s.

SANTINI, JOSEPH

A nineteenth-century New Orleans bartender best remembered for creating the Brandy Crusta, a luxurious sour with a thick sugar rim and long, twining "horse's neck" lemon twist, and an ancestor to the more-famous Sidecar. Santini owned a bar called Jewel of the South, which he opened in 1855 and sold in 1869. Some of Santini's and the Brandy Crusta's fame can be attributed to the drink's inclusion in Jerry Thomas's seminal 1862 cocktail manual. In 2019, a new bar called Jewel of the South opened in New Orleans in tribute to Santini.

SAUNDERS, AUDREY

An American bartender and bar owner who ranks as one of the formative influences of the cocktail renaissance in the United States. A protégé of Dale DeGroff, she went on, through her co-ownership of Pegu Club in New York, to foster master bartending protégés of her own, perhaps more than any other American bartender save Sasha Petraske. Born in Port Washington, Long Island, Saunders came to bartending late, as a second career, after attending a seminar held by DeGroff. She asked to be tutored, and DeGroff took her under his wing, taking her along on various unpaid bartending gigs. She cut her teeth at the bars Beacon and Tonic, developing her drink-making skills and a culinary approach to cocktails that were often collaborations with the kitchen. DeGroff continued to help her. When he opened the short-lived Blackbird in 1999, he brought Saunders along, and when the stately old Bemelmans Bar in the Carlyle hotel, where DeGroff was consulting, asked for a successor, he recommended Saunders. It was there, in the early aughts, that Saunders's star began to rise and she became a cocktail

AUDREY SAUNDERS

authority much quoted in the press. She invented modern classics like the Old Cuban and became exposed to the London cocktail scene via Carlyle collaborations with the Ritz.

When Julie Reiner and her partners decided to open a follow-up to their successful Flatiron Lounge, they enlisted Saunders, who agreed, as long as she could steer the ship. Pegu Club, which opened on Houston Street in 2005, was the apotheosis of her vision of bartending and cocktail creation. Rarely behind the bar, she instead shaped a bar staff in her exacting image. While many of the opening staff were already seasoned cocktail bartenders, they left Saunders's employ with their reputations and skills further burnished, and most opened their own bars. The cocktail list, meanwhile, was almost entirely Saunders's creation, focused on forgotten classics (the Pegu Club, Jimmy Roosevelt) and her own inventions (Tantris Sidecar, Earl Grey MarTEAni, Little Italy, French Pearl, and others). She was notorious for trying out dozens of variations of every cocktail before settling upon one that was suitable to stand as the Pegu Club house recipe. Saunders played a role in the popularization of unsung ingredients, such as apple brandy, rye, Suze, true maraschino cherries, and, particularly, gin, which amounted to her spiritual mission. Saunders's focus over the years continued to be Pegu Club, even after she moved to the Pacific Northwest following her marriage to cocktail expert Robert Hess. Unlike her colleagues, she did not publish a book. Still, she remains a singular influence in the cocktail community.

SAZERAC

One of the preeminent cocktails of all time, despite spending a long stretch of its existence as the pet drink of New Orleans. It is a simple drink, though one requiring an ornate build, and is the last major cocktail in circulation to be often constructed in the nineteenth-century manner of using two glasses. While one old-fashioned glass is chilled with ice, in a second glass, sugar is muddled with water and Peychaud's bitters. Rye is then added and the mixture is stirred over ice until chilled. The first glass is then emptied of ice and given a rinse of absinthe or Herbsaint. Into this glass the liquid contents of the second glass are strained. To finish, a lemon twist is expressed over the surface of the drink and discarded. The dark-brownish-red liquid that remains is the simplest looking beverage imaginable, but one whose flavor contains many layers and great depths.

Though in popular legend it's often mistakenly credited as one of the first cocktails, the Sazerac didn't actually make its debut on the bar stage until very late in the nineteenth century. Recent scholarship by historian David Wondrich revealed that the drink wasn't mentioned in print until 1899. It was associated with a famous New Orleans bar called Sazerac House, which had a special way with their standard Whiskey Cocktail, in that it contained Peychaud's and a dash of absinthe. Wondrich lays credit for the popularizing of the Sazerac's Whiskey Cocktail, later just the Sazerac Cocktail, at the feet of the bar's co-owners, Vincent Miret and Billy Wilkinson, who operated the bar in the years on either side of the turn of the twentieth century. At the dawn of the cocktail renaissance, it was popularly believed that the Sazerac began as a cognac cocktail, named after the Sazerac de Forge et Fils brand of cognac, and that it evolved over time into a rye cocktail. This myth was partly drawn from the 1937 book *Famous New Orleans Drinks and How to Mix 'Em* by Stanley Clisby Arthur. Because of this misunderstanding, many earnest mixologists made their Sazeracs with brandy to display their purity of purpose. (The New Orleans–based Sazerac Company, which knows better, still preaches this fable to sell its cognac brand.) The truth is, the Sazerac has always been made with rye whiskey, and the cocktail was named after a bar, not a brand of cognac.

For the first few decades of its career (interrupted by Prohibition, of course), the Sazerac was a drink of national reputation that could be drunk anywhere. However, during the late twentieth century it slowly but surely became a regional cocktail, enjoyed mainly in New Orleans, probably since a couple of its ingredients—Peychaud's bitters and Herbsaint—could be found only there. That said, within New Orleans it was enjoyed nearly everywhere. When the cocktail convention Tales of the Cocktail began in 2002, bartenders from the rest of the country, and the world, discovered or rediscovered the Sazerac and brought the drink back to their hometowns (also with a smuggled supply of the Peychaud's needed to make it). By 2007, the Sazerac commanded a national stage once again, helped along by the more widely available Peychaud's, the return of absinthe to legality, and the rebirth of the rye whiskey category. In that way, the Sazerac stands as a virtual poster child of the cocktail revival, because none of those ingredients would have been resurrected without the help of cocktail bartenders. In 2008 it was christened the official cocktail of New Orleans.

2 ounces rye

1 barspoon
simple syrup

4 or 5 dashes
Peychaud's bitters

Absinthe

Fill one rocks glass with ice.
While it is chilling, combine
the rye, simple syrup, and
bitters in a mixing glass half-
filled with ice and stir until
chilled, about 15 seconds.
Empty the first glass of its ice
and rinse the inside of the glass
with a barspoon of absinthe.
Pour out the excess absinthe.
Strain the rye mixture into
the waiting glass. Express a
lemon twist over the drink
and discard.

SCAFFA

A category of drink that is served at room temperature. The genre stretches
back to the nineteenth century—examples are found in Jerry Thomas's 1862 bar
manual—but has never proven particularly popular in any era.

SCHMIDT, WILLIAM

A German-American bartender in New York who became one of the most celebrated drink compounders in the United States in the latter nineteenth century
and authored the ornamental and philosophical cocktail treatise *The Flowing
Bowl.* The man who eventually became known by the poetic nickname of "The
Only William" began working behind the bar at an early age and practiced his
trade in Chicago before becoming an institution in lower Manhattan at such bars
as the Brooklyn Bridge House and Times Café. He had a close relationship with
the press, which wrote up his musings on drink making. Schmidt returned the
favor by naming drinks after the *New York Herald, The World, The Sun,* and *The
Evening Sun,* as well as creating cocktails called The Press and The Correspondent.
By 1888, one paper reported, "William Schmidt, the bartender near the Brooklyn
bridge, has a greater reputation for making mixed drinks than any other bartender in New York. His liquid combinations have an airiness, a beauty, a degree

S

WILLIAM SCHMIDT

of ornament and a quality of deliciousness that make him easily the king of drinkmakers." By the time of his untimely death in 1905 at the age of fifty-six, he had graduated to the status of "leading mixer of drinks in the country." He was known for a meticulousness of technique, grace of motion, and thoughtfulness of service. As to his line of work, he never thought of himself as a bartender, but rather as a professional and an artist. A bartender must be a "man of original ideas," he wrote in his book. "A Bartender ought to be leading and not led." His drink recipes were highly detailed and possessed the ornate quality of his time. He was particularly renowned for his gin fizz. He died of dementia in a hospital on Ward's Island. In response, one paper wrote a poem about him.

SCHUMANN, CHARLES

A figure as influential in Germany as Dick Bradsell was in England, Schumann was born in 1941. A multilingual boxer, author, bartender, and, later, model for Hugo Boss, he gained a following as a bartender at Harry's New York Bar in Munich. In 1982, he opened Schumann's American Bar, which became one of the most significant cocktail bars in Europe, influencing more than one generation of continental bars and bartenders. At a time when hotel bars were the norm in Germany, the free-standing Schumann's was a novelty. Schumann took training seriously. Employees, who wore crisp white uniforms, began with washing glasses and slowly moved up the chain of command until they were ready to mix drinks for guests. The bar's impact could be seen in establishments as far flung as Pravda and Employees Only in New York and Der Raum in Melbourne. Beginning with *American Bar,* first published in 1991 and, in the United States, 1995, he furthered his influence, putting out cocktail books when few bartenders were. Later in his career, his antiquated views of who should and shouldn't work in a bar—expressed in multiple interviews—earned him accusations of sexism. When the World's 50 Best Bars organization gave him the Industry Icon Award in 2019, an international backlash, kicked off by New York bar owner Julie Reiner—with whom Schumann has sparred in the documentary *Schumann's Bar Talks*—led Schumann to return the prize.

SCOTCH WHISKY

One of the great spirits in human history, but a bit of an also-ran in terms of cocktails. As cocktails were an American invention, bourbon and rye were favored by mixologists. The Whiskey Cocktail (progenitor of the Old-Fashioned) and the Manhattan were made with American whiskey. Scotch began to gain a foothold in the late nineteenth century, with the Rob Roy following the Manhattan as a classic in its own right. The Morning Glory Fizz from the 1880s was another rare early scotch cocktail that succeeded. The scotch and soda became a sensation in the late nineteenth century, and thereafter scotch remained a favorite in simple highballs that pair the strong-flavored spirit with one other copacetic ingredient, be it club soda or ginger ale. When scotch was mixed in cocktails, it was almost always of the milder, lighter blended variety. Some blended-scotch cocktails that had an impact in the twentieth century include the Bobby Burns, Blood and Sand, and Cameron's Kick. Frank Sinatra's Rat Pack helped popularize the Rusty Nail (scotch and Drambuie) in the 1960s. As single-malt scotch was a rare item in the United States until the late twentieth century, it was rarely used in mixed drinks. Indeed, even after it became popular in the States, it stayed out of cocktails, its character too strong to mix well with other ingredients. A notable exception is Sam Ross's Penicillin, which used both blended scotch as a base and a float of smoky Islay scotch. Owen Westman also made good use of Islay scotch in his Laphroaig Project. To a certain extent, the righteous attitude of scotch drinkers has held the spirit back in cocktail bars, as devotees consider any mixing of their choice elixir to be sacrilege.

SEELBACH COCKTAIL

One of the greatest ruses in cocktail history. This faux pre-Prohibition cocktail was cooked up in 1996 by bartender Adam Seger to gin up publicity for the bar at the historic Seelbach Hotel in Louisville, where he was bar director at the time. Seger sold the drink as a lost house classic. The media ran with the story. Soon, the recipe—bourbon, triple sec, Angostura and Peychaud's bitters, served in a flute and topped with sparkling wine—was appearing in books and being served from London to Berlin as a revived pre-Prohibition cocktail. Only in 2016 did Seger come clean and reveal his deception. The Seelbach hotel still has the drink on its menu, but with an asterisk.

SEELBACH COCKTAIL

1 ounce bourbon

½ ounce triple sec

7 dashes Angostura bitters

7 dashes Peychaud's bitters

5 ounces sparkling white wine

Combine all the ingredients except the sparkling wine in a mixing glass half-filled with ice and stir until chilled, about 15 seconds. Strain into a flute. Top with the sparkling wine. Express an orange twist over the drink and drop it into the glass.

SHAKEN COCKTAILS

A wide genre of cocktails that are prepared by shaking them with ice in a cocktail shaker. Shaken cocktails include sours made with juice and any drinks made with dairy products or eggs. The rationale behind shaking is that drinks that contain juice, dairy, and eggs require a vigorous jostling to sufficiently integrate with spirits. However, for most of the mid- and late twentieth century, shaking was used by most bartenders to mix up all cocktails, regardless of their components. Some believe shaking results in a colder drink. It does not, but it may make a drink colder faster. Veteran bartenders often switch to shaking when a bar gets busy as it can shave seconds off the preparation of a cocktail. Some drinkers like the flow of ice shards on a drink's surface that only shaking can deliver.

SHERRY

A Spanish fortified wine with a long history, if not exactly a preeminent place, in cocktails. Sherry's single greatest hit, cocktail-wise, is the Sherry Cobbler, which reigned supreme for most of the nineteenth century. It remains not only the most famous drink to use sherry as a base but the most famous member of the cobbler family. Other lasting sherry cocktails include the Bamboo and the Adonis, which can be regarded as a sherry Martini and sherry Manhattan. By the late twentieth century, sherry had fallen out of favor and was widely regarded as something sweet that your grandmother drank, rather than a dry wine of infinite subtle variations. In the twenty-first century, sherry received renewed attention from bartenders, who worked it into many of their new creations, particularly, in the 2020s, in Martini variations as a substitute for or complement to vermouth. Despite its many champions, however, sherry is still a specialized taste, and drinks like the Bamboo and Sherry Cobbler remain the choice of the epicure.

SHOOTER

A compact cocktail in the form of a shot, particularly popular from the 1970s through 1990s. It is typically consumed in one go. Shooters are not known for their subtlety, in either composition, appearance, or name. They are favored by youth, taken in the spirit of fun and in the interest of immediate impact. Prominent examples include the B-52 (coffee liqueur, Bailey's Irish Cream, Grand Marnier), Kamikaze (vodka, triple sec, lime juice), Alabama Slammer (amaretto, orange

S

juice, sloe gin, Southern Comfort), Flaming Dr. Pepper (amaretto, rum, beer), and Redheaded Slut (Jägermeister, cranberry juice, peach schnapps). Modern examples that hail from the cocktail-revival era include the Pickleback (whiskey and pickle brine), Hard Start (Fernet-Branca and Branca Menta), and CIA (Cynar and applejack).

SIDECAR

A Jazz Age drink of European pedigree, and cognac's main stake in the classic cocktail sweepstakes. The Sidecar, made of brandy, lemon juice, and Cointreau, has retained name recognition for a century while never quite achieving top-tier ranking among cocktails. Harry's New York Bar in Paris is the top contender for having invented the drink, though the jury is out on that. It did appear in owner Harry MacElhone's 1922 book *Harry's ABC of Mixing Cocktails* and his 1927 book *Barflies and Cocktails*—the recipe asking for one part each of brandy, lemon juice, and Cointreau. That equal-parts formula has given way to more brandy-forward versions over the years. As early as Harry Craddock's *Savoy Cocktail Book,* more brandy was called for. And whether the drink should or should not have a sugar rim remains in dispute. Early accounts of the drink attributed it to one "MacGarry, the celebrated bartender of Buck's Club" in London.

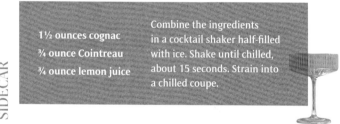

SIDECAR

1½ ounces cognac
¾ ounce Cointreau
¾ ounce lemon juice

Combine the ingredients in a cocktail shaker half-filled with ice. Shake until chilled, about 15 seconds. Strain into a chilled coupe.

SIESTA

A spin on the Hemingway Daiquiri that replaces the gin and maraschino liqueur with tequila and Campari. The drink was created by bartender Katie Stipe at Flatiron Lounge in New York in 2006. It was an early example of a modern tequila cocktail and has since been served the world over. It has also inspired its share of variations, including a Siesta Swizzle, served at the Raines Law Room, and a frozen Siesta at El Quijote, both in Manhattan.

1½ ounces tequila
¾ ounce lime juice
¾ ounce simple syrup
½ ounce grapefruit juice
¼ ounce Campari

Combine all the ingredients in a cocktail shaker half-filled with ice. Shake until chilled, about 15 seconds. Strain into a chilled coupe. Garnish with a lime wheel.

SINGAPORE SLING

A tropical gin concoction with an ingredient list and origin story as confused and confusing as any in cocktail history. Perhaps only the Zombie equals it in its history of recipe variation and bastardization. The undying story is that it was invented in 1915 by a bartender named Ngiam Tong Boon at the Long Bar inside the Raffles Hotel in Singapore, for decades a stopping place and watering hole for actors, writers, diplomats, jet-setters, and tourists—though there is plenty of reason to doubt Raffles' story. In its early years it was sometimes called a Singapore Gin Sling, and it's named a Straits Sling by Robert Vermeire in his 1922 book *Cocktails—How to Mix Them,* in which he writes that it's a "well-known Singapore drink." By the 1930s, the drink was being served stateside, the romantic alliteration and assonance of its lilting name doubtless working in its favor. An indication as to how often it was made poorly is the number of ads and articles that attested to certain bars making it "correctly." The arrival in the 1930s of Singapore Sling "mix" certainly didn't help matters. Trader Vic threw up his hands, offering two very different versions in his 1972 guide. Because of its uncertain formula—who knows if you're ever drinking it as intended?—the Singapore Sling holds little currency in today's cocktail market. Most recipes call for gin, Cherry Heering, Bénédictine, lime juice, Angostura bitters, and sometimes pineapple juice, grenadine, and Cointreau. The Cherry Heering gives the drink its iconic pink hue.

S

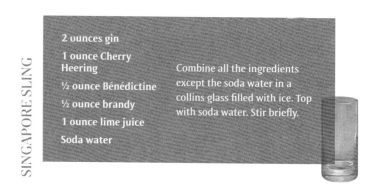

2 ounces gin

1 ounce Cherry Heering

½ ounce Bénédictine

½ ounce brandy

1 ounce lime juice

Soda water

Combine all the ingredients except the soda water in a collins glass filled with ice. Top with soda water. Stir briefly.

SINGLE VILLAGE FIX

A simple sour made of mezcal, lime juice, and pineapple gum syrup created in 2008 by bartender Thad Volger, an early advocate of mezcal in San Francisco, and first featured on the menu at Beretta. The drink was an entry in the mezcal cocktail category that began to emerge in the late aughts.

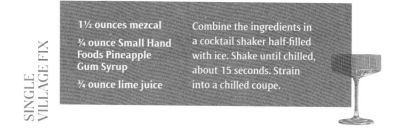

1½ ounces mezcal

¾ ounce Small Hand Foods Pineapple Gum Syrup

¾ ounce lime juice

Combine the ingredients in a cocktail shaker half-filled with ice. Shake until chilled, about 15 seconds. Strain into a chilled coupe.

SLOPPY JOE'S BAR

A bar in Havana that became the preferred destination of thousands of thirsty Americans fleeing the scourge of the Volstead Act. It was owned and run by Jose Abeal y Otero, a native of Galicia, who opened a bodega and bar in 1917 as La Victoria. When regulars began calling it Sloppy Joe's—stories as to how the name came about vary—Abeal adopted it. The easily remembered, likable name worked like a charm. Once Prohibition set in, the corner bar, with its dramatic two-story arches on two sides, open-air entrance, and long mahogany bar, became the favorite watering hole of countless Yankees just off the cruise ships. Soon celebrities became regulars as well, and the media-savvy

SLOPPY JOE'S BAR

Abeal dutifully named drinks after them. Abeal made it easy for everyone to come, staying open twenty-four hours a day and offering a free welcome drink to all comers. Joe's had its own brands of cigars and rum and put out a free-of-charge cocktail recipe booklet. The bar was a tourist trap par excellence, avoided by most Cubans. In 1930, Abeal cashed out, selling his share of the bar to his three brothers-in-law, and returned to Galicia. The bar continued on. Its last Hollywood hurrah was being featured in the 1959 movie *Our Man in Havana,* starring Alec Guinness. Following the Cuban revolution that same year, American trade stopped, and the bar soon closed for good. It stood intact for decades, a ghost bar. In 2013, after a long renovation, it finally reopened under new management, but as a shell of itself and devoid of its former charm and popularity. The Havana Sloppy Joe's is unconnected to a bar of the same name in Key West, which gained its own sort of fame post-Prohibition as a haunt of Ernest Hemingway. That bar also still exists, but again in a form and spirit—as well as address—unlike its original incarnation.

SMITH, TODD

A San Francisco bartender who took what he learned at Enrico's and Cortez and amplified it 500 percent with Bourbon & Branch, an elaborate reservation-only speakeasy he opened with three partners inside a formerly notorious dive bar and onetime actual speakeasy in the Tenderloin district. The opening menu, of Smith's design, was sixty-seven drinks long. In 2014 he, Ryan Fitzgerald, and Erik Reichborn opened the considerably more low-key ABV in the Mission District. Smith is the creator of the Black Manhattan cocktail.

SMUGGLER'S COVE

A tiki bar opened in San Francisco in 2009 by Martin Cate, a student of the writings of tiki historian Jeff "Beachbum" Berry. Smuggler's Cove was Cate's follow-up to Forbidden Island, a pioneering tiki bar he ran in Alameda from 2006 to 2009. Unabashedly ambitious, with a three-tier design of maritime bric-a-brac, an enormous selection of rums, and exacting versions of classic tiki drinks, the bar was a smash success of national renown from the start. The bar's reputation was further cemented with the publication of a *Smuggler's Cove* book in 2016, which won a James Beard Award.

SNAQUIRI

A pre-daiquiri daiquiri, taken as a snack, or a shot, or just plain taken. Credit for its creation goes to bartender Karin Stanley while at Dutch Kills in Brooklyn. In the late 2010s, miniature cocktails, especially Martinis, became a minor craze. (My own contribution to this was the Snackerac, a mini Sazerac, hatched at the Seattle bar Roquette in October 2022.)

SNIT

A short glass of beer that reflexively accompanies a Bloody Mary in bars in the upper Midwest. Also, the state into which a Midwesterner will get if they don't receive one.

SOUR

An expansive category of mixed drinks that includes some of the most famous and popular cocktails of all time, including the daiquiri, Margarita, Whiskey Sour, and Cosmopolitan. The prevailing ratios of many given sours are two parts spirit, one part citrus, and one part sweetener, though measurements vary depending on the desired strength, sweetness, or tartness of the drink. The Brandy Crusta from mid-nineteenth-century New Orleans is generally thought to be the antecedent of most sours to follow, particularly the Sidecar.

SOUR MIX

A commercially produced, artificial mixer used by bars in the mid- and late twentieth century, and the primary reason classic drinks like the daiquiri, Margarita, and Whiskey Sour developed a bad reputation. Sour mix was meant to mimic the flavor and function of lemon and/or lime juice but never really came close. The mix was so ubiquitous by the latter twentieth century that it commanded a button on the soda gun in many bars. With the arrival of the cocktail revival in the aughts, quality cocktail bars retired sour mix and returned to freshly squeezed citrus.

SPRITZ

A light-bodied cocktail closely associated with Italy and typically composed of a bitter liqueur such as Campari or Aperol, sparkling wine, and soda water. With the renewed focus on low-ABV cocktails in the 2010s, this genre of drink got a new lease on life in the United States.

S

SPROUSE, CLAIRE

A bartender and bar owner who arguably made her biggest impact in the cocktail community with her championing of social issues that affect and plague the bar industry. A native of Texas, she earned her stripes as a bartender in San Francisco, then founded her first cocktail bar in Brooklyn, Hunky Dory. It opened in Crown Heights in 2019 as one of the nascent models of sustainable mixology, an issue she had previously advanced as part of the Tin Roof Community initiative with Chad Arnholt. As Covid descended upon New York, she shifted some of her efforts to gaining the hospitality industry a louder voice in government and ridding the workplace of its various ingrained inequities. Hunky Dory closed in 2021.

STAR

A Manhattan made with apple brandy instead of whiskey, emerging in the 1890s. The drink was rediscovered during the cocktail revival of the twenty-first century. It is often built using equal parts apple brandy and sweet vermouth. The Marconi Wireless cocktail, which came later, is similar, but made with more brandy and less vermouth.

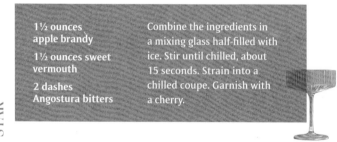

1 ½ ounces apple brandy

1 ½ ounces sweet vermouth

2 dashes Angostura bitters

Combine the ingredients in a mixing glass half-filled with ice. Stir until chilled, about 15 seconds. Strain into a chilled coupe. Garnish with a cherry.

STAR

STAR, EZRA

Former general manager of chef Barbara Lynch's cocktail bar Drink, where she became a prominent figure in the Boston cocktail landscape. Star left her studies in biochemistry in 2010 to join the Drink staff. She left Drink in 2020 for Hong Kong, where she opened a bar called Mostly Harmless.

STARTENDER

A cocktail bartender of the modern mixology era whose fame, brought on by regular media coverage (something old-time bartenders rarely enjoyed), reaches beyond their hometown and origin bar. The lords and ladies of the pop-up bar and the guest shift.

STENSON, MURRAY

A Seattle-based lifer bartender who, late in life, became an elder statesman and mentor figure of the cocktail movement. He established himself in Seattle during a long tenure at Il Bistro but earned a rep as a classic-cocktail master at the Zig Zag Café. Stenson's most lasting achievement was a revival of the Last Word, a pre-Prohibition-era cocktail made of gin, maraschino liqueur, green Chartreuse, and lime juice that he discovered in the 1951 cocktail book *Bottoms Up*. He began serving the drink at the Zig Zag. By the mid-aughts, the Last Word was being served in New York. The drink was an early example of the kind of cross-country, cocktail-info pollination that would become common in the aughts.

STIRRED COCKTAILS

A category of cocktails that is prepared by stirring them with a barspoon in a mixing glass filled with ice. This technique is reserved for drinks that contain solely alcoholic ingredients, such as a Martini or Manhattan. Beyond that, the reasons for preferring stirring over shaking are purely aesthetic, as stirring results in a pristine, clear drink free of the cloudiness and ice shards that shaking imparts.

STONE FENCE

A simple and age-old American mixed drink composed of whiskey and apple cider. The drink appeared in Jerry Thomas's *Bar-Tender's Guide* in 1862 as two ounces of bourbon topped with apple cider and served over ice. Sometimes applejack was used instead of whiskey, and sugar and lemon were occasionally added. In light of its ingredients, it was an intrinsically American quaff and

S

likely of rustic appeal where such things as whiskey, applejack, and cider were in ready supply. A Stone Wall was made with soda water instead of cider, though frequently the recipes for the Fence and Wall became switched around. After repeal, scotch was called for more often, causing the drink to veer into scotch-and-water territory. The drink, being the simplest of highballs, is not one of the bygone beverages that bartenders made a concerted effort to revive during the cocktail renaissance.

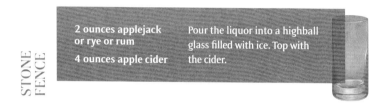

STONE FENCE

2 ounces applejack or rye or rum

4 ounces apple cider

Pour the liquor into a highball glass filled with ice. Top with the cider.

SUFFERING BASTARD

A refreshing highball invented in 1940 by Joe Scialom, a once-famous, now-obscure bartender, while he worked at the Long Bar inside the celebrated Shepheard's Hotel in Cairo. The original highball featured gin, brandy, Angostura bitters, Rose's lime juice cordial, and ginger beer and was devised as a sort of hangover cure for locally stationed Allied troops. Foreign correspondents who frequented the bar helped make the drink famous. It was soon the hotel's signature drink and world renowned. Scialom later riffed on his own invention at the Marco Polo Club in Manhattan, creating the Dying Bastard and Dead Bastard. In both cases, he simply added more and different spirits to the existing drink.

1 ounce gin

1 ounce brandy

½ ounce Rose's lime juice cordial

2 dashes Angostura bitters

4 ounces ginger beer

Combine all the ingredients except the ginger beer in a cocktail shaker half-filled with ice. Shake until chilled, about 15 seconds. Strain into a highball filled with ice. Top with the ginger beer. Garnish with an orange slice and mint sprig.

SWIZZLE

A crushed-ice-laden and slightly mysterious cocktail category. The genre was born in the West Indies, probably in the nineteenth century, and has enjoyed spurts of popularity in various parts of the world from time to time, and was resurrected during the cocktail revival of the twenty-first century. Noteworthy examples include the Queen's Park Swizzle, the Bermuda Swizzle (still wildly popular on that island), and the Barbados Red Rum Swizzle, a onetime staple at Trader Vic's. Most but not all Swizzles are made with rum. These drinks are not shaken or stirred, but rather swizzled with a genuine swizzle stick. The implement in question is an actual stick, snapped off a tree native to the Caribbean. Botanists call it *Quararibea turbinata,* but it is known to locals as the swizzlestick tree. The sticks are about six inches long, with small prongs sticking out at the end, like the spokes of a wheel without the rim, and they are used as a kind of natural, manually operated Mixmaster. Preparing a swizzle takes a little showmanship, which is a large part of the cocktail's appeal. One inserts the swizzle stick in the drink, and with both hands moving in coordination, simultaneously backward and forward, rotates the shaft of the swizzle stick between the palms as quickly as one can.

S

SWIZZLE STICK

SWIZZLE STICK

A name attached to two bar tools, one useful and rare, another pointless and ubiquitous. The first, original swizzle stick was made from a branch of the swizzle-stick tree, which is native to the Caribbean, and is used to mix up Swizzles, the variety of crushed-ice cocktails that take their name from the device. But the original swizzle stick is little known to the greater public. The swizzle stick they know is a long, thin, colorful doohickey—sometimes glass or wood, but usually plastic—that bars and resorts stick into their drinks as a combination advertisement and souvenir. It is little different from a book of matches in that regard. This sort of swizzle stick took hold in the years after Prohibition. Its invention is sometimes credited to Jay Sindler, a Boston man who created the gizmo as a way of fetching out an olive or cherry at the bottom of a cocktail. The company he formed, Spir-It, still exists today as Spirit Foodservice. Though these swizzle sticks can technically be used to prepare a drink, they never are.

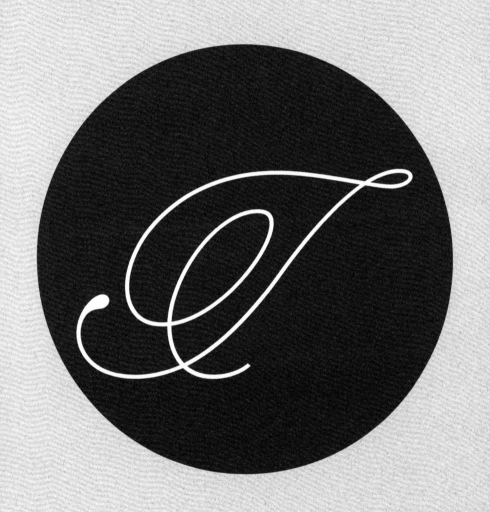

TAILOR

A short-lived Sam Mason restaurant in New York's SoHo neighborhood, whose basement bar, run by Eben Freeman from 2007 to 2009, briefly became a hive of molecular-mixology invention and a bartenders' hangout. Many trendy cocktail techniques that consumed the cocktail world in the 2010s, including smoked cocktails, can be traced back to Tailor. It has been called "the most influential failed bar" in the history of the craft cocktail movement in New York.

TEAGUE, SOTHER

The Florida-born Teague began his career in service as a chef, working as a research and technical chef for television personality Alton Brown. He was on the opening bartending team of Dave Arnold's trailblazing molecular-mixology lab, Booker and Dax. But Teague's legacy lies with Amor y Amargo, a miniscule "bitters tasting room" in New York's East Village. What was intended in 2011

SOTHER TEAGUE

to be a temporary pop-up ended up becoming one of the most successful and lasting bars in entrepreneur Ravi DeRossi's East Village bar empire. Part barware and bitters shop, part cocktail bar (albeit with only a half-dozen seats), Amor y Amargo served drinks that featured bitters, either the dashing kind or the Italian aperitivo and digestivo variety. All drinks were stirred, and citrus was never used. As the leader of this small storefront revolution, Teague has probably educated more people on the subject of bitters than any other bartender in the world. A jovial and loquacious barman of the old style, Teague cut an eccentric and unforgettable figure, with his red-rimmed glasses and winter postal cap. In 2021, Amor y Amargo expanded, opening a dedicated shop. Teague has headed the cocktail programs at several other New York bars but remains most closely associated with Amor. In 2018, he published the book *I'm Just Here for the Drinks.*

TENDER BAR

The Toyko perch, since 1997, of Kazuo Uyeda, one of the most renowned of Japanese cocktail bartenders.

TEQUILA

The most famous of spirits distilled from the agave plant, as well as the most famous spirit to come out of Mexico, where it is one of the country's most successful and high-profile exports. Though it is but one spirit made from agave—and a rather rigid, limited one at that, as it must be made from the blue agave plant, and in only a handful of sanctioned regions of Mexico—it is the one the world first embraced and, even in the current age of mezcal adoration, is still the most famed.

Its global renown is an achievement of only the last century. Tequila consumption outside of Mexico, and particularly its use in cocktails, did not occur until after the repeal of Prohibition. Americans, of course, were more than willing to cross any border or sea during Prohibition, if booze was on the other side, and beyond the Mexico border they found tequila. Its reputation among timid Americans as a spirit with a kick and disagreeable temperament began early. "The only liquor I have ever tasted that I regard as worse than tequila is slivovitz," wrote the otherwise sage David A. Embury in 1946. Since Americans are inclined to put anything in cocktails, tequila eventually found its way into mixing tins. Word of the Tequila Daisy began to appear in the 1930s. This was like a Margarita, but with grenadine, not curaçao. Other drinks pushed by tequila importers in the 1950s include the Tequila Sour,

Tequila and Tonic, Matador, El Diablo, Rosita, and, eventually, the Margarita, the one tequila drink to slay them all and the cocktail that delivered the spirit to the masses. The Margarita eventually became one of the most popular cocktails in the world.

Tequila sales skyrocketed in the 1970s. During that decade, the Tequila Sunrise had a brief heyday. In Mexico, tequila was more commonly drunk either neat or in the form of a Paloma, a brisk highball that didn't become common elsewhere until the 2010s. Tequila's rep as a spirit fit only for shots, however, did not begin to turn until the 1990s, when Julio Bermejo, a restaurant owner in San Francisco, began to preach about the inherent greatness of quality 100 percent agave tequila and began to serve many brands at his restaurant, some in the form of his own Tommy's Margarita (no curaçao, but with the inclusion of agave syrup and fresh lime juice). Tomas Estes performed a similar role in the UK. By the late aughts, bars and bartenders began to take tequila more seriously as both a sipping and mixing spirit, and dedicated agave bars began to open. More tequila cocktails were invented in the aughts and 2010s than at any time in history. Furthermore, the world market became flooded with dozens of new tequila brands, some of them good, but most just opportunistic. Celebrity-backed tequilas took over in the 2010s after actor George Clooney's Casamigos brand launched in 2013. The mezcal mania that followed stole a good deal of tequila's thunder, but the spirit's fortunes remained robust. It was soon nipping at the heels of vodka as the United States' most popular spirit, a circumstance that would have been unimaginable a generation previous.

TEQUILA DAISY

An early tequila cocktail that called for tequila, lime juice, and grenadine. It is closely related to the Margarita, which would eventually eclipse it in popularity, and the two were often confused in the first half of the twentieth century.

TEQUILA SUNRISE

An early example of a cocktail using tequila as a base, invented in the 1920s at the Agua Caliente, a racetrack and resort in Tijuana that was popular with Americans during Prohibition. Early recipes called for tequila, orange juice, grenadine, and crème de cassis. It started making appearances in the U.S. in the '30s but didn't really catch on until the '70s, when a cassis-free version was embraced as the Rolling Stones' cocktail of choice during their 1972 U.S. tour. The next year, the Eagles had a hit with "Tequila Sunrise." Rock and roll has been very good to this drink.

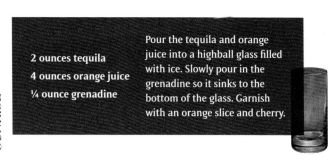

2 ounces tequila
4 ounces orange juice
¼ ounce grenadine

Pour the tequila and orange juice into a highball glass filled with ice. Slowly pour in the grenadine so it sinks to the bottom of the glass. Garnish with an orange slice and cherry.

THOMAS, JEREMIAH P.

The father of American mixology, who earned that title by publishing in 1862 *The Bar-Tender's Guide,* the first cocktail book to codify the cocktail bartender's art in black and white for all to see and potentially practice. Jerry Thomas is the figure we picture today when we think of the star nineteenth-century bartender—theatrical, well-dressed, bejeweled, mustachioed, and well-paid; the star attraction of any bar, performing feats of liquid magic using silver-plated barware. He was quite famous during his day and commanded long obituaries when he passed in 1885.

Thomas was born in 1830 in tiny Sackets Harbor on the shore of Lake Ontario in upstate New York. His days there would be the last time his life was small-time. He first learned the bartending art in New Haven as a teenager. An adventurer and world traveler from an early age, he worked as a sailor and participated in the California Gold Rush. Peripatetic and restless, he commanded bars in New York, San Francisco, Nevada, St. Louis, Chicago, Charleston, and many other cities. His final successful bar, and his most famous, opened in 1866 on Broadway between 21st and 22nd Streets in Manhattan. The walls were covered with his collection of Thomas Nast illustrations. He was bankrupt in his later years, possibly due to bad investments.

The drink he was most famous for was the Blue Blazer, in which he tossed flaming whiskey from one vessel to the other; indeed, the best-known illustration of him shows Thomas in the midst of creating this drink. He claimed in later interviews to have invented the Tom and Jerry—a boast easily believed by many, given the drink's name—but the punch was created well before he was born. He did, however, create the Japanese cocktail, which is still made today. Although his book was reprinted a couple of times, by the mid-twentieth century his reputation and accomplishments had been thoroughly erased from public memory.

JEREMIAH P. THOMAS

Thomas played a critical role in the beginnings of the American cocktail revival. Restaurateur Joe Baum instructed his Rainbow Room bartender Dale DeGroff to dig up a copy of Thomas's book and use it as his guide for putting together the cocktail menu. But Thomas was not fully restored to his rightful place as a colossus of the mixing art until the 2007 publication of *Imbibe!,* a thorough history of Thomas's career, as well as early American mixology in general, by David Wondrich. An enlarged edition was brought out in 2015. Following the resurrection of Thomas's story, there was increased interest in other pre-Prohibition bartender-authors. The Jerry Thomas Speakeasy, the most famous cocktail bar in Rome, is named after him. The Bitter Truth company produces a Jerry Thomas Bitters. Thomas is buried in Woodlawn Cemetery in the Bronx, where his grave, long overlooked, is now a tourist attraction featured on cemetery maps.

THRASHER, TODD

A northern Virginia–based bartender who gave the Washington, DC, area its first craft cocktail bar when he opened the speakeasy-style PX in a second-floor space in Alexandria, Virginia. Born in Alexandria, Thrasher began working in restaurants after dropping out of college in 1991, eventually making Pisco Sours and Caipirinhas at chef José Andrés's Café Atlantico. In 1999 his work was written up in *Food Arts*. Three years later, he helped open Restaurant Eve. PX (which stands for Person Extraordinaire) came in 2005, a Milk & Honey–like bar created by a man who had never seen Milk & Honey. A single blue light indicated the entrance. Thrasher made homemade tonic, Bloody Marys with tomato water, and house-pickled cocktail onions, and used other experimental DIY bar techniques, all ahead of their time. In 2018 he turned distiller, selling Thrasher's Rum at the Potomac Distilling Company in D.C. In 2019 he closed PX.

THROWING

A technique for mixing cocktails in which the ingredients are tossed at a great height from one vessel filled with ice, through a strainer, to another vessel. The method is associated primarily with Cuba and Spain, though it made a comeback worldwide in the 2020s. Beyond providing a great show for the customer, thrown drinks are thought to be lighter and more aerated in texture than shaken or stirred drinks. For this reason, the technique is sometimes reserved for cocktails that contain wines like vermouth and sherry, which benefit from exposure to air. For decades, throwing was particularly associated with Boadas Cocktails, a bar in Barcelona. Miguel Boadas, who founded the bar in 1933, brought the technique back from Havana, where he worked at El Floridita. The main knock against throwing is that it renders a cocktail less cold than it might be otherwise. However, the patrons on the receiving end of thrown cocktails will probably not notice.

TIKI-TI

A single-story, hole-in-the-wall tiki bar in the Silver Lake section of Los Angeles that for many years served as a standard-bearer of tiki cocktailing and a living throughline to the tiki glory days and recipes of Don the Beachcomber. It was founded in 1961 by Ray Buhan, a Philippines native who had worked for Donn Beach for years. Ray was eventually joined by his son Mike and grandson Mike Jr.

TIKI-TI

The bar's signature drink, Ray's Mistake, came to be in 1968 when Ray Buhan poured the wrong syrup into a different drink.

TI' PUNCH

A mixture of rhum agricole, sugar, and lime that is drunk in Martinique. The "Ti'" is short for "petit." It was little known outside the French Caribbean, where rhum agricole is made, until the globe-trotting bartenders of the cocktail revival brought it elsewhere. The cocktail is built in the glass, and while simple, the devil is in the details. The lime usually takes the form of a small disc of rind, the size of a half dollar, rather than a twist or wedge. The sweet element can be raw sugar or cane syrup. The drink is typically served at room temperature, but ice is not unheard of. Still, the dominant flavor is and should be the grassy, unaged agricole. If you make it wrong, rum importer and Ti' Punch zealot Ed Hamilton will come after you.

T

1½ ounces 100-proof rhum agricole

¼ barspoon Petite Canne sugar cane syrup

Small slice of lime

In a small glass, drop a small slice from the side of a lime. Add about ¼ barspoon of Petite Canne Sugar Cane syrup, then 1½ ounces 100-proof rhum agricole. In the French islands, the order of ingredients is important. Lime, sugar, rhum.

Petite Canne Sugar Cane syrup is 72 percent raw sugar from Martinique. I searched the U.S. and couldn't find anything close to this syrup. None of the dozen sugar syrup producers in the U.S. would make anything like this because they don't have the raw sugar. I can import sugar cane syrup but I can't import raw sugar without being a member of the sugar cartels that control sugar quota imports to the U.S.

There are other syrups from Martinique, but be sure to look at the ingredients and viscosity. All have less sugar and contain other things like aromatized spices and caramel.

Limes vary considerably. The limes found on Martinique are generally smaller than the large Mexican limes we get in the U.S. and the skin is thinner.

If you use a wedge of lime, the 100-proof spirit, which acts as a solvent, will make the drink bitter. While it is easy to think of the rind as the bitter part of the lime, the pulp in the lime gives up its bitter oils much faster than the rind. The essence of the Ti' Punch, petite punch, is that the sugar and lime are there to complement the 100-proof rhum agricole and not cover it up.

TOM AND JERRY

A rich holiday elixir, this hot relative of eggnog flourished in America in the nineteenth and early twentieth centuries. It is frequently (though not definitively) credited to Pierce Egan, the English chronicler of sports and popular culture. The milky broth, which is fortified with rum and brandy and accented with baking spices, was once so popular that it inspired an ancillary trade in Tom and Jerry punch-bowl sets. You can still spot them in antiques stores, typically emblazoned with the drink's name in Old English type. (A bar in Manhattan, called Tom and Jerry's, has a large collection of such bowls.) Up until Prohibition, Tom and Jerry bowls would dependably appear in taverns across the United States every December, whenever it got cold enough, and would remain in circulation throughout the holiday season. After repeal, they remained popular but gradually faded from view. The drink's appeal retained a grip in the Midwest, where winters are long. You can buy Tom and Jerry mix, either fresh or powdered, in Midwestern grocery stores yet today. A few restaurants and bars are still known

TOM AND JERRY

for the drink, including Miller's Pub in downtown Chicago and Bryant's Cocktail Lounge in Milwaukee, which opens a dedicated Tom and Jerry room every December. Cocktail renaissance leaders like Dale DeGroff and Audrey Saunders reintroduced the public to the drink in the twenty-first century.

TOM COLLINS

Perhaps the ultimate highball, and one of history's most enduring cocktails. Made of gin, sugar, lemon juice, and soda water, served over ice, it was historically prepared with Old Tom gin, which is sweeter than London dry gin, but the drink works well with both forms of the spirit, and after Old Tom gin largely disappeared after Prohibition, it was exclusively made with London dry.

A peculiar methodology is used in mixing up a Tom Collins. Though it contains fresh juice, which usually dictates that the drink must be shaken, it is nonetheless often built in the glass in which it is served. But shaking the drink and then straining it into an ice-filled highball works as well, and arguably leads to a better-integrated cocktail. The drink has roots that can be traced back to England, where it was called the John Collins and made with genever. Once it jumped the pond, the drink was made with Old Tom and renamed the Tom Collins, probably owing to the gin being used. The Tom Collins's other claim to fame is the most entertaining cocktail origin story of all time. Basically, it was born of a practical joke. Back in 1874, the gag went, barflies took to egging on a gullible mark by telling him that one Tom Collins was talking trash about him and could be found at a neighboring saloon should the dupe want to settle the score. Off the injured party would go, only to find out that ol' Tom had moved on to another tavern. And so the merry chase went until the sucker wised up.

Vastly popular in the mid-twentieth century, the Tom Collins doesn't get a lot of play in bars, either the old-school or the newfangled, these days; it's often dismissed as nothing but fizzy lemonade. It is one of the select few drinks to have a glass named after it: the collins glass, also known as a highball glass.

2 ounces Old Tom gin
1 ounce simple syrup
¾ ounce lemon juice
1 ounce soda water

Combine all the ingredients except the soda water in a cocktail shaker half-filled with ice and shake until chilled, about 15 seconds. Strain into a collins glass filled with ice. Top with the soda water. Garnish with a cherry and lemon wedge "flag."

TOMMY'S MARGARITA

A simplified version of the Margarita invented by Julio Bermejo at Tommy's Mexican Restaurant in San Francisco. To showcase the quality of 100 percent agave tequila, Bermejo 86'd the curaçao in the drink, used fresh lime juice, and substituted agave syrup for simple syrup. It is, in fact, as some have pointed out, simply a Tequila Sour. All these changes to the drink evolved over several years, but by the early 1990s, the drink was fully formed. By the early 2000s, it was established as a modern classic, almost as well known as the Margarita itself.

2 ounces reposado Tequila
1 ounce lime juice
½ ounce agave syrup

Dip half of the rim of a rocks glass in lime juice and then salt. Set aside. Combine the ingredients in a cocktail shaker half-filled with ice. Shake until chilled, about 15 seconds. Strain into the prepared rocks glass filled with ice. Garnish with a lime wedge.

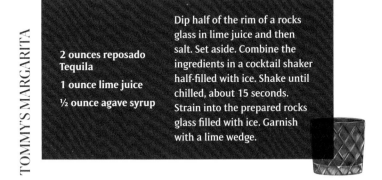

T

TRADER VIC'S

A chain of tiki restaurants that began in Oakland, California, and eventually girded the world, becoming the only real competition to Don the Beachcomber, the chain that kicked off the tiki phenomenon. Vic was Victor Jules Bergeron Jr., born in 1902 in San Francisco. In 1934 Bergeron opened a small restaurant called Hinky Dink's. This he eventually renamed Trader Vic's. Inspired by trips to Hollywood's Don the Beachcomber and El Floridita in Havana, he went full tiki and found success. Bergeron first started to franchise his concept with a restaurant in Seattle in 1949. He later partnered with hotelier Conrad Hilton, who opened new Trader Vic's restaurants in his various hotels. The original Oakland location eventually closed and a bigger place opened in nearby Emeryville, which still stands. The chain soon grew to twenty-five locations. Bergeron's most famous concoction is the Mai Tai, tiki's most popular drink, though Beach contested the claim. Unlike Donn Beach, Bergeron published a cocktail book with recipes, *The Bartender's Guide,* in 1947, which proved influential with bartenders in decades to come. An updated version came out in 1972. As tiki's popularity waned in the 1970s and '80s, the Trader Vic's chain dwindled, but it began to expand again in the twenty-first century as the tiki fad was revived in the 2010s. There are now more than a dozen locations. Vic's is particularly popular in the Middle East.

TRIDENT

This unusual mixture of aquavit, Cynar, fino sherry, and peach bitters was created by Seattle cocktail enthusiast Robert Hess in 2002 as an "obscured Negroni" and a way to showcase a few of his favorite unsung ingredients. He brought the recipe to the Zig Zag Café, where it was put on the menu. Bartender Brian Miller, a Seattle native, then brought the drink to the Pegu Club in New York, where he worked. And thus a layman, with the help of a few professional bartenders, handily pulled off the rare trick of creating a modern classic cocktail.

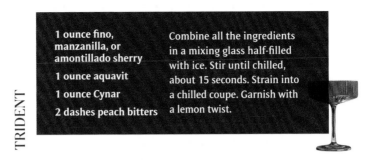

TRIDENT

1 ounce fino, manzanilla, or amontillado sherry

1 ounce aquavit

1 ounce Cynar

2 dashes peach bitters

Combine all the ingredients in a mixing glass half-filled with ice. Stir until chilled, about 15 seconds. Strain into a chilled coupe. Garnish with a lemon twist.

TRINIDAD SOUR

An improbable drink, using as its base one and a half ounces of Angostura bitters—an ingredient usually used as an accent in drinks like the Old-Fashioned and Manhattan. The cocktail further piled on the crazy with the addition of an ounce of orgeat, the almond syrup most associated with the Mai Tai. Smaller amounts of lemon juice and rye rounded out the heady mixture. According to Giuseppe González, its bartender inventor, it was created in 2008 at Clover Club, a cocktail bar in Brooklyn. (Julie Reiner, the owner of Clover Club, does not recall this being served at the bar.) John Gertsen tried the drink and took it to Drink, his bar in Boston. When González moved to Dutch Kills in Queens, he made the cocktail frequently. Like the Chartreuse Swizzle, it is expensive to make. Nonetheless, by the mid 2010s the drink was internationally known.

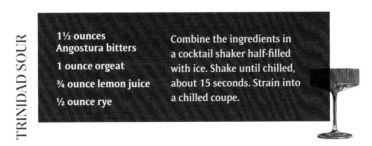

TRINIDAD SOUR

1½ ounces Angostura bitters

1 ounce orgeat

¾ ounce lemon juice

½ ounce rye

Combine the ingredients in a cocktail shaker half-filled with ice. Shake until chilled, about 15 seconds. Strain into a chilled coupe.

TURF CLUB

A Martini relative that first appeared in print in the 1880s. The recipe for it ping-ponged about for a number of years until settling down as something containing gin, dry vermouth, and dashes of absinthe, maraschino liqueur, and orange bitters—a formula very close to the subsequent Tuxedo No. 2. The drink faded from view as the Martini made its climb to cocktail supremacy, though it still has a few modern-day champions.

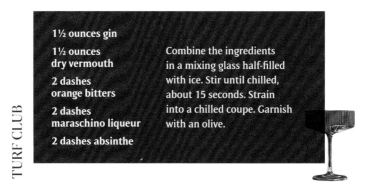

TURF CLUB

1½ ounces gin

1½ ounces dry vermouth

2 dashes orange bitters

2 dashes maraschino liqueur

2 dashes absinthe

Combine the ingredients in a mixing glass half-filled with ice. Stir until chilled, about 15 seconds. Strain into a chilled coupe. Garnish with an olive.

TUXEDO

A Martini variant that proliferated in two forms in the early twentieth century. The first, generally thought to be the original, is a dry drink made with gin, sherry, and orange bitters. The second, called Tuxedo No. 2 (after the title it was given in the 1930 *Savoy Cocktail Book*) and generally more luscious in character, is made with gin, vermouth, maraschino liqueur, and absinthe. In the 2010s the drink experienced a small comeback.

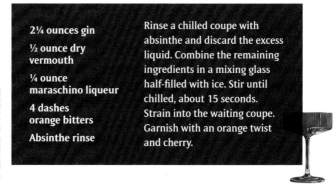

TUXEDO NO. 2

2¼ ounces gin

½ ounce dry vermouth

¼ ounce maraschino liqueur

4 dashes orange bitters

Absinthe rinse

Rinse a chilled coupe with absinthe and discard the excess liquid. Combine the remaining ingredients in a mixing glass half-filled with ice. Stir until chilled, about 15 seconds. Strain into the waiting coupe. Garnish with an orange twist and cherry.

20TH CENTURY

A blend of gin, Lillet blanc, crème de cacao, and lemon juice, the 20th Century cocktail ironically didn't show its face until 1937, well into the century. It was named after the famous train that ran from New York to Chicago, not the hundred-year span. The drink was attributed to Charles A. Tuck, a career British bartender who went on to publish a cocktail book in 1967. It's basically a riff on the Corpse Reviver No. 2, and the unlikely presence of the crème de cacao really does rocket the drink into another flavor world entirely. Though it's never quite had a heyday, the drink has never quite faded away either and has its fans.

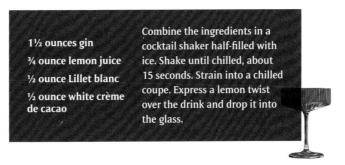

1½ ounces gin

¾ ounce lemon juice

½ ounce Lillet blanc

½ ounce white crème de cacao

Combine the ingredients in a cocktail shaker half-filled with ice. Shake until chilled, about 15 seconds. Strain into a chilled coupe. Express a lemon twist over the drink and drop it into the glass.

T

UENO, HIDETSUGU

A Japanese bartender who, as the owner of Bar High Five in Tokyo, ranks as one of the most recognizable figures in the Tokyo bartending world. He began bartending in 1992 and worked under Hisashi Kishi at the Star Bar before opening Bar High Five, which has no menu, in 2008. He is particularly renowned for his skill in carving ice into diamonds. Unlike some of his colleagues in the Japanese bar world, he travels often, judging cocktail competitions and lecturing on bartending. He is easily identifiable by his signature pompadour hairstyle.

UNDERBERG BITTERS

A sui generis brand of German digestive bitters that became a darling of bartenders of the cocktail revival in the aughts, when the cocktail world was rediscovering heritage bitters brands. The company was founded by Hubert Underberg in the 1840s. Underberg's tiny, single-serving bottles, with their tan wrappers and green caps, set the brand apart from other bitters. It was rarely used as an ingredient in cocktails, but racks or boxes of Underberg bottles became common sights behind cocktail bars, and the bitters were often dispensed as friendly shots in the manner of a bartender's handshake. For a time in the 2010s, the Brooklyn bar Prime Meats sold more Underberg than any bar in the United States.

UYEDA, KAZUO

One of the best-known Japanese bartenders of the late twentieth century and early twenty-first, Uyeda is the proprietor of the Ginza cocktail bar Tender Bar, which he opened in 1997, and is well known as the originator of the controversial hard shake, an intricate and picturesque technique for shaking drinks. Uyeda began his bartending career in 1966. Private and hermetic, he has never been the public personality some of his colleagues have become, keeping his own counsel, tending to his own bar, concentrating on the perfection of classic cocktails such as the Martini and Gimlet, and rarely visiting other bars or traveling. Indeed, a rare visit he made to New York, hosted by entrepreneur Greg Boehm in 2010, was largely regarded as a classic case of lost in translation, with Uyeda and the American bartenders in attendance failing to make a connection. He is the

KAZUO UYEDA

author of the book *Cocktail Techniques,* published in 2000, which was translated into English in 2010.

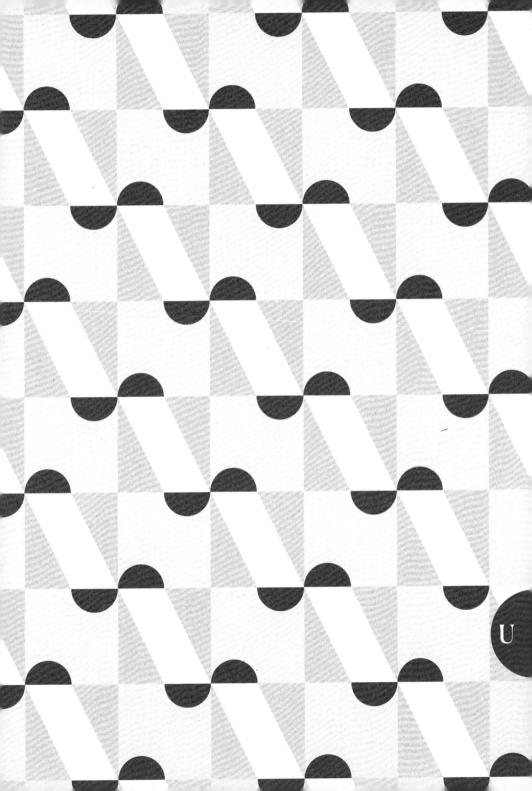

VARNISH, THE

A speakeasy-style bar tucked in a room at the back of French dip haven Cole's, The Varnish was the first truly important craft cocktail operation in Los Angeles when it opened in 2009. It was a collaboration between Milk & Honey founder Sasha Petraske; his lieutenant, bartender Eric Alperin; and L.A. restaurateur Cedd Moses. It possesses all the earmarks of a Petraske joint, from the meticulously crafted drinks to the dim lighting to the accent on decorum, though, unlike its mother bar, it does offer a menu and live music.

THE VARNISH

VELÁSQUEZ, CARINA SOTO

A native of Colombia and a leading player in the Paris cocktail scene, Velásquez runs, with her partners, an empire of cocktail bars in Paris, including Glass (now closed), Le Mary Celeste, Hero, and, most significantly, Candelaria, a taqueria and bar that opened in 2011 and specializes in agave spirits.

VERMOUTH

A category of aromatized, fortified wine with a long tradition in Europe, where it is usually drunk straight or on the rocks or as part of a Spritz. There are three major styles: sweet, also known as red; dry, also known as white; and bianco or blanc, which splits the difference between the two, being both white and sweet. Though all three styles are made in several countries, traditionally dry vermouth is associated with France and sweet vermouth with northern Italy. Flavors and styles vary widely, of course, depending on the base wine that is used and the cocktail of botanicals (always kept secret by companies).

Vermouth's long-prominent role in the world of cocktails began in the 1870s, when the wines became more widely available in the United States. Soon, bartenders were experimenting with them, combining them with spirits. The Manhattan cocktail was the first major success in this fast-growing field of drink, with the Martinez, Martini, Turf Club, Metropolitan, Star, Irish Cocktail, Rob Roy, Negroni, and myriad more following soon after. There is, in fact, a strong argument to be made that the Martini got its name from the Martini vermouth company. Vermouth's reputation suffered after the repeal of Prohibition, as bars mishandled the products, letting them sit out and get oxidized. This led to a false public perception that vermouth tasted bad and ruined drinks, and that helped push along the mania for drier and drier Martinis. The wine's standing was not restored until the advent of the cocktail renaissance, when "refrigerate your vermouth" became one of the battle cries of the mixologist, and unsung Italian brands like Carpano Antica and Punt e Mes were championed. Also pushed was the newly in-vogue Fifty-Fifty Martini, which was half dry vermouth. In the wake of the cocktail wave, the first American-made vermouths in decades appeared, and heritage brands from Europe finally made the journey to North America, most significantly the Dolin line, which offered an alternative to the dominant dry of Noilly Prat and the fallback sweet of Martini & Rossi, as well as introducing American drinkers to the possibilities and versatility of blanc vermouth, which was invented in the late nineteenth century in Chambéry, in southeastern France. The rise of low-ABV and Italianate drinking in the 2010s further elevated the fortunes of vermouth.

VESPER

A fictional cocktail that made the leap into real life. The Vesper was born in the pages of Ian Fleming's 1953 spy caper *Casino Royale,* in which James Bond concocts the recipe—gin, vodka, Lillet blanc, and a long lemon twist—out of thin air and instructs the bartender to make one. The cocktail didn't find a breathing audience until the aughts, when *Casino Royale* was remade as the 2006 movie starring Daniel Craig, and cocktail bartenders began offering it as a less-offensive alternative to the "shaken, not stirred" Vodka Martini that Bond wannabes kept lobbing their way.

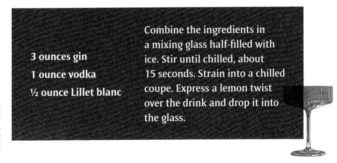

VESPER

3 ounces gin

1 ounce vodka

½ ounce Lillet blanc

Combine the ingredients in a mixing glass half-filled with ice. Stir until chilled, about 15 seconds. Strain into a chilled coupe. Express a lemon twist over the drink and drop it into the glass.

VIEUX CARRÉ

Along with the Sazerac, Ramos Gin Fizz, and Brandy Crusta, one of the great, enduring New Orleans cocktails—though far younger, having come along in the 1930s. It is strongly associated with the Carousel Bar inside the Hotel Monteleone in the French Quarter, where bartender Walter Bergeron invented it. It combines some of New Orleans's favorite things, including rye, brandy, and Peychaud's bitters, into a concoction that is not too far from a Manhattan, but much richer, owing to the inclusion of Bénédictine. Its profile received a good boost in the twenty-first century owing to enterprising young bartenders in service of old cocktails with pedigrees.

V

1 ounce rye

1 ounce cognac

1 ounce sweet vermouth

¼ ounce Bénédictine

1 dash Angostura bitters

1 dash Peychaud's bitters

Combine all the ingredients in a mixing glass half-filled with ice. Stir until chilled, about 15 seconds. Strain into a chilled rocks glass over one large ice cube. Express a lemon twist over the drink and drop it into the glass.

THE VIOLET HOUR

Along with the Drawing Room, the Violet Hour, which opened in 2007, was the first important craft cocktail bar to open in Chicago. Headed up by bartender Toby Maloney, who had worked at Milk & Honey and Pegu Club in New York, it brought modern attitudes toward cocktails to a blue-collar city more accustomed to beer and shots and steak house Martinis. The bar served as training ground for a generation of bartenders who went on to open or run their own important Chicago cocktail bars, including Brad Bolt, Stephen Cole, Kyle Davidson, Michael Rubel, and Nandini Khaund. Several modern classic cocktails were born there, including Art of Choke, Bitter Giuseppe, and, in an early iteration, the Paper Plane.

VODKA

The mainstay spirit of Russia and Poland, which never had much of a foothold in the cocktail world until the mid-twentieth century, when its promise of odorless, tasteless, frictionless drinking landed it in such mid-century foundational drinks as the Moscow Mule, Screwdriver, and Bloody Mary. By the 1970s and '80s, it had successfully supplanted gin in several staple drinks, with customers increasingly opting for Vodka Martinis, Vodka Collins, vodka and tonics, and more. During the 'tini craze of the 1990s, the majority of so-called "Martinis" being sold at bars had a base of either vodka or flavored vodka. The latter subcategory exploded, kudzu-like, from the 1980s on, to the point where a back bar could be filled—and often was—solely with the flavor variations. One of the defining cocktails of the era, the Cosmopolitan, had a base of lemon-flavored vodka (Absolut Citron, to be specific).

THE VIOLET HOUR

THAD VOGLER

During this period, an increasing number of vodka brands successfully marketed themselves to the public as premium brands and status symbols, including Absolut, which became one of the first vodka brands to be called for by name in bars, as well as Belvedere and Grey Goose. In the early days of the cocktail revival, and particularly in England, vodka still found a place behind the bar at the best cocktail dens, even becoming the base of a few modern classics, such as the Espresso Martini, Russian Spring Punch, and Drink Without a Name. But by 2000, at least in the United States, the spirit became persona non grata, viewed as the characterless enemy of sophisticated mixology. Some influential early cocktail bars, such as Milk & Honey and Pegu Club, which were intent on reeducating the drinking public, refused to carry vodka, or heavily discouraged drinkers from ordering it. By the 2010s, such attitudes had relaxed a bit. Still, vodka was few bartenders' first choice when creating an original cocktail.

VOGLER, THAD

A tall, Yale-educated iconoclast who drifted into the San Francisco service world against his better judgment and proceeded to tear apart all preconceived ideas about the industry and how it conducted itself. By the mid-aughts, he had set up lauded bar programs at Slanted Door, Beretta, and Heaven's Dog, among other places. He'd rip out soda guns at bars he managed and go out of his way to get products that had a creditable pedigree. By the time he opened his own place, Bar Agricole, in 2010, he had pared down his back bar to a bare minimum, carrying only spirits whose provenance he trusted and approved of. His cocktail list, too, was minimal, focusing on classics with skeletal profiles, each of which he workshopped down to the last detail, and eschewing fancified original creations. Because of his preference for artisanal spirits yet untouched by corporate taint, he developed particular interests in mezcal, rhum agricole, calvados, and brandy. Over time he built a small empire, including Trou Normand, dedicated to French spirits, and a rum bar, Obioso. All shuttered in 2020 during the Covid-19 pandemic, though Bar Agricole returned in 2022. In 2017, Vogler turned author, writing *By the Smoke and the Smell,* a principled memoir about his various pursuits of quality spirits and his concerns with the liquor and bar businesses. In 2022, he launched his own line of spirits, some sourced, some created from scratch.

WARD EIGHT

The only famous cocktail to have come out of Boston, and one that has perennially fallen short of the title "beloved." It is basically a Whiskey Sour with the addition of grenadine as the sweetener and orange juice. It is said to have been created in 1898 at the Locke-Ober, one of Boston's oldest and most famous restaurants and a political hangout, but stories vary. Though widely known and a regular actor in cocktail books published over the decades, the Ward Eight never rose above a second-tier minor classic. Nor was it embraced by the bartenders of the cocktail revival. In a notorious incident, the best young bartenders of Boston convened one night in the aughts to ascertain the best possible recipe for the cocktail, only to conclude that the Ward Eight was unsalvageable.

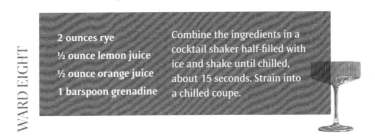

WARD EIGHT

2 ounces rye
½ ounce lemon juice
½ ounce orange juice
1 barspoon grenadine

Combine the ingredients in a cocktail shaker half-filled with ice and shake until chilled, about 15 seconds. Strain into a chilled coupe.

WARD, PHIL

A Pittsburgh native who, after moving to New York, immediately displayed a preternatural talent for mixology. He headed the programs at three of the most prominent Manhattan cocktail bars of the aughts—Flatiron Lounge, Pegu Club, and Death & Co.—before opening his own spot, the influential Mayahuel, the first significant agave spirits–oriented cocktail bar in New York. He is widely credited with pioneering the "Mr. Potato Head" school of mixology, in which new cocktails are created by plugging new ingredients into established drink templates. This approach resulted in a flurry of popular Ward creations, including the Elder Fashioned, Final Ward, Division Bell, and, most famously, the Oaxaca Old-Fashioned. As famous for his contrary, curmudgeonly personality as his mixing skills, he has in recent years turned his back on bar ownership and devoted himself primarily to bartending.

PHIL WARD

WHITE LADY

A cocktail strongly associated with the American Bar at the Savoy hotel, which makes sense, since the recipe first appeared in Harry Craddock's *Savoy Cocktail Book* in 1930. Made of gin, Cointreau, and lemon juice, it is basically a gin Sidecar. It was famous enough by 1932 that Cointreau regularly used the recipe in ads. An egg white is often included in the mix.

WHITE LADY

1 ½ ounces gin

¾ ounce Cointreau

¾ ounce lemon juice

Combine the ingredients in a cocktail shaker half-filled with ice and shake until chilled, about 15 seconds. Strain into a chilled coupe.

WHITE LYAN

A trailblazing, boundary-shifting London bar that operated in Shoreditch from 2013 to 2017 and largely made the reputation of its owner and chief philosopher, Ryan Chetiyawardana (who actually did study philosophy, along with biology and

WHITE LYAN

art), who would go on in the aughts to become the most influential bar figure in England. Its approach was not about add-ons, but about subtraction. The bar confronted the customer nearly unarmed. It was equipped with no ice, no cocktail shakers, and very few bottles of liquor beyond its branded house spirits, which it bought directly from distillers. White spirits were made to Chetiyawardana's specifications. Aged stock like whiskey was blended and then diluted with White Lyan's own water: filtered London tap water that had been spiked with a custom mineral content. The cocktails were premixed, bottled, and refrigerated, rather than stirred over ice. During its short run, the bar was widely praised and influential. Its short life would presage Chetiyawardana's habit of opening and closing popular bars at a rapid rate.

WHITE RUSSIAN

A simple, heavy-going cocktail made of vodka, cream, and coffee liqueur, its popularity rose in tandem with that of vodka in the 1960s. In 1998 it was given a new lease on life, which shows no sign of ebbing, with the release of the Coen Brothers film *The Big Lebowski,* whose laid-back protagonist, Jeffrey "The Dude" Lebowski, drinks White Russians almost exclusively, calling them, affectionately, "Caucasians." It was preceded historically by the Black Russian, which is merely vodka and coffee liqueur, but—just as the Brandy Alexander did to the original Alexander—the White Russian has long since eclipsed the older drink. Both are "Russian" because of the presence of vodka, a spirit once exclusively associated with Russia.

WHITE RUSSIAN

1½ ounces vodka
¾ ounce Kahlúa
¾ ounce heavy cream

Combine the ingredients in a cocktail shaker half-filled with ice and shake until chilled, about 15 seconds. Strain into a chilled old-fashioned glass.

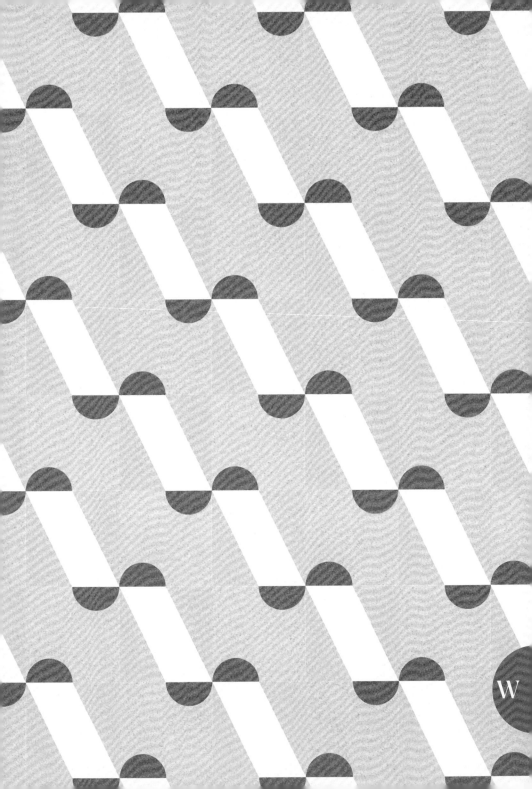

ZIG ZAG CAFÉ

A Seattle bar owned by Ben Dougherty and Kacy Fitch. Hidden away along a steep public stairway called the Pike Hillclimb, it established itself as a cocktail oasis in the city, largely due to the presence of veteran bartender Murray Stenson. The Last Word became the house drink when Stenson discovered the obscure pre-Prohibition cocktail in a vintage cocktail book and began serving it.

ZIG ZAG CAFÉ

ZOMBIE

ZOMBIE

Arguably the most famous, and certainly the most notorious, of all tiki cocktails. It was invented by Donn Beach, founder of the trailblazing tiki bar Don the Beachcomber, in the 1930s. It was often imitated, but never duplicated, since Beach guarded his drink recipes jealously, forcing others to only guess at what went into his most famous concoctions. The only thing that ties all the various Zombies together was the enormous amount of rum that went into each—almost always including a shot of overproof rum—as well as its reputation as a knockout punch of a drink. The running gimmick was that there were only two allowed per customer, as woe betide anyone who had a third. The recipe might have been permanently lost to time if not for the sleuthing of tiki historian Jeff "Beachbum" Berry, who in

2007, after years of tracking the Zombie's history, came upon the original recipe, dated 1934, and written down in the notebook of a Beachcomber waiter named Dick Santiago. The formula, now widely accepted as the original Zombie, includes four ounces of three rums (including overproof rum), lime juice, falernum, Don's mix (white grapefruit–cinnamon sugar water), Pernod, grenadine, bitters, and crushed ice, all tossed in a blender.

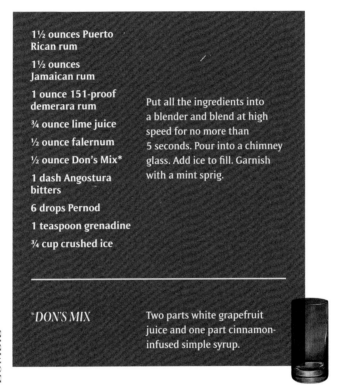

1½ ounces Puerto Rican rum

1½ ounces Jamaican rum

1 ounce 151-proof demerara rum

¾ ounce lime juice

½ ounce falernum

½ ounce Don's Mix*

1 dash Angostura bitters

6 drops Pernod

1 teaspoon grenadine

¾ cup crushed ice

Put all the ingredients into a blender and blend at high speed for no more than 5 seconds. Pour into a chimney glass. Add ice to fill. Garnish with a mint sprig.

*DON'S MIX

Two parts white grapefruit juice and one part cinnamon-infused simple syrup.

ACKNOWLEDGMENTS

Thanks, first of all and most of all, to Ten Speed Press publisher Aaron Wehner who, during the first fraught months of the Covid-19 pandemic, when I was quarantining in my Brooklyn apartment, suggested I write this encyclopedia. The offer was a life preserver in an ocean of uncertainty. Great thanks, as well, to the great team at Ten Speed, including my patient editor Kim Keller, Julie Bennett, Betsy Stromberg, Annie Marino, David Hawk, and Chloe Aryeh. Special thanks to Suzanne Dias, whose illustrations adorn this volume. Love and gratitude, as always, to my wife, Mary Kate Murray, son, Asher Simonson, and stepson, Richard Santana. And thanks, I guess, to the Roman authorities at Fiumicino International Airport who, in May 2022, seeing I had tested positive for Covid, sent me to the Sheraton Parco de' Medici, a nearby hotel turned hospital/jail, where I quarantined for the next eleven days. Having nothing to do, and a nonfunctioning television, I wrote fully one-sixth of this book there. Finally, thanks to every bar, bartender, spirit, bar tool, drinks writer, drinker, or cocktail that ever existed. You have kept me entertained and interested for the past twenty years and have made the world a better place on a daily basis.

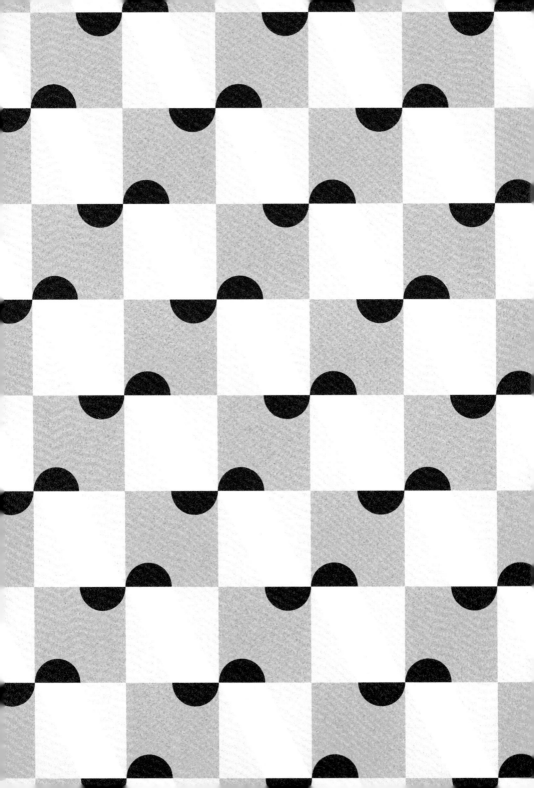

ABOUT THE AUTHOR

ROBERT SIMONSON is the author of six previous books about cocktails and cocktail history, including *The Old-Fashioned* (2014), which kicked off an ongoing cottage industry of single-drink cocktail books; *A Proper Drink* (2016), the first and so far only history of the current cocktail renaissance; *3-Ingredient Cocktails* (2017); *The Martini Cocktail* (2019); *Mezcal and Tequila Cocktails* (2021), and *Modern Classic Cocktails* (2022). Both *3-Ingredient Cocktails* and *The Martini Cocktail* were nominated for James Beard Awards; *Mezcal and Tequila Cocktails* won a 2022 IACP Award; and *The Martini Cocktail* won a 2020 Spirited Award. Simonson is also the recipient of a 2019 Spirited Award for best cocktail and spirits writer and a 2021 IACP award for narrative beverage writing. He writes about cocktails, food, and travel for *The New York Times*, where he has been a contributor since 2000. He is a primary contributor to *The New York Times Essential Book of Cocktails*. Simonson is the coauthor with Martin Doudoroff of two apps, "Modern Classics of the Cocktail Renaissance" and "The Martini Cocktail." He is also the author of the prominent Substack newsletter *The Mix with Robert Simonson*. He lives in Brooklyn with his wife, Mary Kate, and their children, Asher and Richard.

INDEX

Published in the United States by Ten Speed Press, an imprint of Random House, a division of Penguin Random House LLC, New York.
TenSpeed.com

Ten Speed Press and the Ten Speed Press colophon are registered trademarks of Penguin Random House LLC.

Typefaces: Linotype's Memento and Commercial Type's Pilat and Candy Darling

Library of Congress Cataloging-in-Publication Data
Names: Simonson, Robert, author.
Title: The encyclopedia of cocktails : the people, bars, and drinks, with more than 100 recipes / by Robert Simonson.
Description: California : Ten Speed Press, [2023] | Includes index. |
Identifiers: LCCN 2022056365 (print) | LCCN 2022056366 (ebook) |
ISBN 9781984860668 (hardcover) | ISBN 9781984860675 (ebook)
Subjects: LCSH: Cocktails. | LCGFT: Cookbooks.
Classification: LCC TX951 .S58362S 2023 (print) | LCC TX951 (ebook) |
DDC 641.87/4—dc23/eng/20221128
LC record available at https://lccn.loc.gov/2022056365
LC ebook record available at https://lccn.loc.gov/2022056366

Hardcover ISBN: 978-1-9848-6066-8
eBook ISBN: 978-1-9848-6067-5

Printed in China

Acquiring editor: Julie Bennett | Project editor: Kim Keller
Production editor: Joyce Wong
Designer: Annie Marino | Production designers: Mari Gill and Faith Hague
Production manager: Serena Sigona
Copyeditor: Kristi Hein | Indexer: Elizabeth Parson
Publicist: David Hawk | Marketer: Chloe Aryeh

10 9 8 7 6 5 4 3 2 1

First Edition